Cambridge Studies in French

General editor: MALCOLM BOWIE

Also in the series

Cambridge Studies in French

CORNEILLE, CLASSICISM AND
THE RUSES OF SYMMETRY

CORNEILLE, CLASSICISM AND THE RUSES OF SYMMETRY

MITCHELL GREENBERG

Professor of French, Miami University, Ohio

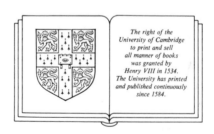

The right of the
University of Cambridge
to print and sell
all manner of books
was granted by
Henry VIII in 1534.
The University has printed
and published continuously
since 1584.

CAMBRIDGE UNIVERSITY PRESS

CAMBRIDGE

LONDON   NEW YORK   NEW ROCHELLE

MELBOURNE   SYDNEY

Published by the Press Syndicate of the University of Cambridge
The Pitt Building, Trumpington Street, Cambridge CB2 1RP
32 East 57th Street, New York, NY 10022, USA
10 Stamford Road, Oakleigh, Melbourne 3166, Australia

© Cambridge University Press 1986

First published 1986

Printed in Great Britain at
the University Press, Cambridge

British Library cataloguing in publication data
Greenberg, Mitchell
Corneille, classicism and the ruses of symmetry.
– (Cambridge studies in French)
1. Corneille, Pierre – Criticism and
interpretation
I. Title
842'.4   PQ1779

Library of Congress cataloguing in publication data
Greenberg, Mitchell, 1946–
Corneille, classicism, and the ruses of symmetry.
(Cambridge studies in French)
Bibliography.
Includes index.
1. Corneille, Pierre, 1606–1684 – Criticism and
interpretation. 2. Classicism. 3. Symmetry in
literature. 4. Historical drama, French – History and
criticism. 5. Tragic, The, in literature. I. Title.
II. Series.
PQ1779.G7   1986   842'.4   86–6836

ISBN 0 521 32554 4

GG

Pour Julia et pour Marie-Claire

Et comme notre esprit, jusqu'au dernier soupir,
Toujours vers quelque objet pousse quelque désir . . .
                              (*Cinna*, II, i, 367–8)

CONTENTS

GENERAL EDITOR'S PREFACE

This series aims at providing a new forum for the discussion of major critical or scholarly topics within the field of French studies. It differs from most similar-seeming ventures in the degree of freedom which contributing authors are allowed and in the range of subjects covered. For the series is not concerned to promote any single area of academic specialization or any single theoretical approach. Authors are invited to address themselves to *problems*, and to argue their solutions in whatever terms seem best able to produce an incisive and cogent account of the matter in hand. The search for such terms will sometimes involve the crossing of boundaries between familiar academic disciplines, or the calling of those boundaries into dispute. Most of the studies will be written especially for the series, although from time to time it will also provide new editions of outstanding works which were previously out of print, or originally published in languages other than English or French.

PREFACE

On September 12, 1642, in Lyons, Place des Terreaux, the headsman's ax falls anew, punishing Henri d'Effiat, Marquis de Cinq-Mars, for the crime of 'lèse-majesté'. As if to conjure away premonitions of the uncertainties that always accompany a new regency, uncertainties that threaten the edifice of Absolutism so laboriously constructed during their joint reign, Richelieu and Louis XIII insist on the execution of Cinq-Mars and his co-conspirator, de Thou, as a final spectacular demonstration of royal authority. This execution is only the latest in a series that throughout the 1620s and 1630s radically underlined the decline of the nobility and the concomitant rise of 'raison d'Etat': Marillac's death was perhaps the most unjust, Montmorency's the most pathetic. Surely, however, Cinq-Mars' execution fired the imagination of his contemporaries, and of history, as the most tragic.

Of the many versions of the conspiracy, trial and execution of d'Effiat we possess, Vigny's fictional narrative *Cinq-Mars* is particularly compelling in its Romantic excess:

'Qu'attends-tu? que fais-tu là?' dit-il [Cinq-Mars] ensuite à l'exécuteur qui était là et n'avait pas encore tiré son couperet d'un méchant sac qu'il avait apporté. Son confesseur, s'étant approché, lui donna une médaille; et lui, d'une tranquillité d'esprit incroyable, pria le père de tenir le crucifix devant ses yeux, qu'il ne voulut point avoir bandés. J'aperçus les deux mains tremblantes du vieil abbé Quillet, qui élevait le crucifix. En ce moment une voix claire et pure comme celle d'un ange entonna l'Ave maris stella. Dans le silence universel, je reconnus la voix de M. de Thou, qui attendait au pied de l'échafaud; le peuple répéta le chant sacré. M. de Cinq-Mars embrassa plus étroitement le poteau et je vis s'élever une hache faite à la façon des haches d'Angleterre. Un cri effroyable du peuple, jeté de la place, des fenêtres et des tours, m'avertit qu'elle était retombée et que la tête avait roulé jusqu'à terre. (*Cinq-Mars*, pp. 371–2)[1]

The paraphernalia of death and the figures of rhetoric are combined in this narration to represent the drama that is at the heart

of seventeenth-century tragedy. The execution — that face-to-face with death — underscores the immense dissymmetry between Sovereign and subject.[2] In a brief instant those strands that constitute the diverse networks of power and pleasure structuring society are concentrated in one spectacular show of force. Curiously, it is precisely this spectacle that is denied Classical representation. The 'bienséances' exile death to the wings of the theater. The spectacle of death is never allowed onto the stage of tragedy and the center of the tragic is forever condemned to another scene, to another place.

What could not take place on the seventeenth-century stage is allowed to happen in Romantic fiction. Vigny's retelling of the most powerful example of Absolutist prerogative brings these two irreconcilable 'scenes' together. In the tumult of the carnival organized by Richelieu to inaugurate his new residence, in the nighttime blurrings and interminglings of a populace's unleashed quest for pleasure, an incongruous encounter figures the origin of the narration we have just read. On the 'Pont-neuf', next to the newly erected statue of Henri IV, two spectators are thrown together and find themselves isolated from the movement that swirls about them. The two friends (for they are 'friends') use this moment of calm and recognition to criticize the political events of these last days of the Cardinal's reign. What fortuitous stroke of genius led Alfred de Vigny to end his novel with this chance encounter? Was it simply coincidence that made him place the narration of Cinq-Mars' spectacular death in a letter that the English poet John Milton hears read to him by his friend, the French dramatist Pierre Corneille?

By situating Corneille as the spokesman of his narrative's tragic conclusion, Vigny's novel makes him embrace the two scenes of seventeenth-century Absolutism: the executioner's block and the theater. Although apparently separate, these two worlds are, as Vigny's narrative suggests, joined by the scaffold that upholds them both. Separating the victim from the mob, the scaffold makes of the execution a spectacle. As a support for the stage it serves as a constant reminder that the theater is yet another locus where sovereign power is exercised.

The lines of power separating victim, executioner and witness are never radically distinct: they are always ambivalent, always reciprocal. It is precisely this ambivalent space in which all the participants are joined, this space of reversibility and co-mingling, that most adequately veils and reveals the ubiquitous power of the

Sovereign. Sovereignty emerges from this ritual of death where the guilty body that has violated the integrity of the ruler is punished. And who in the multifaceted crowd is not capable of an offending gesture? Who among us is not always also the criminal, a potential victim in the eyes of the Law?[3]

If the scaffold is always a spectacle of power, a theatricalization of power, may we not suspect that the theater, and here I am speaking most particularly about the tragic theater that Corneille so triumphantly institutes, is also the space of an execution? Here, in the theater, the distance separating Sovereign and subject is paradoxically both the greatest and the least. Is it not here, in the crossing over, in the mingling of the scenes of execution and tragedy that we, with Vigny, must situate Corneille?

More than twenty years ago S. Doubrovsky reminded us that Corneille's theater was 'historical'. At the same time he cautioned readers of Corneille not to misunderstand the meaning of 'history'.[4] Surely Corneille's plays are of their time, but they are not only a retelling of evenemential or social history.[5] Rather they 'mirror' their moment, holding themselves up as a model of what in the world remains pure immanence. What this means, of course, is that tragedy is never just a mimesis but also, and perhaps more important, a poiesis. The consequences of the way tragedy and history interreact, the way, that is, that different discourses come together at different critical moments to form new clusters of interpretation, new ways of seeing, will bear heavily on the reading of Corneille this study proposes.

In a recent book, *L'Ecriture de l'histoire*, Michel de Certeau argues powerfully for seeing historiography as an exercise of ideological control. He points out the difference between actual historical action − the past − and the political and ideological implications of its narration. In its effort to resurrect and yet contain the past, to make the dead speak, think or act, history, as a form of rhetoric, constantly invests the past with its own present:

Le discours sur le passé a pour statut d'être le discours du mort. L'objet qui circule n'est que l'absent, alors que son sens est d'être un langage entre le narrateur et ses lecteurs, c'est à dire entre des présents. La chose communiquée opère la communication d'un groupe avec lui-même par ce 'renvoi' au tiers absent qu'est son passé.[6]

History is dialogue with the dead where the present asks questions about itself and listens to its own answers. The narrative strategies de Certeau circumscribes as pertaining to 'history' are shared, I

would argue, with 'literary history'. Texts are inscribed within both cultural and ideological frameworks that authorize the way they can be seen, the way they can be 'plausibly' analyzed, the way, that is, they are made to speak to and for us.

The readings of Corneille's tragic universe that I offer here form my own dialogue with his world. This statement, however, demands some elaboration. First of all I am not primarily concerned with studying Corneille in his 'historical' context: this is not a book about Corneille and the seventeenth century, but rather a book about Corneille, the seventeenth century and us, a book, in other words, that asks how the past engages us in its tragedy and how we, in turn, embrace it.

We continue to stage these tragedies because of the pleasure they give us. It is the examination of this pleasure that constitutes the central explorations of my book. It is my contention that pleasure is an effect of subjectivity, as that subjectivity is informed by the intermeshing of several networks – the networks of sexuality, of authority, and of representation. I find it intriguing that the notion of subjectivity as an ideological construct received, in the seventeenth century, its first and most powerful articulation in the tragedies of Corneille. Whether or not the Cornelian hero's 'moi' corresponds to, or reflects, the Cartesian 'ego' is less important than the coincidence of their simultaneous emergence. This coincidence does signal the arrival of a different and novel articulation of the self. This articulation, in turn, implies not only a restructuring of the individual but also the concomitant restructuring of the way that individual exists in and colonizes the world – a reformulation, in other words, of how the world is at once represented and made to represent this self.

The articulation of subjectivity, as both an ontology and a legacy, has been at the center of recent critical speculation: the putting into question of those presuppositions upon which the notion of an integral subject can or cannot come into being has been, at least since Nietzsche, the mark of 'modernity'. It will come as no surprise, therefore, that in my dialogue with Corneille I have recourse to diverse critical idioms (psychoanalysis, in its Freudian and post-Freudian forms, epistemology as represented most notably by Foucault, the various recent discussions by French feminists on sexuality and difference, and finally contemporary social analyses of the theater) that are the discourses most involved with unraveling the puzzle of subjectivity and representation. These heterogeneous idioms are invoked not as some irrefutable

'Authority', as if they, finally, could yield us the 'Truth' about Corneille that has remained hidden for the past 300 years. Rather, they are discourses that, by constantly putting into question the possibility of ultimate truth, enable me to dialogue with Corneille where he is most compelling and most problematical. In a study that wishes to trace those shifting borders of power and pleasure that allow Corneille's tragedies to continue to speak to us, to involve us in their world, to make, in other words, their past present, these discourses seem the most apt at engaging Corneille's texts where they engage us, in the unstable margins defining and undermining our articulation of ourselves in the world. At the same time, they also enable us to affirm this articulation, in its evanescence, as pleasure.

INTRODUCTION

'Toutes nos passions ne savent qu'obéir.'

Cornelian tragedy emerges during the 1630s and 1640s and radically alters the course of French and European theater. More important still, this new tragedy, standing apart from those inchoate forms of representation that we have come to identify with the term 'baroque', imposes Classicism's Law upon chaos, its concept of ideality on materiality, and elaborates a radically different model of human subjectivity.

The period that forms the contextual framework inside which Cornelian tragedy evolves has been diversely studied as a period of transition − of transitions in esthetics (from baroque to Classical), in the political and social structures governing French life, and, finally in the ideological parameters informing discursive reasoning itself.[1] Among recent critics who have attempted to theorize this transition, M. Foucault's concept of 'epistemic' change, precisely because it embraces the internal contradictions of this epoch while proposing a general method for its comprehension, remains a forceful argument for grasping the interrelation of social, esthetic and discursive practices that constitute what we have come to identify as the Classical epiphany of Cornelian dramaturgy.

Corneille's dramatic breakthrough occurs during that era Foucault has called 'la période du grand renfermement', whose defining trait would be its compulsion to enclose and exclude. The world is separated into distinct and identifiable areas of social, psychological, linguistic and sexual differences.[2] At first glance, the universe Corneille created in his great tragedies seems both to corroborate and to celebrate this brave new world of difference. The Cornelian universe has been lionized as the realm of light. Its clarity is the resplendence of division, of sharply delimited, unconditional boundaries. Shadows are not allowed to adhere to the contours of ideals or heros. In this world choices, when they are given, are absolute: one is either Roman or Alban, Horace or Curiace, for Emilie or for Auguste. It is in the absolute brilliance of their

1

choices, choices which always seem irrevocable, ultimate confrontations with a personal and political truth, that the 'moi' of the Cornelian hero stands out and is so sharply framed.

The relation between text and context, between the world in which Cornelian dramaturgy emerges and the subject of that dramaturgy, engages us in a dizzying play of mirrors. We can best approach the analysis of this relation by considering the dialectical nature of the rapport that unites the theater (as both text and production) to its audience. A successful dramatic text always responds in some mysterious fashion to its public's expectation. It is always the fulfilment of the audience's desire, even if that desire remains unknown to the audience, even if the audience would be incapable of articulating it.[3]

It is precisely to this ambivalent locus – the theatrical experience as the space of a reciprocal desire – that we must look to pinpoint accurately the mutual imbrication of history, ideology and representation that is at work in the Cornelian world.[4] We must dwell in this space in order to understand the 'archeology' of this desire as it articulates both seventeenth-century history and politics and by so doing establishes the link between its own time and ours. The first question we must ask ourselves, therefore, as we enter into our discussion of the Cornelian world, is: what is this desire that we can perceive only in its fulfilment, only, that is, in the plays? – and, then: why and in what way(s) does this response give us pleasure?

Surely the coincidence of the rise of the Absolutist Monarchy with the representation of Cornelian subjectivity has not gone unnoticed. Critics as diverse as P. Bénichou, B. Dort, S. Doubrovsky and R. J. Nelson have attempted to draw parallels between the birth of the Cornelian hero and the emergence of a centralized State.[5] It is not my intention here to go over that well-mapped terrain. I would only like to identify a few 'markers' in this terrain that prove to be particularly relevant to the following discussion.

The move to Absolutism traces a shift from fragmentation to integrity. For the first quarter of the seventeenth century France still reeled from the turmoil of the preceding fifty years. The Religious Wars had rent the nation not only into two religious camps, but into sundry antagonistic political factions. The shock of these wars and of the havoc created by them produced a sense of discontinuity and disintegration whose resonance echoes in the major writers of the later sixteenth century: Ronsard, Montaigne, d'Aubigné. All of them give voice to the fear that France no longer existed.

Introduction

Perhaps the rhetorical exercise that most effectively expresses these fears is the metaphor of France as a fragmented body, more specifically the fragmented body of the Mother:

> O France désolée! ô terre sanguinaire,
> Non pas terre, mais cendre! ô mère, si c'est mère
> Que trahir ses enfans aux douceurs de son sein
> Et quand on les meurtrit les serrer de sa main?
> Tu leur donnes la vie, et dessous ta mammelle
> S'esmeut des obstinez la sanglante querelle;
> Sur ton pis blanchissant ta race se débat,
> Là le fruit de ton flanc faict le champ du combat.
>
> (D'Aubigné, *Misères*, vv. 89–96)[6]

This image is powerful even as it is banal. Primarily we are given an image of excess and of decomposition. Transforming France into the Mother, these writers transform the Mother into a wasteland. Exposing the naked body of the Mother to the reader's gaze transgresses the same taboo, participates in the same destruction that puts an end to France. Our transgression not only destroys the image of the 'nation', but, by so doing, also successfully eradicates a millenary association that linked the concept of the State to the body of the Sovereign and to that Sovereign's special relation to God.[7] The images of late sixteenth-century literature break any possible link between the 'Sovereign body' and a corporate State. The apparent undermining of this dream has consequences that are far more revealing than a glance at a rhetorical exercise would seem at first to indicate. Beyond the rhetoric is an entire history, an ideological history, where the religious, judicial and social networks of the nation are interwoven in the 'image' of the integral body of the monarchy. We have learned from the classic demonstration of Kantorowicz that the elaboration of this image throughout the Middle Ages was essential for grounding the monarchy in Christianity, for, that is, establishing through the Christic parallels the link between God the Father and his representative on earth, the 'most Christian King', who ruled by divine right. At the beginning of the seventeenth century, however, the dream of a unifying, protective and available presence underlying all social organization – familial, political, religious – seems to exist, if at all, as a negative, unattainable fantàsy.

By insisting, however, on the decomposition of the maternal body, the writers of the sixteenth century reveal both their own investments in the dream of a patriarchal monarchy and their desire to save it, to save the corpus of the State from its own destruction.

3

When they reverse the image of France into the destroyed and self-destructive 'terre mère' the possibility of any subjective grounding, rather than being entirely swept away, is displaced, transformed into isolated, suffering fragments. The nation has become a wound that demands to be healed, to be made entire again, to be subjugated to the order of an Integrity that escapes it.[8]

At the beginning of the reign of Louis XIII, although the wars were long over, their echoes still resonated throughout French society. This society was a stranger to itself, neither completely foreign (to what it had been before the wars) nor entirely familiar. Imperceptibly it had been altered.[9] It is in the instability of this context that the appeal of and to Absolutism takes root. We are aware of the long road that leads from Thomas Hobbes and Jean Bodin to Richelieu. This road is not straight, nor can it be said to begin arbitrarily with these two theoreticians of the early sixteenth century. Machiavelli stands behind them, and behind him an entire network of political and theological speculation that, from the Middle Ages, prepared the way for the renewed metamorphosis of the monarchy in the resplendence of Louis XIV.[10]

Nevertheless, we can state fairly accurately that it was during the 1620s and 1630s that the last stones of the Absolutist edifice were added by Richelieu.[11] These stones supported the scaffold upon which the bodies of the King's subjects were sundered so that the integral Body of the State could be reconstructed. Richelieu's achievement, the new Absolute State, is bolstered, primarily, by the spectacular manipulation of fear, a fear of the implacable Law that can be visited on any subject. It is our own vulnerability, our own death/dispersion, that is directly related to the maintenance and worship of the intact body of the monarch, become an absolute Integrity:

> The absolutist theory depicted a regime organized by perfect unitary sovereignty. This tradition stressed the central role of the monarch himself as the ordering principle of all social life, the ultimate source of authority and energy within the state . . . Absolutism required on the one hand an intense personalization of Kingly power, an incarnation of pure authority in a single human individual to be adored and obeyed, and on the other abstraction from any human qualities in the tangible symbol of the state, pure authority and public purpose organized without human frailty.
>
> (Keohane, *Philosophy and the State*, p. 17)

There can be no doubt that this King–Father, who joined the political to the religious, and from whose own mystical union with God flowed the unity of France, was the object of desire, the

revered and feared object of desire of the majority of the French people.[12] They looked to the king to reconstitute the unity that eluded and taunted them.

Absolutism then may be seen as desire, and desire as a metaphor that hides and reveals a totality that shines in the person of the king, his own physical body. It shines so brightly that it blinds those who behold it. This apogee of desire, the deification of the king, a king who is both a body, a physical presence in the world, and yet not of the world, becomes in Classical ideology a metaphysical imperative. This body lost in its own radiance finds its most adequate metaphor of itself, the representation of a representation, in that other image of self-contained, self-absorbed brilliance, the sun,

the noblest of all . . . which by virtue of its uniqueness, by the brilliance that surrounds it, by the light it imparts to other heavenly bodies that seem to pay it court, and by equal and just distribution of this same light to all the various parts of the world, by the good that it does everywhere, constantly producing life, joy and activity everywhere, by its perpetual yet always imperceptible movement, by never departing or deviating from its steady and invariable course assuredly makes a most vivid and a most beautiful image for a great monarch.

(Louis XIV, *Mémoires*, pp. 103–4, quoted in Keohane, p. 251)

The desire that underlies Absolutism is a drive toward integrity, toward the figure of the One, the center, self-contained and self-generating. It is the plenitude that nourishes, engenders all life, all movement. It begets all order, all hierarchy and in that begetting is a source of joy, of pleasure: the King as Sun, and the Sun as Father.[13] In this new paternity the rent body of the Mother is not only sutured, but Integrity renders maternity redundant. The body of the Mother is obfuscated by the brilliance of the King, and France, 'une mère affligée', becomes the 'Fatherland' ('la patrie').

Absolute Monarchy, then, would be impossible without a metaphoric substructure of Patriarchy, without the structuring of familial organization around the center/Sun of the Father. Politics becomes a family affair where the State doubles the family, where each is inseparable from the mirror image of the other. In the confines of this double enclosure the King is first and foremost 'le père du peuple'.

The unity of the Father is the unity of exclusion. All that contravenes, or is opposed to, its mimesis is exiled to the frontiers of representation, to its outside. An obsessive drive against dispersion, a constant dread that chaos–disruption is always ready to

break loose in the world, a horror of the loss of control, is the constant negative other of Paternal order. Integrity is achieved only with the greatest vigilance, the greatest sacrifice. This sacrifice is part of the desire, part of the pleasure of the ambivalent dialectics between Law and chaos, between mastery and submission, between suffering and rapture, that is at work in the esthetics of tragedy. The juncture of these apparent antitheses, the focal point of the tragic, is also a vanishing point. The moment of tragic bliss is always a point of no return, is always a repetition, a re-turn of something always other and yet the same, of some other pleasure, on some other scene.

Despite their regal trappings, Corneille's great plays circumscribe a tragic locus which repeats familial enclosure. Cornelian tragedy, like Greek tragedy, finds its most fertile ground, its real inspiration, in the mise-en-scène of familial binding. In Corneille's theater, however, it is impossible to separate the family from the State. Corneille's tragic universe is inherently a political world where the family is constantly called upon to mirror the State.[14] In this theater which ignores the separation of the world into private and public spheres all existence is invariably political.

We might pause here to reflect that if in Corneille all existence is political, this statement can be turned around to argue that this political existence insofar as it engages the very heart of the family's constitution − marriage − is in one very important sense sexual. The joining of the subject to the family and the family's continuity through the subject in marriage occupy the epicenter of all dramatic tension in Corneille. 'Cet hyménée . . . importe', the admonition of the Infanta in the *Cid*, echoes throughout the great tragedies as a hollow plea. In all of these plays the marriage that motivates the tragic dilemma is either deferred, left in suspense (*Le Cid, Horace, Cinna*), or occurs before representation, informs the other scene of tragedy, as its past, its other (*Polyeucte*). It is this union, this bringing together of two 'natural' partners to form a new harmonious symmetry, that is finally left hanging.

When the dramatic locus is the most narrow, when desire and obstacle, transgression and punishment can all be located within the narrow confines of 'la proximité du sang', in the binding and undoing of those most sacred ties, ties of love and of family, tragic pleasure/pain reaches its most exquisite proportions. At the same time it is these ties that, although capable of being rent, can never be abandoned, that provide us with our first insight into the particular pleasure of Cornelian theater and the involvement of this pleasure in Absolutism.

Introduction

The theater as spectacle constitutes a privileged locus in which diverse strategies of power and pleasure are essayed and affirmed. These strategies elaborate the parameters inside which the experience of the world, an experience that is always an experience of representation, makes possible the elaboration of subjectivity. It is this subjectivity in turn that reflects in its pleasure the power structures of representation that corroborate its own mode of self-apprehension. More so than any other form of art the theater, the theatrical space, is most obviously dialectical in the ambivalent structuring of the dichotomy separating spectacle and spectator. Despite the ever-present ramp (real or imaginary) that divides stage from audience, actor from spectator, the space of illusion from the reality of the parterre, the theater's essential mystery both recognizes and denies these separations.[15] Audience and actors are embraced within the theatrical space: each is potentially capable of assuming the role of the other. Although the classic dictum 'all the world's a stage' became a cultural topos at the end of the sixteenth and at the beginning of the seventeenth centuries, its acuity was not dampened. In a world given to the spectacular imbrication of symbols of power with the subjects of that power, Corneille's epoch certainly viewed the world as a stage. It also knew that the stage reflected a perfectly coherent world. Actors and spectators held up mirrors to each other. Caught in a mise-en-abîme of representation, the theater in its illusoriness inscribes the spectators within its own frame of reference, within its own desires, and pleasures them.

In order to approach an elucidation of the pleasure shared in the Cornelian universe we will always have to repeat the double gesture of theatricality: we must confront an analysis of the internal dynamics of the tragic plot (the essential dilemma of the Cornelian family/State) with what in that plot reflects the desires of its audience – of those spectators who are silently, but not passively, participants in its representation.

The interreaction of actor and spectator, the confusion of illusion and reality, and their reversal are the most (politically) dangerous aspects of theatrical pleasure, containing the greatest potential for political unrest.[16] If the theater produced an uncontaminated pleasure, a release of unfettered desire, it would probably not be so privileged an art. In a recent book, M. H. Huet has analyzed the role of the theater during the French Revolution and its manipulation by the different governing coalitions. She concludes that

The Revolution's constant concern with making the people into a public did not necessarily correspond to any form of political liberalism; . . . it

7

was inscribed in a tradition that consists in repressing by means of spectacle. To make a spectator of the people, while making sure that the possibility of a spectator–actor reversibility remains carefully controlled, is to maintain an alienation that is the real form of power.

(*Rehearsing the Revolution*, p. 35)

Curiously, the leaders of the Revolution which deposed the monarchy by the highly ritualized sundering of the King's body (the beheading of the 'père de peuple') resorted to the same type of pleasure to control its citizens as did that same monarchy at its beginnings. In order to see beyond what appears to be an historical and esthetic contradiction, in order to speculate on the continual appeal of the theater across the centuries, and across societal upheavals, I suggest we turn to a discourse that is rooted both in familial trauma and in that trauma's representation as tragedy. Perhaps more than any other theory that one could invoke to elucidate literary texts, psychoanalysis is most at home in the theater. Surely, a discipline that enjoys so intimate a relation with *Oedipus* and *Hamlet*, that has so laboriously and minutely constructed a theory of subjectivity as dependent on a never-resolved desire for and struggle against the Father and his Law, can afford us a privileged approach to the theater in general, and to Cornelian tragedy in particular. Rather than appear as a discipline foreign to Corneille's great creations, psychoanalytic discourse might be regarded as continuing, in another register, the dialogue with this enigmatic Other, God–Sovereign, who continues to inhabit our dreams and desires as well as those of Corneille and his contemporaries. The Emperor changes clothes, speaks another language, and remains as attractive and powerful as ever.

The work of Freud and his followers suggests that the theatrical scene functions very much like the dream scene.[17] Like a dream, the play articulates, in the individual and collective unconscious of the spectators, the dialectic of Law and desire. The particular imbrication of politics and desire in Corneille's theater involves the spectator in a plot that also functions as a fantasy of sacrifice and death. Through the illusion of representation pleasure is produced in the spectator as he is implicated in the epiphany of tragedy. Like dreams, the theater functions as both the projection and the satisfaction of desire. Play-acting, like dreaming, figures the dangerous intrusion of the passions into the universe of the Law. It also, however, figures the reappropriation of these passions by the Law. The theater as immolation allows us to participate in the ambiguous pleasure of affirming the obstacles of desire while

transgressing them.[18] In this way, Anne Ubersfeld suggests, the stage allows the transgression of the ideology it represents and also the concomitant recuperation of that ideology's strictures:

Le théâtre a le statut du rêve: une construction imaginaire dont le spectateur sait qu'elle est radicalement séparée de la sphère de l'existence quotidienne . . . [Le spectateur] . . . peut se permettre de voir fonctionner les lois qui le régissent sans y être soumis, puisqu'elles sont expressément visées dans leur réalité contraignante.[19]

The enigma of theatrical pleasure resides in its ambivalence; it is both liberating and confining.[20] This paradox has tantalized philosophers and aestheticians from antiquity to the present. Since Aristotle's sybilline pronouncements on 'catharsis' this enigma has essentially been reduced to determining how the suffering of the hero produces pleasure in the spectator. In his brief paper 'Psychopathic Characters on the Stage', Freud proposed a solution to this enigma by speculating that the pleasure of the spectator in seeing the hero, who 'first and foremost rebels against God or against something divine', is essentially masochistic: 'pleasure', he wrote, 'is derived, as it seems, from the affliction of a weaker being in the face of divine might, a pleasure due to masochistic satisfaction' (*Standard Edition*, VII, p. 306). For Freud, the pleasure of the spectator would be intimately linked to a masochistic terror, a terror that in itself is inseparable from a sadistic turn: spectator and actor revolve in a spectacle of execution where each is victim, each tormentor.[21]

Freud's speculations on the actor–spectator relationship which he couches in the vocabulary of sexuality point to and reinforce our initial assumption that the theater represents the locus of an exercise of sovereignty. This conjunction of heterogeneous discourses becomes even more revealing when we realize that Corneille himself in his theoretical writings seems to corroborate the perspicacity of Freud's intuition. Corneille did not have to wait for the twentieth century to know that the intensity of tragic pleasure increases in direct proportion to the symmetrical intimacy binding victim and torturer: 'C'est donc un grand avantage, pour exciter la commisération, que la proximité du sang et les liaisons d'amour ou d'amitié entre le persécutant et le persécuté, le poursuivant et le poursuivi, celui qui fait souffrir et celui qui souffre' (*Discours de l'utilité et des partis du poème dramatique*, p. 42).

In general, when we consider Classical structures as they were elaborated during the reigns of Louis XIII and Louis XIV, and

Cornelian theater in particular, we realize that it is this drive to symmetry, a symmetry that is always a mystification, that underpins their elaboration. Symmetry, sexual and esthetic, becomes the invisible scaffold upon which Classicism is erected.[22] In its perfection, this most invested of esthetic criteria camouflages a violence that is at its center. The symmetry of Classicism functions to obfuscate an original dissymmetry that is the mainspring of all Absolutist political theory. This dissymmetry can be made apparent only in moments of tragic epiphany or in the moment of execution. On a first level, at least, the 're-connaissance' of Classical symmetry is always a 'méconnaissance': it disguises the ponderous and total difference that separates the Sovereign from his subject(s). The harmony of form hides the violence of ideology.[23]

This violence is re-structured in the Cornelian universe, where the world is presented as divided into a symmetrical, if unequal, sexual division. Serge Doubrovsky has commented on the separation of the Cornelian world into male and female camps, camps which are, according to him, clearly opposed in their 'essence'.[24] It has been argued by recent feminist critics that the equation of a biological separation of the sexes to an essential distinction of masculinity and femininity is a 'metaphysical illusion'.[25] This illusion is made possible by the repression of an ambiguous locus of sexual 'indifference', of a bisexuality in which both sexes participate, which marks them both, but which, it seems, males in a patriarchal culture repress more thoroughly.[26]

Feminist theorists, particularly those who speak from within the institution of psychoanalysis, add yet another twist, a powerfully de-centering twist, to the role and importance of the metaphor of the Father in western representation. It is, they speculate, only from the male perspective of repression that an 'essence' of virility and its obverse, femininity, can be enunciated.[27] This proves to be a compelling argument in attempting to analyze Corneille's tragic universe, for in the patriarchal order that defines the world of Cornelian drama, the power of this repression acquires the force of Law. It informs the possibilities and limits of human freedom according to an implied sexual difference. The way this difference struggles with its own uncomfortable relation to the Law structures the tragic potential of the great plays.

In a patriarchal culture such as we see elaborated in Corneille the masculine is the standard for all conduct in social interreaction. Femininity is never articulated in any way which is not already inextricably bound to the politics of virility. It is always seen as masculin-

ity's 'less', its negative other. Freud, perhaps the most famous in a long line of commentators, remarked that because femininity was always dependent for its definition on its relation to masculinity, it was not, per se, definable. Nevertheless, in his essay 'Femininity' (*Standard Edition*, XXII) and in other, particularly later, writings he attempted such a definition. Recently these works of Freud's have been the subject of cogent analyses by both L. Irigaray (*Speculum de l'autre femme*) and S. Kofman (*Freud et l'énigme de la femme*). Glossing Freud's essay, Irigaray suggests that any definition of the 'feminine' must necessarily be based on an 'essential' splitting of the world into two symmetrical halves. Her commentary on Freud's writings would seem to reveal in him the same underlying structures that Doubrovsky's reading of Corneille has also uncovered. She continues to argue that this splitting, a mirroring, is always done from the privileged male perspective. In this perspective a simple idea of symmetry, as a self-apparent, 'natural' and, therefore, neutral phenomenon, is shown to be heavily invested with sexual bias. Symmetry is studied as the creation of mutually reflected opposition: the other one sees is the self one projects:

Le désir du même, de l'identique à soi, de soi (comme) même et encore du semblable, de l'alter ego et pour tout dire de l'auto . . . et de l'homo . . . de l'homme domine l'économie de la représentation. La 'différence' sexuelle est tributaire d'une problématique du même, elle est encore et toujours déterminée à l'intérieur du projet, de la projection, de la sphère de la représentation du même. La différentiation en deux sexes part de l'à priori du même.[28]

In the universe of the 'hommological' that this representation of sexual difference elaborates, a universe where all difference and therefore desire is reduced to a reproduction of the same, the only real 'difference' allowed the feminine, the only Other that becomes its particularizing mark, is its situation as 'outside'. This Other, Irigaray suggests, is outside speech, outside desire, and finally outside representation. Effectively this 'outside' equates femininity with Death:

Dans ce désir proliférant du même la mort sera le seul représentant d'un dehors, d'un hétérogène, d'un autre. La femme assumera la fonction de la mort (du sexe) du châtrage, dont l'homme s'assurera ainsi autant que faire se peut la maîtrise, l'assujetissement.[29]

The hypothesis with the interesting parallels it suggests between Corneille and Freud allows us, on the one hand, to view Cornelian tragedy as a particular form of patriarchal representation rooted in seventeenth-century Absolutism and, on the other, to see its

rapport with a more general tendency in the western representation of human sexuality that it joins and enriches. These parallels allow us to suggest that in any discussion of the 'essential' opposition of the characters in Corneille, when we speak about the women as females in representation we immediately forget that what we are discussing is a masculine projection of likeness on them. It is their masculinity rather than their femininity (which remains outside representation) that we are accepting as a 'given'. Secondly this implies that as textual icons the women in Corneille are always in a position of both less and more — less than a man and more as an undefinable excess.[30] Finally, for the male characters, those characters who are defined as whole (One), we must not forget that their integrity is won at the price of a sacrifice, of a sacrifice of a primary 'indifference' that is too threatening to survive social restraints.[31] Nonetheless this 'indifference' continues to exist, even as it is repressed, also beyond representation, joining them to the women in an indifferent, unrepresentable space of excess, the tragic locus of Death.

The violence that is repressed in Classicism's illusions of symmetry returns at the center of the tragic dilemma in Corneille's great plays. It is here in this representation, a representation that traces the parameters inside which subjects, as political and sexed beings, are linked to the totalizing gaze of Law, that we can begin to understand the hold that this theater has on us, begin to understand the 'plaisir à Corneille'. This pleasure powerfully affects us because, in essence, what is played out in Corneille's Classical universe is the family romance of the emerging bourgeois subject. André Green has described all tragedy as 'la représentation du mythe fantasmatique du complexe d'Oedipe que Freud désignera comme complexe constitutif du sujet'.[32] While I do not wish, here, to argue for the universality of the Oedipal schema, as Green does, I do wish to situate this schema in a very definite social/esthetic context, a context that appears clearly during the first third of the seventeenth century and makes its way to us.[33] Corneille's tragic universe has its origins in the France that sees the development of what can be considered the first (modern) totalitarian State; the idea of national power and glory is structured around an official idolatry of the Monarch/Sun. At the same time the universe Corneille creates in his tragedies reflects and elaborates, consciously and unconsciously, on the rewards and difficulties of institutionalized Patriarchy. It might even be said, as we shall see, that it is this reflection that is at the heart of the tragic scenarios. It is

in the mutual imbrication of text and context, in their overlap, that the image of the modern 'self' emerges.[34] I do not, therefore, feel that we are being reductive if we read the origins of this emergence through an analysis of its end, if we read Corneille with Freud or Freud with a feminist critique: Corneille's tragedies inform the narrative of familial closure inside which the Classical 'subject' evolves from Classicism to Freud and from Freud to us.

It is only when we see through the trappings of plot that always situate Cornelian drama in far-removed cultures and historical moments to the underpinnings of its archeological structures that we can attempt to analyze its hold on us. When we realize that the repetitions at the center of Cornelian tragedy are the same repetitions in which we are involved the cultural and historical gaps can be bridged. We can begin to understand our involvement in the scenarios of power and pleasure that this 'foreign' universe stages for us.

I have speculated that the theater functions like a dream. When at the center of that dream we place a family romance, we can see how Cornelian theater exerts a powerful pull on the audience. Our very position as spectator is in itself a condensation of numerous forces that for the moment of the tragedy come together informing the 'spectating subject', who paradoxically is never an individual but, as S. Heath puts it, is a 'multiple instance': 'The spectator . . . is distinct from, is not equivalent to, the spectating individual, the individual in the act of spectatorship, who may come into its invited place. It should be stressed, moreover, that the spectator . . . is a multiple rather than a single instance.'[35] This suggests that in the theatrical space a spectator is freed of the quotidian defenses against experience that structure him or her as an individual subject, a particularly sexed − as male or female − subject. For the brief time of illusion, involved as we are in the fantasmatic family romance, we are transported back to a fragmented time, a time before the imposition of a particular type of sexual Law. We are all participants in a tragic scene, where, 'freed' from our repressions, we can identify with characters of both sexes and of all ages. In the dream-like fascination of theatrical denegation the spectator pleasures in his identifications with the actors and with his fellow spectators. This pleasure of being omnisexual is, however, irreconcilably connected with the pleasure of being fragmented, of being unsexed. It is too dangerous a position to prevail and too politically menacing not to be recuperated by other, more powerful structures that reinscribe this pleasure in its own sacrifice.

Corneille, Classicism and the ruses of symmetry

Classical theater releases enormous amounts of repressed energy but also, and here is perhaps a clue to its great genius, by its conventions and by its institutional role, recuperates them, makes them safe for the individual and for society. The theater functioning inside the parameters of ideology sutures sexuality and politics in representation. Despite the liberating aspects of one level of this representation, it cannot help but re-enforce its own parameters. In a certain sense what this suggests is that theatrical illusion is also always a disillusion, that there is really no illusion at all.[36]

It strikes me that here, particularly, is a clue to the pleasure we find in Corneille, a pleasure that is essentially re-assuring to a subject formed within the limits of family. It will perhaps come as no surprise that within those limits the repression so necessary for the subject to exist is re-iterated in the plays themselves. The pleasure that is ours in these plays is perhaps related to a certain narcissism which constantly reflects the mirror of our own investments in a never-ending repetition. This repetition indicates to us that it is only through this pleasure that a certain masochistic desire for repression can be both admitted and denied.

It will be the task of the following chapters to pursue and uncover the different aspects repression as a consequence of and desire for Absolutism takes in Corneille. The essays that comprise the body of this study attempt, each in its own way, to explicate the mirror that the Cornelian universe holds up to us where sexuality as ideology is inextricably intermingled in its own tragic representation. What is at stake in this study is not so much Corneille as a curious mime of his time, but rather Corneille as the creator of brilliant icons that take their places at the focal point of our dramatic imagination. It is for this reason that I have decided to go against a trend in recent Cornelian criticism. I am not, here, interested in tracing the entire Cornelian oeuvre that spans more than half a century of writing for the French stage. I have made a deliberate choice to structure my reading around the four 'great' tragedies. It is these plays, that, for reasons that I hope will become apparent, continue to dialogue with us, continue to move us as theater, continue to be staged and admired as reflections of ourselves, of our culture. I have, nevertheless, placed these works within a tragic 'context'. They are introduced by a schematic explanation of *Médée*, Corneille's first tragedy, and followed by a concluding essay on *Nicomède*, *Rodogune* and *Suréna*. The tragic world of the central chapters represents, not unambiguously, the interrelation of sexual and political roles in the patriarchal family/

State. It is only when we see the workings of this Absolute quest for totality that we can also try to demonstrate what is at stake in the pleasure we take in these tragedies. The violence that is inherent in them is the same violence at the origin of modern Law and thus of the modern subject. It was Corneille who first elaborated this violence with such seductive elegance as to command our pleasure and our obedience. The great tragedies serve as a troubling reflection of our continued investments in systems of repression that we, perhaps as much as the Frenchmen of 1640, both desire and fear.

1
MYTHIFYING MATRIX: CORNEILLE'S *MÉDÉE* AND THE BIRTH OF TRAGEDY

'. . . que peut faire une femme?'

Corneille enters the tragic universe through the door of myth. By choosing to stage, as his first tragedy, Medea's infanticide, Corneille both affirms a belief in (literary) genealogy, of his own place in progression (Euripides, Seneca, Corneille), and plunges back into a universe that pre-exists history. C. Lévi-Strauss has taught us that one of the essential attributes of myth is its 'eternal' quality, a quality which negates 'time' and ignores 'progress':

> Un mythe se rapporte toujours à des événements passés: 'avant la création du monde', ou pendant les premiers âges, en tout cas, 'il y a longtemps'. Mais la valeur intrinsèque attribuée au mythe provient de ce que les événements censés se dérouler à un moment du temps forment aussi une structure permanente. Celle-ci se rapporte au passé, au présent, au futur.
> ('Structure du mythe', p. 231)[1]

Situated at an eternal moment of conflict before the imposition of the Law, before the radical separation of the universe into the domains of nature and culture, and co-terminous with the scission of the sexes, myth traces the shifting parameters of these undefined borders. At its most extreme the mythic universe defies all order and seeks refuge in the illogical mode of the magical and the sacred.[2] It is a world whose outlines come into focus in brief flashes of narration only to be engulfed, once again, in the vast expanses of the unrepresentable.

Perhaps the fascination for myth, especially in those cultures that have already passed into 'history', passed beyond, that is, that horrifying moment which marks the instauration of the Law, is precisely the power that the myth retains to transcend those barriers that enclose culture. The projection of myth as spectacle (tragedy) fascinates because it plays out for us, over and over again, excessive desires that culture has only, with great effort, contained. These desires remain, however, vital and aggressive in the unconscious −

16

both in the collective unconscious of the audience and, to a different degree, in the individual psyche of each spectator who participates in this mythic 'speculation'.[3]

For a limited time this 'speculation' allows those desires and fears that have been harnassed by culture to resurface within the minds and bodies of the spectators, to stand as their mirror, their Other − the negative determinant − the unrepresentable force that informs, in its negation, their being in the world:

Par le dédoublement de la représentation: représentation le mythe, représentation de la représentation: la tragédie, par cette incarnation qui donne à la fable une seconde vie (comme le rêve rend la vie aux pensées qu'il met en scène), le mythe qui était dans l'épos un discours proposé à la représentation se mue dans la tragédie en discours imposé par la représentation. Il devient discours de l'Autre.[4]

The staging of desire is the articulation of the silent discourse of the Other. As spectacle, however, myth must function within the parameters of paradox: it supposes the established presence of the interdiction that founds desire − the interdiction of incest − and must project itself as 'mimesis' of a moment before this interdiction. Perhaps for this reason it finds its most fertile ground in the mise-en-scène of familial binding. The origins of family, its constitution and disintegration as recounted in myth, provide the most compelling of tragic scenarios because it is here, in this vortex of conflictual passions, that the desiring subject is most radically affected in those sexual, political and economic structures in which s/he is most invested. It is here that the subject becomes the object of the most violent threat to his own dispersion:

La famille est (donc) l'espace tragique par excellence. Sans doute parce que les noeuds d'amour, donc de haine, sont en elle les tous premiers en date et en importance. . . . L'espace tragique est l'espace du dévoilement et de la révélation sur les relations originaires de la parenté.[5]

These 'original' relations are never simple. They force the spectator out of time, and make him stand in his own pre-history, at a moment before repression, before s/he entered into a state of 'difference', of sexual difference, within the sphere of signification. On one essential level myth is always the attempt to explain (sacrifice) an initial indeterminacy, an inherent (poly-)sexuality, of the constitution of the subject as a sexed, that is a masculine or feminine, being, and to explain why this difference is essential to cultural order. The evolution from indifference to difference is a violent one, implying a threat of death, of mutilation and of chaos,

where the subject constantly is being dispersed along the axes of its own fragmentation. It is for this reason that 'myth' stages, in its narration, the conflict between the most elementary of oppositions (male–female) and their own mediation in enunciation. In this scenario the sexual opposition metaphorizes a more essential metaphysical coupling, the opposition between materiality and ideality.[6] These metaphorized conflicts are constant and, ultimately, remain unresolvable, but it is the myth's function to offer itself as their possible mediation.

This mediation is progressive. It is never terminable, never complete, yet it mirrors and repeats the socializing role of the family. As a unit the family mediates the demands of society and individuality. It becomes the model of all cultural investments that conflict with individual libidinal investments. For this reason the family as myth and the myth of family enter the space of representation as the 'already there' of the tragic, the 'already there' of the violence of sexual desire and the passion of this desire pushed to its limits, to the destruction of those limits, to the end of the 'self'.

Violence, of course, is at the very heart of *Médée*. In choosing to center his first tragedy around the fury of betrayed love, Corneille reveals a penchant for a particular type of the tragic he will later, in his 'great' plays, eschew. In the *Discours*, written almost thirty years after *Médée*, Corneille specifically states that politics, not love, must be the motivating force of tragedy. Tragedy's true nature demands a plot in which major questions of State – the end of a dynasty, the death of a great king, the destruction of an empire – are hanging in the balance. Love can only be allowed into the tragic universe as incidental to these events. It must take an ancillary role and leave the main spotlight to political concerns.[7]

Quite clearly *Médée* does not do this. Although we are aware of a political undercurrent in its plot, an undercurrent to which I will return, the crux of this tragedy is sexual desire, jealousy and revenge. It is a tragedy of excess, a play of unbridled emotions. It is probably not for nothing that in this, his first tragedy, Corneille chooses as his subject the passions, fears and murderous powers of a woman scorned. This first venture into the tragic universe presents us with an 'original' drama, a prototypical 'family romance' in which the conflicting tensions are so great, the resolution so utterly traumatic to the political universe, that its violence will cast a long shadow over the tragedies to come.

As the author most associated with the elaboration of the Classical edifice, an edifice which reflects while representing the

Law, Corneille poses as the first stone of this edifice a tragedy that refuses this Law. By placing at the entrance of his own tragic universe a work, a myth, that portrays the reign and victory of excess, Corneille institutes that excess as the desire/fear his great tragedies must mask. It is with the troubling conundrum of *Médée* that the subsequent tragedies must struggle as they elaborate the strictures of symmetry and order that are attained only through repression — the repressions of *Médée*, of Medea.

It would betray the essential paradox of myth if we were to look only at the *story* of Jason and Medea, to look at Jason and Medea as simple allegorical incarnations of the struggle between nature and culture along the lines of sexual division. These characters are situated at an ambiguous moment that predates the imposition of sexual difference. The mythic time exists before the imposition of the Law of sexual distinction, and also it is co-terminous with this imposition.[8] What this implies is that the myth on one level affirms 'sexual indifference', affirms an inchoate world of desire, a state of (bi-)sexuality, that has not as yet been channelled into a masculine/feminine split. At the same time, it also denies this ambivalence: characters are represented as already 'recognizable' sexed human beings structuring the world as a symmetrical, sexual division. This is the logical aporia where myth (as narration) leads us. We are compelled, in a fetishizing gesture, both to deny and to affirm sexual differences, both to affirm and to deny any initial moment of poly-sexuality and its immediate sundering into the sexual (that is, cultural) roles, in order to make some order.[9] What this means for our understanding of the myth–tragedy of Medea and Jason is that we must always bear in mind that Medea and Jason do represent 'Mother' and 'Father', that they are female and male in the universe that the myth delineates, but also that this dichotomy is set into larger opposing camps, into the camps of nature and of culture. In these camps the natural is associated with a 'feminine' essence, whose history in metaphysics is identified with 'matter', and in which 'culture' is associated with the masculine, a concept, in turn, essentialized as 'form' or 'ideal'. The conflict in *Médée* is posed as the struggle between matter and form, between materiality and ideality.[10]

The universe of *Médée* in which this struggle takes place is structured by a legal code which is a guarantor of Patriarchy. It is a code that vouchsafes a system of exchange — the devolution of property/power — among males, and guarantees genealogy as a 'metaphoric' investment that both affirms and denies death (castra-

tion) as the basis of Law. In order for this denial to be constantly veiled, in order in other words for its 'mauvaise foi' never to be brought to consciousness, males invest their libido in an economy of reproduction, a reproduction of a constant chain of new males that guarantees their primacy. It is this obsessive desire for reproduction, or the re-presentation of their own image, that haunts both Créon and Jason, those representatives of legality in *Médée*. It enables them self-assuredly to appropriate their descendance to themselves in order to guarantee their continuity. Genealogy – the transference of power – can be read as an essential step in the formulation of culture because it assures the predominance of metaphor (masculine idealization) over the dispersion of metonymy (female materiality) in the reduplication, through the male child, of the 'Same'.[11] It is in order to assure his reduplication, and thus his 'immortality', that Créon (without male descent) desires and agrees to the divorce of Jason and Médée. He wants Jason to marry his own daughter and assure him a progeny to whom, as he says, he can

> laisser ma couronne à mon unique race,
> Et cet espoir si doux, qui m'a toujours flatté,
> De revivre à jamais en sa postérité.   (v, iv, 1406–8)[12]

Créon is in a particularly difficult situation for a Greek (and, one assumes, a seventeenth-century French) male. He has no male heir. His only child is a daughter, Créuse. No one assures, therefore, the continuation of Créon. Without male descent Créon himself is a defective, incomplete man. Greek legal codes foresaw such a predicament and rose to the challenge male-less inheritance posed to Greek society: in these aberrant cases Solon's law on the 'epikleroi' allowed the father to substitute a surrogate for himself. This surrogate, marrying the heiress, assures the father's continuity while avoiding the scandal of incest: 'On sait en quoi consiste l'épiclérat: un père privé de descendance mâle peut suppléer à cette carence en devenant nominalement le père de l'enfant que sa fille pourra avoir' (Green, *Un oeil en trop*, pp. 244–5).[13] Créon must have a surrogate, a 'self–son' substitute. In earliest times this task was usually entrusted to the closest male relative of the father (perhaps to the father himself) but in less remote moments this role devolves upon a stranger (Jason): 'Au lieu d'épouser le plus proche parent du père, c'est dans les contes, à un aventurier de naissance royale mais sans patrimoine que la fille s'unit. Celui-ci est le plus souvent banni de son pays en raison d'un meurtre' (Green, p. 245).

Jason, the noble 'outcast', alienated from his own community, arrives at the gates of Corinth 'unattached'. He becomes the perfect surrogate, the conduit that guarantees Créon's survival.

This initial and essential desire for posterity motivates masculine rivalry and competition for power: Créon wants to have his line continued; Jason wants the power of a throne ('Un sceptre est l'objet seul qui fait ton nouveau choix'). It also forms the basis of the legal code that is so vehemently destroyed in *Médée*.

The play opens with a questioning of the investments of this legal code. Médée is presented and presents herself as a victim of injustice. By repudiating her, Jason is breaking a judicial vow:

> Souverains protecteurs des lois de l'hyménée,
> Dieux garants de la foi que Jason m'a donnée,
> Vous qu'il prit à témoins d'une immortelle ardeur
> Quand par un faux serment il vainquit ma pudeur,
> Voyez de quel mépris vous traite son parjure,
> Et m'aidez à venger cette commune injure. (I, iv, 201–6)

Rhetorically Médée's entrance is a plea for justice; she has been wronged and her initial reaction is to pose her demand for reparations in terms of the legal code inside whose parameter she has moved. Médée shows both the confusion and the rage of the woman who has been 'had' by a system based on her alienation and appropriation. Jason's repudiation of her is doubly significant: not only is Médée rejected sexually – Jason prefers another (younger) woman – but Jason's divorce casts Médée out of the 'polis'. She is deprived of her place within the community and becomes, by this ostracism, an outcast. Outside this community her humanity is denied, her demonic 'natural' legacy enhanced; Médée, dehumanized, becomes a monster:

> Où me renvoyez-vous, si vous me bannissez?
> Irai-je sur le Phase, où j'ai trahi mon père,
> Apaiser de mon sang les mânes de mon frère?
> Irai-je en Thessalie, où le meurtre d'un roi
> Pour victime aujourd'hui ne demande que moi?
> Il n'est point de climat dont mon amour fatale
> N'ait acquis à mon nom la haine générale;
> Et ce qu'ont fait pour vous mon savoir et ma main
> M'a fait un ennemi de tout le genre humain. (III, iii, 776–84)

In the system of exchange that the play articulates, Médée, suffering the ingratitude of her husband, also suffers the alienation of

her identity. Having renounced for Jason her father/Law, she becomes a 'nonperson'. Now with neither father nor husband she is condemned to wander family-less in a 'no-man's' land of the unknown.

The conflict in the play, its tragic center, will involve the question of guilt and innocence within this system of exchange. It is a question that necessarily involves the very foundation of culture as it emerges from nature. It also, and co-terminously, involves questions of sexual identity and subjectivity as products of Law rather than as givens in nature. By so doing, it brings into question the metaphysics of sexuality and power that this tragedy-myth articulates.

Médée has been accepted into the 'polis' (culture) upon the sacrifice of her 'nature'. She has abandoned her difference to participate in a system of exchange that assures male prerogative. Médée's position is charged with the ambiguities of a legal code that functions as a sexual investment of power. Her situation is paradoxical because she suffers as a wife–woman in a system which she has accepted to the detriment of her own force. Médée is scorned by a culture that has imposed impotence upon her in return for a certain idealized role − maternity − within community. She has been allowed into the 'polis' only after agreeing to leave her powers at its borders. In exchange she assumes the role of Mother. Médée has been allowed into Corinth on the condition that she be a 'woman' − that is, that she accept the 'lack' masculinity needs in a woman and its supplementation in maternity.[14] In her defense, Médée claims to have been scrupulous in maintaining her role in this exchange. 'Votre simplicité,' she tells Créon, 'n'a point été déçue.'

> Quand votre coeur, sensible à la compassion
> Malgré tous mes forfaits, prit ma protection
> Si l'on me peut depuis imputer quelque crime,
> C'est trop peu de l'exil, ma mort est légitime:
> Si non, à quel propos me traitez-vous ainsi?
> Je suis coupable ailleurs, mais innocente ici. (II, ii, 483–8)

At the play's opening, she is brought face to face with this system's sham, and her own loss. Confronted by Créon, the representative of this Law, Médée reacts by refusing to submit further to it. Reassuming her nature, Médée affirms her power. This affirmation denies the illusion of any original lack, any weakness, and threatens the self-deluding foundation upon which male culture is based.

In order to give the lie to the bonds of a community based on inter-

diction and renouncement Médée reaffirms the role that she has temporarily abandoned at Corinth. In her fury, Médée's rhetoric transforms her into a monster/witch whose unnatural power hauntingly conjures up the frightening image of the 'phallic' woman, the uncastrated 'mother', an object of both fear and desire.[15] Médée represents the fantasy of unbridled, threatening power that recognizes no Law:

> Ce corps n'enferme pas une âme si commune;
> Je n'ai jamais accepté qu'elle me fit la loi,
> Et toujours ma fortune a dépendu de moi.   (III, iii, 882–4)

Médée declares herself to be beyond (or before) the Law. Her anarchical stance is inimical to any ideal of 'community' based on privation. Médée does not, cannot, curb her desire. It is this rampant passion that has led her to overthrow the nascent order of a cultural system by bringing her into constant conflict with its symbolic head. Médée has deposed the Father (both her own, Pélie, and Créon) and is cast in the role of eternal parricide/regicide. She becomes the outside limit of any order of culture. Her passion (her excess) is her crime, and this crime, as Créon tells her, is her ostracism:

> Repasse tes forfaits, repasse tes erreurs,
> Et de tant de pays nomme quelque contrée
> Dont tes méchancetés te permettent l'entrée.
> Toute la Thessalie en armes te poursuit;
> Ton père te déteste et l'univers te fuit.   (II, ii, 388–92)

Médée, object of the Father's opprobrium, is an external exile from the human community. That community cannot exist without the renunciation of individual (feminine) desire and without this renunciation being immediately idealized as Law. This 'legality' becomes a standard of exchange that joins together those who have accepted repression. Community, the myths tell us, is the imposition of form on matter, a political construct which is sexualized or a sexual construct that is immediately politicized by the association, ancient and seemingly universal, of the female to matter and the male to form. It is this double gesture that *Médée* stages and undoes for us.

Médée represses a power greater than any man's. When Jason refuses to flee with her from Corinth, arguing that they could never escape the combined forces of two kings, her response, 'Bornes-tu mon pouvoir à celui des humains?', uncovers his weakness, his

23

lack of faith, and her force. Jason, of course, should know better. He has been the principal beneficiary of Médée's talents. Rather than being controlled by men, Médée holds them in her sway. It is she rather than any of the men in the play who is the epitome of potency, but this potency, so frightening, cannot be 'real' (human). Médée is potent because she is unreal, a sorceress, an 'unnatural' combination of the temptress and the Fury: Corneille has her describe herself as the eternal image of the succubus:

> Moi-même (en les cueillant) je fis pâlir la lune,
> Quand, les cheveux flottants, le bras et le pied nu,
> J'en dépouillai jadis un climat inconnu.   (IV, i, 982–4)

Her floating hair, silhouetted against the pale moon, signals her as a new Medusa. Like Medusa she is a symbol of both life and death, flaccidity and virility. Hers is the power that men fear and desire, the power and call of indeterminacy, of a return to a state of pre-subjectivity, to a state before difference.[16]

It is precisely in her role as an essential ambivalence that Médée both kills and creates, both devours men and empowers them with her own potency. Médée uses her gift of sorcery both to destroy and to occasion culture. She is situated as a primal force − 'nature' − but nature as the symbolic inscription of femininity. Médée is unpredictable, she is pure 'matter', and both desires and repels 'form'.

In the first exchange between Jason and Pollux, Corneille underlines the fact that Médée's fame was initially acquired by her ability to restore potency and reverse the normal decline of the male:

> J. – Mon père, tout caduc, émouvant ma pitié
>   Je conjurai Médée, au nom de l'amitié . . .
> P. – J'ai su comme son art, forçant les destinées
>   Lui rendit la vigueur des ses jeunes années. (I, i, 51–4)

What Médée effects for Jason's father, physically, she effects metaphorically for Aegée. He, too, is an old, declining monarch who is fettered by the real chains of his prison. Though he is powerless and at the door of death, Médée restores his 'courage':

> Ni grilles ni verrous ne tiennent contre moi.
> Cessez, indignes fers, de captiver un roi;
> Est-ce à vous à presser le bras d'un tel monarque?

Et vous, reconnaissez Médée à cette marque,
Et fuyez un tyran dont le forcement
Joindroit votre supplice à mon bannissement;
Avec la liberté reprenez le courage.   (IV, v, 1218–24)

It is not only the old men whom Médée stimulates. The young
heroes, too, the Argonauts, are entirely indebted to her for the successful conclusion of their quest. It was Médée, not any force of
superior skill or cunning of theirs, who was responsible for the rape
of the Golden Fleece:

      seule, j'ai par mes charmes
Mis au joug les taureaux et défait les gensdarmes.
Si lors à mon devoir mon désir limité
Eût conservé ma gloire et me fidélité,
Si j'eusse eu de l'horreur de tant d'énormes fautes,
Que devenoit Jason, et tous vos Argonautes?
Sans moi, ce vaillant chef, que vous m'avez ravi,
Fût péri le premier, et tous l'auroient suivi.
Je ne me repens point d'avoir, par mon adresse
Sauvé le sang des Dieux et la fleur de la Grèce:

        .   .   .

Tous vos héros enfin tiennent de moi la vie.[17]
                 (II, ii, 429–38, 441)

With her superhuman powers Médée is a threat to all systems of
hierarchy devised by culture. She triumphs by reversing, or ignor-
ing, the order the world has defined as 'natural'. As sorceress,
Médée is an 'unnatural' presence − a negative, destructive force.
She restores the father, but she can also eliminate him. She betrays
her own father, and uses her sorcery to reverse the 'natural' order
of filial piety, encouraging the daughters of Pelias to their most
unfilial of tasks:

A force de pitié ces filles inhumaines
De leur père endormi vont épuiser les veines:
Leur tendresse crédule, à grands coups de couteau,
Prodigue ce vieux sang, et fait place au nouveau;
Le coup le plus mortel s'impute à grand service;
On nomme piété ce cruel sacrifice;
Et l'amour paternel qui fait agir leurs bras
Croiroit commettre un crime à n'en commettre pas.
Médée est éloquente à leur donner courage.   (I, i, 81–9)

The concept of 'natural' or 'unnatural' for Médée is of course

spurious. Médée is a metaphor for the primary ingredients of life, the four elements, earth, fire, air and water:

> Sa vengeance à la main, elle n'a qu'à résoudre,
> Un mot du haut des cieux fait descendre la foudre,
> Les mers, pour noyer tout n'attendent que sa loi;
> La terre offre à s'ouvrir sous le palais des Rois;
> L'air tient les vents tous prêts à suivre la colère,
> Toute la nature esclave . . .   (III, i, 701–6)

>   tu vois en moi seule et le fer et la flamme,
> Et la terre et le mer et l'enfer et les cieux.   (I, v, 322–3)

She can either concentrate these elements into a single force, giving life, the creation of an individual (Jason's father), or disperse them into the original chaos of nothing. As such, like Dionysus, she is an ambivalent 'matrix', origin and end of all suffering, all tragedy.[18]

Although she controls the elements, the single element that is most closely associated with her throughout the play, her birthright as granddaughter of the Sun, is fire:

> Mais, pour exécuter tout ce que j'entreprends,
> Quels Dieux me fournissent des services assez grands?
> Ce n'est plus vous, enfers, qu'ici je sollicite;
> Vos feux sont impuissants pour ce que je médite.
> Auteur de ma naissance, aussi bien que du jour,
> Qu'à regret tu dépars à ce fatal séjour,
> Soleil, qui vois l'affront qu'on va faire à ta race,
> Donne-moi tes chevaux à conduire à ta place:
> Accorde cette grâce à mon désir bouillant.
> Je veux choir sur Corinthe avec un char brûlant;
> Mais ne crains pas de cette chute à l'univers funeste;
> Corinthe consumé garantira le reste;
> De mon juste courroux les implacables voeux
> Dans ses odieux murs arrêteront tes feux.
> Créon en est le prince, et prend Jason pour gendre:
> C'est assez mériter d'être réduit en cendre.   (I, v, 255–70)

Her look burns. When Créon gazes into Médée's eyes and sees the fire that is blazing there he must turn away:

> Voyez comme elle s'enfle et d'orgueil et d'audace!
> Ses yeux ne sont que feux, ses regards que menace!
>   (II, ii, 377–8)

She emits an all-consuming fire that embraces both Créon and

Créuse. Both are consumed. In the blaze of Médée's passionate revenge their bodies become their own pyre:

> elle sent aussitôt une ardeur qui la tue:
> Un feu subtil s'allume, et ses brandons épars
> Sur votre don fatal courent de toutes parts;
> Et Jason et le Roi s'y jettent pour l'éteindre;
> Mais (ô nouveau sujet de pleurer et de plaindre!)
> Ce feu saisit le Roi: ce prince en un moment
> Se trouve enveloppé du même embrasement.
>
> (v, i, 1306–12)

We can only explain the hold Jason has on Médée if we do see their burning passion as an essential mediation of forces that pre-exist representation (forces of matter) but that representation (the myth as narration, the narration as a tragedy) presents to us embodied in a 'love' story. Any reader familiar with the literary antecedents of Corneille's *Médée* must be aware that one of the major differences between Corneille and his models is the larger role Corneille attributes to Jason. Compared with his predecessors, Corneille allows Jason to participate more fully in his own downfall.[19] By expanding Jason's role Corneille elaborates a far greater symmetry between his male and female protagonists than had existed in his literary antecedents. This attempt re-structures the myth, and demands our attention because it is here, in the creation of this character, that we see for the first time the desire of a particular period and of a particular author invested in the insistence upon a 'symmetrical' sexual coupling.

It would be difficult to understand the tragic-passionate crux of the myth as Corneille portrays it if we could not look behind what is so obviously the rather one-dimensional character of Jason. On the level of representation (Jason as 'role') the character appears to be essentially a 'matamore', a self-involved, self-obsessed braggart who is, in every way, inferior to his wife. Not only is Jason inferior to her, he is entirely indebted to her. As we have already noted, all of the heroic exploits of Jason and his Argonauts are attributed to Médée. It is she, rather than they, who is the 'hero'. What the play leaves to Jason, therefore, is his braggadocio, his swaggering self-assurance which projects a certain sexual power that is the reflection of a particularly obvious form of narcissism.

In a (strange) reversal of roles Jason's narcissism, as it is here represented by Corneille, corresponds closely to Freud's analysis of the same phenomenon in beautiful women. It is a narcissism that reflects the subject's complete enclosure upon itself. It is this tan-

27

talizing image of a perfect, self-sufficient whole that becomes the universal object of desire. In a sense, therefore, Jason's narcissism is 'feminine' and it is this 'femininity' that makes him attractive to women. There is a strange chassé-croisé here in which the bisexual nature of males and females, a nature that is not admitted into culture, resurfaces in the subtext of representation.[20]

Jason's only force in the play, his only interest, is this narcissism that impels his enormous sexual power. Jason attracts women, attracts Médée, because he, unlike them, represents sexuality as a promise of plenitude: Jason's narcissism functions as the projection of a sexual image, an image which paradoxically is a containment, an imposition of form. It is this closure (a representation of ideality) that the women (unformed matter) desire. Jason's chief claim to fame does not lie in his heroism but in his attraction. From the very beginning of the play, Jason is presented as a priapic force. He, too, like Médée, is a force of nature. Unlike Médée's, however, Jason's sexuality is essentially channeled into a political scheme. It is always a force that inspires desire, but it also sublimates this desire to political ends. Jason always seduces to advance his career in the world. It is through his sexual power that Jason creates an image of hero/master that he projects out into the world and which is affirmed by the desire he inspires in others. Jason's real (and only) heroism is his subjugation of female desire to his desire for power. In the context of *Médée* the representation of Jason situates his sexuality within the realm of a history that figures the progress of Law over nature. Jason is, as the male, both weaker and stronger than the females: he is weaker in his overall power, but stronger in directing and controlling the power he has as repression. Through his sexuality Jason creates politics:

> Aussi je ne suis pas de ces amants vulgaires;
> J'accommode ma flamme au bien de mes affaires;
> Et sous quelque climat que me jette le sort,
> Par maxime d'état je me fais cet effort.
> Nous voulant à Lemnos rafraîchir dans la ville,
> Qu'eûssions nous fait, Pollux, sans l'amour d'Hypsipyle?
> Et depuis à Colchos, que fit votre Jason,
> Que cajoler Médée, et gagner la toison?
> Alors, sans mon amour, qu'eût fait votre vaillance?
> Eût-elle du dragon trompé la vigilance?
> Le peuple que la terre enfantoit tout armé,
> Qui de vous l'eût défait, si Jason n'eût aimé?
> Maintenant qu'un exil m'interdit ma patrie,
> Créuse est le sujet de mon idolâtrie;

Et j'ai trouvé l'adresse, en lui faisant la cour
De relever mon sort sur les ailes d'Amour.　　　　(I, i, 29–44)

The attraction of Jason's narcissism coupled with a reputation for amorous conquest makes of him a symbol of fecundity, a new Priapus. Jason is a 'hero' because he dompts monsters: he masters and subjugates the 'monster' that is female sexuality, that uncontrollable, chaotic force of unformed matter. He domesticates this force and implants on it his own mark. He is the male principle that molds matter into culture. Despite his failings, Jason represents the superiority of ideality over materiality, of reason over passion, of men over women. Women, because they desire him, subjugate themselves to him. It is their sexual submission to Jason that makes of him the 'standard' of communal life. His virility, his sexual prowess, captures and subjugates matter and channels its excess into the repression of culture. In this way Jason's exploitation of his potency makes of him a true 'hero of culture', a 'Sovereign'.[21]

Jason exists and has value as the object of universal desire, a desire Médée shares. Her attraction/desire for Jason (and of this desire there can be no doubt; Médée's relation to Jason is totally passional, while his for her is completely political) has led her to accept a form of self-imposed servitude. For him she has come from the far outlands of the world, from barbarous Scythia, and established herself within the confines of civilization. This geographic shift from 'Barbary' to Corinth corresponds to a primary metaphysical change. Coming into culture (history), Médée submits to the rule of the male, submits to his Law, and for a time being, the time of sexual fulfilment, is content with the inferior role that is assigned to her.

Once in Corinth, however, both Créuse and Créon also desire Jason.

> Que vous dirai-je plus? Mon bonheur ordinaire
> M'acquiert les volontés de la fille et du père;
> Si bien que de tous deux également chéri;
> L'un me veut pour gendre et l'autre pour mari.
>
> (I, i, 109–12)

Jason joins the sexual to the political, making them inseparable. He yokes the masculine and the feminine within the sphere of his own sexual potency. As the representative of this 'order', of the sovereignty of form over matter, Jason needs the confirmation of its reproduction as his own validation. Jason needs his children because paternity is the verification of the power of metaphor, the

hold of reason over matter. His children are the proof of Jason's political power, his ability to re-produce form to maintain his sovereignty as this re-presentation.[22] Jason needs these 'testicular'[23] witnesses of his own 'triumph' which, imposed diachronically, validates paternity as genealogy, genealogy as the basis of culture, and culture as the order, the declension of the same, a proof of his eternity.[24]

For this reason Jason insists on keeping *his* children. By demanding that they remain with him in Corinth, that they do not accompany their mother into exile, he is effectively denying their (and his) link to the female, denying their connection to matter and situating them solely within the masculine domain. They are his investment in order, in legality. Instead of leaving them as the mediating union between the male and the female (but is this mediation ever possible?) Jason attempts to eradicate them as in-difference, and to use them as proof of his own sovereignty. This is, of course, tantamount to the suppression of Médée. It is this suppression that will prove intolerable (the myth will not be sacrificed to 'history'), that will return, in its fury, to give the lie to the pretension of Law, to any system of exchange that would exclude 'dépense', to the very existence of culture itself.

All the characters in the play who are situated within the polis and whose investments reside within culture can retain their status only by imposing on an other the guilt they all share. Although Médée and Jason bear equal responsibility for their fate, and although Créon also becomes their accomplice when he admits them into his kingdom and grants them asylum, it is Médée who is made to bear the burden of their past. In the realm of (masculine) political expedience the female, the mere receptacle of the male, is expendable. She is easily replaced. Médée must be sacrificed to the rule of the Father in order for Jason to advance his own interests, the interests of culture.

It is obvious that the legal system which serves as the standard of culture in the universe of the play is designed to function for Patriarchy. The Law of the Father which is articulated by Créon operates on the exclusion of the feminine, an exclusion which in *Médée* takes the form of ritual banishment. In order to prepare for his ascension to royal power, Jason must be cleansed of guilt. The only way to do this is to make of Médée the 'pharmakos', the sacrificial victim who carries evil out of the city. All the characters who are defined within Patriarchy are joined by their commitment to legality. They all have recourse to the Law, to repression, to ex-

cuse their sacrifice of Médée. For each of them she is made to bear the entire responsibility of those events from which Jason profited. He, however, is exonerated of all blame:

> M. – O d'un injuste affront les coups les plus cruels!
> Vous faîtes différence entre deux criminels!
> Vous voulez qu'on l'honore, et que de deux complices
> L'un ait votre couronne, et l'autre des supplices!
> Créon – Cesse de plus mêler ton intérêt au sien.
> Ton Jason, pris à part est trop homme de bien.
>
>   .   .   .
>
> Le séparant de toi sa défense est facile;
> Jamais il n'a trahi son père ni sa ville;
> Jamais sang innocent n'a fait rougir ses mains;
> Jamais il n'a prêté son bras à tes desseins. (II, ii, 455–64)

> Créuse – Laissez agir, grand roi, la raison sur votre âme,
> Et ne le chargez point des crimes de sa femme,
> J'épouse un malheureux, et mon père y consent,
> Mais prince, mais vaillant, et surtout innocent.
>   (II, v, 625–28)

> J. – Il manque encor ce point à mon sort déplorable,
> Que de tes cruautés on me fasse coupable. (III, iii, 857–8)

It is obvious that the three witnesses in Médée's trial are prejudiced representatives of a system of desire as Law that can perpetuate itself only by the communal suppression of an intrusive, alien other. Médée is cast out of community, she is made to bear the burden of her refusal to accept an 'original lack', that women should acknowledge, of her own subjugation to Jason and to culture. Despite her own claims to innocence (or at least to the innocence of her motive, passion; she acts only out of Love), Médée, by the same gesture that disculpates Jason, is univocally condemned as evil.

This condemnation is, in the context of this tragedy, a form of hubris and it is this hubris that brings about Jason's and culture's downfall. It is Jason's error to attempt to suppress as alien, to banish beyond the confines of the city, what is actually also an integral part of itself/himself. Médée, as 'nature', inheres in Jason, but it is this unacknowledged fact, too fearsome to contemplate, that must undergo repression. This point of 'hubris', the instance

31

of repression, situates the passage of myth and history, the interaction of legality and nature, in the narration of *Médée*. At this juncture, the mythic sub-text of the narration becomes co-terminous with the historical/legal dimension of the narrative (that is the role of myth as mediation − to be both at once) and attempts to reassert its irrepressible ambiguity.

As 'myth', neither Jason nor Médée is reducible to essential antitheses, neither male nor female. Each partakes in 'essential' attributes of both sexes, as defined in culture − both are sexual forces that are complementary and interconnected. They represent impulses in which difference, sexual difference, overlaps. It is this space of overlapping, of indeterminacy, that representation (narration, history) attempts to deny in favor of difference (that is, in favor of the Law). Only as they enter culture (as objects of narration) are Médée and Jason representable as separate essences, essences which are immediately sexualized and politicized. In culture, their inherent ambivalence, the way they both partake of a primary bisexuality, is denied. The tragedy, the representation of myth, stresses this conflict, which is the conflict of culture − which might even be the definition of culture − that is the denial of an inchoate sexuality and its separation into 'sexuality', a separation which cannot be accomplished without the violent repression of desire in scission.

The conflict of differentiation (the questioning of the ambiguous space of mediation) is accused most radically when each partner attempts to claim as his/her own the metaphors of their mediation, the children. Both Médée and Jason want to keep the children, but for different reasons, different libidinal investments. For Médée the children reflect Jason; they are the mirror in which Médée can gaze and see not herself, but Jason:

> Souffre que mes enfants accompagnent ma fuite;
> Que je t'admire encore en chacun de leurs traits,
> Que je t'aime et te baise en ces petits portraits;
> Et que de leur cher objet, entretenant ma flamme,
> Te présente à mes yeux aussi bien qu'à mon âme.

(III, iii, 918–22)

Médée loves her children because they are an image of Jason. They represent him to her and thus we might say that they stand in for Jason, and more particularly for Médée's own subjugation to Jason. The children are Jason's male prerogative. They represent what she desires in him and what is denied her − his ability to reproduce himself, to form, impose order on matter. The children

are indeed Médée's 'fetish'; they point to Médée (in Law) as self-imposed castration. In her worshipping of them as portraits of Jason (= same) they become the symbol of her (matter's) subjugation to him (ideality). And they also deny this subjugation: they also stand for the 'phallus' (power, integrity) that Médée has relinquished by becoming (their) 'mother', accepting her place with Jason in culture. The children are both the sign of her castration and its refusal. Médée, the 'phallic' woman, had accepted castration, had abandoned her power to the Law, but the Law has returned it to her (mastered) in her maternity.

For Jason, too, as we have already seen, the children function as a fetish. Representing his own ability to re-produce himself, they deny his own lack of power in nature. This lack of power is, of course, sublimated in the children as substitutes of himself. They are guarantors of his continuity within the Law. They are proof of his position as progenitor of history.

The children are the most highly invested of a series of mediating objects (the Golden Fleece, Médée's dress) that both deny and affirm nature and culture, myth and history. They are the most vulnerable of objects, the objects in which the battle between nature and culture (between male and female) will be most effectively played out.

We should not forget that Corneille's text underlines the children's role as mediators: they are made to go back and forth between Médée and Créuse, between Médée and Jason, between Jason and Créon. They are the shuttle going back and forth between exile and polis. It is precisely because of their role as mediators that each parent thinks of their destruction as a way of destroying his/her other without destroying himself/herself. In Corneille, both parents contemplate the murder of the children, Jason as well as Médée:

> J. – Instruments des fureurs d'une mère insensée,
> Indignes rejetons de mon amour passée,
> Quel malheureux destin vous avoit réservés
> A porter le trépas à qui vous avoit sauvés?
> C'est vous, petits ingrats, que malgré la nature,
> Il me faut immoler dessus leur sepulture.
> Que la sorcière en vous commence de souffrir:
> Que son premier torment soit de vous voir mourir.
> Toutefous qu'ont-ils fait qu'obéir à leur mère?
>
> (v, v, 1529–37)

In his rage, Jason wants to sacrifice his children in order to punish

Médée – but Médée the 'sorceress', Médée denizen of nature, the force that mocks him. He contemplates their murder as a way of negating, or at least affecting, the power that escapes his control and therefore continually risks giving the lie to the Law.

Médée, on the other hand, comes to contemplate destroying her children as a final attack on Jason inside the Law:

> Il aime ses enfants, ce courage inflexible:
> Son foible est découvert, par eux il est sensible;
> Par eux mon bras, armé d'une juste rigueur,
> Va trouver des chemins à lui percer le coeur. (IV, v, 945–8)

and again:

> Que n'a-t-elle déjà des enfants de Jason,
> Sur qui plus pleinement venger sa trahison!
> Suppléons-y les miens; immolons avec joie
> Ceux qu'à me dire adieu Créuse me renvoie.
> Nature, je le puis sans violer ta loi:
> Ils viennent de sa part, et ne sont plus à moi.
> Mais ils sont innocents; . . .
> Il sont trop criminels d'avoir Jason pour père;
> Il faut que leur trépas redouble son tourment;
> Il faut qu'il souffre en père aussi bien qu'en amant.
>
> (V, ii, 1331–40)

By destroying the children Médée effectively attacks the foundation of Jason's hold on politics, on repression, on the Law. Médée correctly identifies the children as the symbol of her alienation in culture. In both instances ('ses enfants'; 'Ils viennent de sa part et ne sont plus à moi') she disassociates herself from her children because they are the integral link to Jason's position in the polis, and to her condemnation by it. By deciding to destroy them, Médée relinquishes her role as 'mother', the imposition on her, by the order of Patriarchy, of her 'maternal' nature – the brand of her castration. By one spectacular act of destruction Médée not only kills her children, but also effectively destroys the fetters of the Law, and the base upon which rests the culture of the (play's) universe.

Médée begins her attack on the Law by destroying Créon and Créuse. Corneille gives this destruction to us as a blazing spectacle of Médée's nature/power. This spectacle which is offered to our gaze is meant to galvanize us, to point out the immense disparity that exists between the victim (culture) and the executioner (nature–matter).[25] Médée goes on to demonstrate this 'disequil-

ibrium' fully by the final eradication of all Law. As long as the children remain alive there is always a chance for Jason (the Father) to recoup his power, assured by the continuation of his image. Their destruction, however, removes all hope, all idea of continuity, and reduces him to a state of utter impotence. In the last scene we see Jason who, in his grief over the death of Créuse and deprived of those symbols that reflect his own self-sufficiency back to him, is bereft of all the exterior 'forms' that represent him. He no longer has an image, no longer has a self. He has been undone by Médée's power. The hypocrisy that subtends his role in society has been revealed. Faced with the undeniable superiority of Médée, Jason is left defenseless, unable to take any revenge:[26]

> Mais que me servira cette vaine poursuite,
> Si l'air est un chemin toujours libre à ta fuite,
> Si toujours tes dragons sont prêts à t'enlever,
> Si toujours tes forfaits ont de quoi me braver?
>
> (V, vii, 1593–6)

Deprived of the illusion of his political base, deprived of his narcissistic reflection of himself, deprived of his progeny, Jason can only turn his impotent rage against his vacant self. By his suicide Jason surrenders the last vestiges of resistance to Médée. He destroys those limits that (his) culture has so laboriously erected, and, breaking them, returns to the limitless, selfless, indifferent embrace of Death.

Corneille's *Médée* ends on an ominous note for Patriarchy, for order and for control. The last act plays out for us the utter destruction of the Law: Créon and Créuse, symbols of history, of the polis and of the small sphere of culture, have been destroyed. Jason in his melancholic despair, a despair that is the most narcissistic of sufferings, in an ultimate act of desperation does away with himself. This suicide is another new twist Corneille brings to the myth. More important, the children, metaphors of mediation, symbolic terms of the acceptance of castration, of the structuring of desire around the Father, imitation and proof of the triumph of ideality over chaotic matter, of culture over nature, have been obliterated. In her last liberating act Médée has freed herself from the bonds of Law to which she had submitted herself. Nothing remains. All semblance of 'human' community, of the organization inherent in community, has been destroyed in the bloodbath released by Médée.

In the end, only Médée remains, or rather only the image of

Médée as we last see her in the penultimate scene of the tragedy. There, she is no longer the wife, no longer the mother, but she becomes again a mythic, supernatural force, who assumes in her being a power that defies difference, that denies sexuality's symmetrical divisions in which she, as woman, is lost. Coming back into her own, Médée 'supernatural' leaves the scene of representation transported through the air by her dragon-drawn chariot.

Médée leaves this world of representation, and yet remains, by her absence, an effective threat that always lurks in the shadows, in the folds of the Cornelian universe. Perhaps we can see *Médée*, Medea, as both the transhistorical fear of all Patriarchy (*Médée* as myth), and at the same time (*Médée* as tragedy) as the pointed reminder of the dread of dissolution that was particularly poignant, as I have suggested, in French society at the beginning of the seventeenth century. Free and uncontainable, Médée becomes the original object of desire and fear whose repression will constitute the political and sexual tension of the great tragedies to come. These tragedies, reflecting the structures of Classical Patriarchy, always show these structures to be teetering on the brink of an abyss. This abyss, Patriarchy's attraction–repulsion of the feminine, can, as we have seen, undermine the entire edifice of the Father and bring it tumbling down in ruin around him.[27]

2

LE CID: FATHER/TIME

'Que de maux et de pleurs/Nous coûteront nos pères.'

Despite its all-consuming violence *Médée* did not evoke a loud public outcry. Perhaps it was just another in a long line of blood-and-gore tragedies that dominated the Parisian stage in the 1620s and 1630s. Perhaps the public of the day, so accustomed to the constant portrayal of destruction, was too blasé to react to Médée's passion. As we know, such was not the case with *Le Cid*. The ensuing uproar, the 'querelle', embraced the play, its characters and the author in a scandal unprecedented in the annals of the French stage. The public's reaction to the *Cid* was unique in its vehemence, its passion and its division. No other theatrical début, not even *Hernani*'s ushering in the Romantic revolution, was to have such a momentous impact on its contemporaries and on successive generations of admirers as Corneille's new tragi-comedy. From its première to this day, *Le Cid* is marked as 'une pièce à scandale'.

For the last three centuries the history of this scandal and its political, esthetic, philosophical and sociological implications have been exhaustively examined.[1] It is not my intention here to go over that well-mapped terrain. What I would like to underline, however, is that once the storm of protest, the accusations and counter-accusations, subsided, once the Académie had made public its own thoughts on the new play, the crux of the scandal remained as troubling as ever. Implicated in this crux were two distinct but interrelated areas of theatrical tension. On the one hand what most scandalized the play's audience, what sent a shiver of pleasure throughout the parterre, was Chimène's reaction to her predicament, a reaction that immediately marked her as 'unnatural':

Amante trop sensible et fille trop dénaturée. Quelque violence que luy peust faire sa passion, il est certain qu'elle ne devait point se relâcher dans la vengeance de la mort de son père et moins encore se résoudre à epouser celuy quy l'avoit fait mourir. En cecy il faut avouer que ses moeurs sont du moins scandaleuses, si en effet elles ne sont pas dépravées.

(Chapelain, *Les Sentiments de l'Académie française*, p. 39)

On the other hand, Corneille censures himself for his awkward handling of the unity of time. The temporal dimension of the play is described by him as being 'invraisemblable'. It too is not right, not 'natural':

> Je ne puis dénier que la règle des vingt et quatre heures presse trop les incidents de cette pièce. La mort du comte et l'arrivée des Maures s'y pouvaient entre-suivre d'aussi près qu'elles font, parce que cette arrivée est une surprise qui n'a point de communication, ni de mesure à prendre avec le reste; mais il n'en va pas ainsi du combat de don Sanche, dont le roi était le maître . . .
>
> Cette même règle presse aussi trop Chimène de demander justice au roi la seconde fois. Elle l'avait fait le soir d'auparavant et n'avait aucun sujet d'y retourner le lendemain matin pour en importuner le roi.
>
> (*Le Cid*, 'Examen', p. 15)[2]

Corneille attacks the play because of his gaucherie in orchestrating the flow of time. The action of the play − the death of the Count, Rodrigue's expedition against the Moors, his subsequent combat with Don Sanche and finally the King's command that Chimène accept Rodrigue in marriage − is too much. Not only the play's heroine, but also its plot, the representation of Rodrigue's becoming the Cid, and the implications of this metamorphosis for the society of the play, are intrinsic causes of its scandalous nature.

These two essential components of scandal, women and time − the same we met with in *Médée* − form an extended metaphor of monstrosity that sets this play off from the 'Classical' perfection towards which it tends. Needless to say, this 'monstrosity' is inscribed in the very nature of the play, in its ambivalent stance, at once 'tragic' and 'comic', of the hybrid genre. It is this monstrosity that the Classical impulse must control, must eliminate in its own obsessive drive towards the perfection it desires, towards the creation of its own perfect monsters.

When Corneille moves from *Médée* to *Le Cid* he leaves the realm of myth for the domain of history. This move displaces the scene of the drama from a universe existing before time to a world already structured within the limits of a very definite chronology. What was not possible in *Médée*, the triumph of the Law of the Father and the concomitant organization of society in sublimation, is presented as an 'already there' by *Le Cid*. While the world of *Médée* surrealistically represented a stance outside time, the world of *Le Cid* is anchored in the curious interstice of diachrony and synchrony that meet in the embrace of Castillian history. This history is the narration of a 'race' whose roots reach into the past and

whose ambitions send it forth into the future. In this, Corneille's first venture into history, temporality takes the form of genealogy.

Although *Le Cid* is radically different from *Médée*, although it presents a world of order, of succession, of hierarchy and devolution it is not, for all that, a world impervious to chaos. On the contrary, while we are aware of the history of this world we are also aware of its precariousness. Don Fernand, the titular head of this world, is the *first* King of Castille. His power is only recently established and only minimally secured. The uncertainty of his vassals' loyalty, the omnipresent threat of a Moorish invasion, create constant tension. At the beginning of the play the world the King represents and leads is only just emerging from the cauldron of another order, a dying order which is not completely subdued, which coexists with the new, tainting it and all those in it with its own insecurity. It is this tension between the two orders that threatens the entire social and temporal unity Fernand represents, constantly reminding him (and them) that their world can be cast back into chaos. In his introduction Corneille underlines the precarious nature of this situation, stressing the tension that the play must both reveal and disguise: 'on peut considérer que don Fernand étant le premier roi de Castille, et ceux qui en avaient été maîtres auparavant lui n'ayant eu titre que de comtes, il n'était peut-être pas assez absolu sur les grands seigneurs de son royaume' ('Examen', p. 15).

The world of *Le Cid* is on the near side of the margins separating the universe of ordered, progressive chronology from the indifference of disorder. We are in history, but in history that trembles on the brink. The society the *Cid* portrays is young, and it is still prey to uncertainties that transcend the political and are confused with the anxieties of the metaphysical. It is these anxieties that Chimène more than any other of the play's characters embodies. Her role casts an uneasy shadow over the new splendor of the emerging Classical Sun.

While *Médée* showed us the victory of matter (mater) over form (the Father), *Le Cid* is clearly a mise-en-scène of a patriarchal society where we have moved from a frightening world of an all-powerful phallic mother to the smaller, but ever so more rigidly organized stage of the Law. From a world of vengeance, hostility and aggression played out as natural forces exterior to the person of the heroine (but metonymically representative of her) we are now in world where these same passions are interiorized. The conflicts that in the former play could still be resolved in the world with which they were one are in this new play − and this is not the least

39

of its major innovations – all internalized. They have become part of a human psychology of desire and repression. Paradoxically, when we move from the realm of myth to the domain of history, that sphere of the human psyche that ignores chronology, the unconscious, comes to the fore.[3] Co-terminous with this birth is the elaboration of the entire familial–social edifice that both predicates its existence and defines that existence as a conflict of the uncompromising demands of nature and culture.

In its original edition (1637) the play begins with a conversation between Don Gomès and Elvire. Chimène's father and her confidante discuss her future marriage. This first scene clearly establishes the locus of dramatic tension within the space of desire and chronology, at the interstice of 'clanic' history and individuality that defines all of the play's character. Don Gomès enumerates the laws of genealogy that structure the social universe of *Le Cid*. He defines the parameters inside which marriage may or may not be contracted.

These laws that situate the individual within the social order are subtended by a constant reference to time which is metaphorized as the linear descent of male to male. Genealogy in *Le Cid* spatializes temporality. It imposes a metaphorical essence (masculinity) on a metonymical (biological) displacement. It is this shift from metonymy to metaphor in genealogy that allows Patriarchy to exist in history and yet to transcend the particular historical moment. Genealogy creates a transhistorical 'essence' that can be transmitted from man to man.[4]

When he considers the different suitors for his daughter's hand Gomès' judgment of their (market) value expresses itself in terms of past investments and future returns:

> La valeur de son père en son temps sans pareille,
> Tant qu'a duré sa force a passé pour merveille;
> Ses rides sur son front ont gravé ses exploits,
> Et nous disent encore ce qu'il fut autrefois.   (I, i, 33–6)

Rodrigue is a worthy suitor because he contains within himself the proleptic promise of excellence that will be actualized in the world: 'Je me promets du fils ce que j'ai vu du père.' Time, as mortality, is both acknowledged as a reality and immediately denied within a system of sublimation. The individual is destined to a moment, but what is most precious in him, what guarantees his class's pre-eminence, is eternal.

This schema becomes complicated, however, when we realize

that between the exploits of the father and the promise of the son stands the present. It is at this juncture joining the past to the future that Don Gomès situates himself. Gomès, now, is what Diègue was and what Rodrigue will become:

> Et qu'a fait, après tout, ce grand nombre d'années,
> Qui ne puisse égaler une de mes journées?
> Si vous fûtes vaillant, je le suis aujourd'hui;
> Et ce bras du royaume est le plus sur appui.　(ı, iii, 193–6)

Although not of the same family as Diègue, Gomès is clearly of the same 'essence'.[5] They are in fact interchangeable, as are Diègue and Rodrigue, and Rodrigue and Gomès. Each man is what the other was and will become what the other is:

> D. –　　et ton illustre audace
> Fait bien revivre en toi les héros de ma race:
> C'est d'eux que tu descends, c'est de moi que tu viens.
>
> 　　　　　　　　　　　　　　　　(ııı, vi, 1029–31)

> D. (to G.) – Vous êtes aujourd'hui ce qu'autrefois je fus.　(ı, iii, 212)

> I. (to Ch.) – Que ton père en lui seul se voit ressucité.　(ıv, iii, 1180)

Thus from the beginning we are presented with a paradoxical blurring of the chronological parameters of this patriarchy. There is a chain of descent that links all the male characters on a continuum. At the same time there is also a transcending of the idea of descent. Each male – Don Diègue, the patriarch who has served his king and country, who is now at a remove, whose virility is gone, is the symbol of tradition and Law; Don Gomès, the knight at the height of his powers, virile (controlling the object of desire), is jealous of his prerogative and vengeful; Rodrigue, the adolescent male coming into his own (his sexuality, the desire for the father's possession), is on the point of becoming a 'man' – is co-eval to every other male. They are but different moments of one eternal masculine essence. It would be only a little blasphemous to situate this Cornelian trinity alongside the Christian, for structurally they are identical: three (male) persons, but one essence, each proceeding from the other, each becoming the other. Each sums up the others at a particular moment in individual history. Together they form a unity that points to progression in the world, to decay and death, while immediately negating this same progression: the Holy Trinity of Classical theater.[6]

This homogeneity of masculine identity is not unproblematic; on

the contrary, it does imply a necessity for each male to distinguish himself from the others at a particular moment of his own evolution. This distinction is made at the expense of the others. Paradoxically, however, it is at the precise moment of differentiating himself (the moment of 'meurs ou tue' in S. Doubrovsky's schema)[7] that the individual male both challenges the Father and affirms him. In realizing his own potential he both negates his own father and affirms his own allegiance to an ideal Patriarch to whom all must pay tribute. The paradox of the (feudal) system that the play elucidates is that it is only by challenging the other males, by establishing a hierarchy of more or less powerful, of more or less experienced, of more or less necessary to the State, that each man can determine his place in a synchronic chain that reflects and justifies the diachronic.

The obvious differences of these male characters are only a ploy to obfuscate their inherent similarity, and this similarity is too threatening not to be challenged within the parameters of individual desire. Too close an identity blurs distinction, bringing the separate generations into too intimate and too exclusive an intermingling to be tolerated. Such an intense identification can only be threatening in its inherent homo-erotic drive. There is too great a promiscuous mingling of fathers and sons, of the entire chain of older and younger men. It is precisely in order to avoid this threat, to establish clearly defined areas of difference, that rivalry, the challenge of one man to another, intervenes and sets up a system that protects men from the centrifugal attraction that draws them irresistibly to the same, to their annihilation in a homosexual embrace.[8] This attraction is counterbalanced by the imposition of a code of 'individual' honor ('gloire') which displaces itself onto a military–sexual rivalry. The introduction of the woman functions as both guarantor of sexual potency and as the prize validating the superiority of the individual male in the competitions that constantly pit him against all others.

This universe of masculine competition is also introduced to us in the first scenes of the play. This rivalry is constantly at work on all levels, and among all men. It is, in essence, the foundation of the political system as represented in the play. Rodrigue and Sanche are presented as obvious sexual rivals for Chimène:

> Don Rodrigue et Don Sanche à l'envie font paraître
> Le beau feu qu'en leurs coeurs ses beautés ont fait naître.
>
> (I, i, 3–4, 1637 version)

Gomès and Diègue (and even Gomès and the King, as we will see) are political rivals:

> Le roi doit à son fils élire un gouverneur,
> Et c'est lui que regarde un tel degré d'honneur;
> Ce choix n'est pas douteux, et sa rare vaillance
> Ne peut souffrir qu'on craigne aucune concurrence.
> Comme ses hauts exploits le rendent sans égal,
> Dans un espoir si juste il sera sans rival.   (I, i, 43–8)

'To be without rival' is the supreme wish of all the men in this play: to have triumphed over all the others and to exist in a realm free of the contingency of social, political and sexual dependency, to be outside the eternal round of hierarchy, to be outside the Law, to be, that is, co-terminous with the 'Father' to which they all sacrifice.

There can, at times, be lulls in the rivalries that structure this world, especially between men of different generations. Alliances can be contracted, particularly in the form of marriages, that join them together through the mediation of women.[9] Yet these areas of truce, these spaces of masculine contiguity, are never permanent; men must always be ready to mark their difference from others with a compelling show of force. Their honor is always there, and any slight, imagined or real, is terrifying because it means instant and total negation.

It is only after we have understood the profound investment all the males have in this hierarchy, in this sublimation, that Gomès' affront to Diègue can be fully appreciated as the tragic hubris it is. What is least important, perhaps, in this affront is the person of Don Diègue; his age, his honor, his past services are a ploy that disguises the real import of the insult. For beyond the person of Diègue, Don Gomès challenges the entire system of sublimation to which he subjects himself and against which he rebels. In slapping Diègue, Gomès refuses the law of metaphor — and in so doing uncovers the spectre of Death (impotence) that lives within each man. Don Gomès' affront is a threatening gesture because it reveals what the entire society of *Le Cid* must keep hidden.

In the most obvious way (as Doubrovsky has previously noted) Diègue is brought by this affront face to face with his nothingness in time:[10]

> O rage! ô désespoir! ô vieillesse ennemie!
> N'ai-je donc tant vécu que pour cette infamie?
> > > > (I, iv, 237–8)

His monologue articulates the most profound fear. All glory, all honor, all victory is illusory: one blow has undone a lifetime of service:

> O cruel souvenir de ma gloire passée!
> Oeuvre de tant de jours en un jour effacée! (I, iv, 245–6)

By this blow, Diègue's entire past has been cast into the abyss of eternity. It and he are obliterated.

In a sense we might say the Gomès has done what every man wishes to do, but cannot. He has attacked the integrity of the Father, but he has not taken, cannot take, his place. In the society whose evolution the *Cid* represents, Gomès' allegiance is not to the new political order that is emerging, the order of the King, but to an older, more archaic order, that of the communal horde of brothers–vassals.[11] By showing up Don Diègue's weakness, Gomès only underlines the evanescence of his own triumphs and strength. More important still, by revealing Don Diègue's vulnerability, Gomès gives the lie to the entire political system inside which he lives. In a fit of pique, he shows us that the Emperor has no clothes.

Don Gomès has sacrificed altruism for his own personal pleasure. In the context of the play this narcissistic display figures the symbol of his political conservatism. In the evolution of the 'feudal' State that *Le Cid* sketches, in, that is, the institution and affirmation of a particular type of society that transcends the moment and perpetuates itself in time, Don Gomès' relation to the King is analogous to his relation to Diègue: he is a 'bad' son. He cannot accept his role as vassal in the elaboration of this still tenuous new monarchy. His force has been used to support the aggrandizement of the kingdom, but he has not learned to be subservient to it. He refuses to submit to the King's wishes ('Qu'aux volontés du roi ce grand courage cède') but instead prefers the narcissistic illusion of controlling the State, rather than being controlled by it: 'Tout l'Etat périra s'il faut que je périsse' (II, i, 398). His narcissism comes in conflict with his devotion to ideals; it triumphs over them. Gomès refuses to obey the Law:

> Monsieur, pour conserver tout ce que j'ai d'estime,
> Désobéir un peu n'est pas un si grand crime. (II, i, 365–6)

Don Gomès' narcissism recuperates the closure, refuses linearity and progression, in an obeisance to non-difference. It gives pride of place to the individual (synchrony) over the clan (genealogy) and

is all the more dangerous to the political system because, closed in upon itself, its stasis defies the power that invests the King with the aura of the sacred.[12] It disavows his sovereignty:

> Justes cieux! ainsi donc un sujet téméraire
> A si peu de respect et de soin de me plaire!
> Il offence D. Diègue, et méprise son roi!
> Au milieu de ma cour il me donne la loi!   (II, vi, 561–4)

While at first glance this masculine structuring that I have been describing in *Le Cid* might seem to be an arbitrary phenomenon, isolated in this play, I would like to suggest that, on the contrary, it is not arbitrary at all. Rather, it can be seen (as I have implied by my reference to the 'Holy Trinity') to be part of a greater structuring device in western metaphysics that forms one of the ideological parameters of masculine prerogative and, as we shall see, one of the recurring patterns in Corneille's Classical tragedies. What we have begun to see functioning in *Le Cid* conforms with the 'mythic' structuration of masculinity that G. Rosolato has described as a perpetual chain, a chain of 'three generations of man'.[13] According to him, this chain is constituted by father–ego–son and it allows the masculine subject to situate himself in society as both the subject and object of the Oedipal conflict and of its resolution in genealogy. Essential to this conflict – the conflict itself – is the fantasmatic sacrifice of the Father and the immediate sublimation of this fantasy in its incorporation in the subject's libidinal economy as his sense of guilt and, thus, of renunciation. It is at this moment of guilt that each individual male identifies with the Father as being himself at one and the same time subject of the sacrifice and object of that act which allows the child to break out of the closure of the Oedipal triangle and to enter upon the linear evolution of successive generations.[14] What the *Cid* in particular reveals, however, is the shaky passage of one order of obeisance to another. The conflict separating Gomès, Diègue, Rodrigue and Chimène is essentially a political conflict. It represents the birth throes of this new order, of a new system of Patriarchy. It is a system that is inextricably bound to the old order, that contains the old order within itself. Nevertheless its origin, although impossible to isolate, is co-terminous with the destruction of this old order. In *Le Cid* this destruction is represented not by its brutal extinction but by its appropriation – the marriage of Rodrigue and Chimène.

It is for this reason that the marriage of Chimène remains the

central troubling conundrum/scandal of *Le Cid*. On its acceptance or rejection hangs the entire system of genealogy–history that is emerging and that subtends the ideology of essence that the drama plays out. The figure of Chimène introduces into this world of masculine devolution the unsettling, decentering, 'unnatural' force of desire that is recalcitrant to political accommodations, to any 'raison d'Etat'.

Significantly, just as the elaboration of Patriarchy ignores the presence of women as a determining element in historical evolution, just as, in other words, the women remain the invisible nodal point of generation, Chimène is not present on stage in the original version's first scene. The scene that articulates her desire and her future does so in her absence. A strategic shift occurs between the 1637 and the 1660 editions of the play. In the original version Chimène is represented by her confidante. Not only does Chimène not appear on stage but, more radically, this absence effectively denies her any expression of a wish/desire that would signal her as an independent subjectivity. In fact, Elvire clearly states that Chimène has no desire. She presents her as an indifferent object of her suitor's demands. Chimène does not exist as a desiring subject:

> Ce n'est pas que Chimène écoute leurs soupirs,
> Ou d'un regard propice anime leurs désirs:
> Au contraire, pour tous dedans l'indifférence
> Elle n'ôte à pas un ni donne d'espérance.
>
> (I, i, 5–8, 1637 version)

Chimène's only passion is filial; she waits for and wants her father to name her future husband. She waits, in other words, for her father to announce his desire: 'C'est de votre seul choix qu'elle attend un époux' (I, i, 10). In this first version the Count is clearly situated as the arbitrator of desire. He effectively chooses Rodrigue as his future son-in-law and as his replacement vis-à-vis Chimène:

> Je me promets du fils ce que j'ai vu du père;
> Et ma fille, en un mot, peut l'aimer et me plaire. (I, i, 37–8)

In 1660, however, Gomès' speech is now recounted by Elvire. It is transformed from direct to indirect discourse and this change, it would seem, empties it of much of its dramatic force. Telling is, as Corneille himself states in his 'Examen', a much less persuasive dramatic device than showing: 'ce qu'on expose à la vue touche

bien plus que ce qu'on n'apprend que par un récit' (p. 3).
Dramatically speaking, therefore, there is a shift, a rather radical
shift, in the dynamics articulating Law and desire in the two versions of the play. The first version is paradoxically the more ambiguous of the two, focusing as it does the dramatic light on the
desire of/for the Father. It also calls our attention to an indifference, or at least an initial 'blurring', of Chimène at the beginning of the drama.

Perhaps this variation is slighter than it actually appears. Surely
I am not suggesting two dramatically opposed readings of the same
character, an 'indifferent' Chimène and an actively passionate one.
In both cases it is a question of focus. In the first version it is the
Count's desire that is given precedence, in the second Chimène is
spotlighted. What is perhaps more important is the fact that in both
cases we are brought face to face with the fact that there is an essential coincidence of desire. The desire of the daughter is the desire
of the father – 'Il estime Rodrigue autant que vous l'aimez' – and
vice versa. This situation of the congruity of desire is intriguing
enough in its own right, establishing a generational and sexual link
between Gomès and Chimène which forms the tragic vortex of the
play's irresolvable political conflict.

While it might have come as a surprise to us to discover that
Chimène's desire coalesces with her father's, we take it for granted
that as far as she and Rodrigue are concerned, their mutual passion
should be identical. Their love for each other, reflecting their own
positions in the genealogical schema, is perfectly symmetrical. How
could it be otherwise? Each is presented at once as unique: 'Vous
n'avez qu'une fille,' Don Diègue tells Don Gomès, 'et moi je n'ai
qu'un fils.' They are mirror reflections, in sexual difference, and
mutually complementary. The two lineages, with all the weight of
history that has accrued to them, give forth their finest flowers in
this last equation, one son = one daughter. The next step, marriage, the grafting of these two perfect buds to form a new shoot,
is the most logically, economically and socially pleasing of pros-
pects. Through their union not only will the two fathers be united
– 'Leur hymen nous peut rendre à jamais plus qu'amis' (I, iii,
168) – but in their marriage a new and illustrious line of descent
will originate. ('A jamais', of course, pushes this union into a
perpetual renewal in the future.)

Their marriage is the crux of the entire drama, the 'tragedy' of
the play, and the 'comedy' too. It is a union that is constantly invoked by all the characters (Don Diègue, Don Gomès, Rodrigue,

Chimène, the Infanta, the King) and which finally is constantly deferred. It is the absent center of the play which initiates and controls the dramatic action and which ultimately is left, at the end of the play, in the same situation as at the beginning; it is about to be, it will be, at some future date, which is situated beyond representation. It would seem, therefore, that the real tension of the play, its motivating force, is not the marriage, which within a patriarchal system is a definitive act of appropriation, not sexual satisfaction, but rather the tension and frustration of indefinite deferral.

This deferral exists from the very beginning of the play, from Chimène's first utterances after she has listened to Elvire's retelling of her conversation with her father:

> Il semble toutefois que mon âme troublée
> Refuse cette joie et s'en trouve accablée.
> Un moment donne au sort des visages divers,
> Et dans ce grand bonheur je crains un grand revers.
>
> (I, i, 53–6)

Something tells Chimène that satisfaction is not to be her lot. She has a presentiment that this marriage will not occur. It is not, therefore, this marriage, which Corneille does not stage,[15] that can be used as a proof of Chimène's 'unnaturalness'. The marriage does not take place (except in history, which is another story, another 'stage'). There must be a more profound, more deeply perverse reason why the play, despite Corneille's careful denegations and despite the care he took not to shock the delicate feelings of his contemporaries, did shock them.

Rodrigue and Chimène form, of course, the central knot uniting the dynamics of history and desire in the play. They are, in the final analysis, the quintessential reduction, the dramatic icons of all the values and aspirations of the society in which they evolve. Not only are the two presented as complementary, they are also the perfect symmetrical reflections of each other. They are presented as an harmonious interior unity. All their difficulties arise not from themselves, not from their desires, but are imposed from without. Their love is presented as essentially unproblematic to them. We do not witness any evolution of their passion. It is presented as a 'fait accompli' from the beginning (and, therefore, from forever). From the moment the play commences they are shown not only as in love but as perfect lovers. Their passion is exclusive and reciprocal: 'J'aimais, j'étais aimée, et nos pères d'accord' (II, iii, 451). Each

believes in a mutually held set of values, and participates in a commonly held ideology, and each has for the other the same passion. Desire and history seem, at the outset of the play, to be one, a seamless whole.

Chimène and Rodrigue are so patently alike, in such a reciprocal relation, that if they were not 'lovers' one could almost see them as siblings, a perfect brother and sister pair.[16] Is this, in fact, so farfetched? Do they not share the 'same' father? Don Diègue and Don Gomès are interchangeable paternal figures, and their children reflect, as they gaze into each others' eyes, the same desire, the burning desire of the Father.

At the beginning of the play, then, Rodrigue and Chimène, this brother–sister of Patriarchy, are trapped within their mutual reflection of sameness.[17] The only difference that distinguishes them, the only mark that they are not the same, that they are not interchangeable, is a sexual (or rather, biological) one. Chimène is female. I pointedly settle the 'difference' on Chimène because in the world of Cornelian Patriarchy, difference is imposed by one's relation to the Father. In this relation it is the female, not the male, who carries the sign of something other, of something less.

Despite the rivalry, hatred and jealousies that exist between men in the synchronic present, on a more profound level men are always linked to each other by a mutually re-enforced system of knowledge and power. This system is based on the exclusion of the feminine. It articulates a notion of male integrity–unity that functions as a signifier of wholeness. Women, on the other-hand, are always inscribed as a disunity, a break in the integral. It is this difference, a 'difference within',[18] that Chimène, as well as the other Cornelian females, both represent and fight against.

At first glance nothing could be more symmetrical than the predicament in which both Rodrigue and Chimène find themselves. Act III, scene iv, the (in)famous act of confrontation, is structured as a perfect symmetrical duel. The alexandrines are used to their most powerful effect. They restructure in their well-cadenced verses the antagonistic situation that opposes the lovers. Here, for the first time, the difference between the two principal actors is reduced to the barest minimum, the hair's breadth of difference in the final verse they share:

> Ch. – Rodrigue, qui l'eût cru?
>
> R. – Chimène, qui l'eût dit?
>
> (III, iv, 987)

Each interpolates the other in one verse whose entire meaning turns around the opposition that the two articulate and reverse, affirming and denying their own separation within discourse (the switching of the names, the difference falling on past participles).

The scene spotlights the two lovers locked in battle. Chimène presents this battle as a reciprocal obligation, in which their honor battles their passion:

> Tu t'es en m'offensant, montré digne de moi;
> Je me dois, par ta mort, montrer digne de toi.
>
> (III, iv, 931–2)

The ultimate difference is articulated as a reduction of rhyme, of signification 'moi/toi'. The agonistic relation is accentuated at the same time that it is lost. For in this battle that she undertakes, Chimène, less, is already the loser.

In his analysis of the play, S. Doubrovsky, following O. Nadal's lead, shows us that in the clash that opposes these two heroes, Rodrigue relentlessly pursues Chimène in a verbal duel that reduces her to impotence. By refusing the mastery he has accepted, by refusing the ultimate test of 'Death', Chimène is subjugated. Rodrigue puts her in the position of inferior/slave.[19] It is true that Rodrigue leaves this arena a victor (once again). I would, however, like to suggest that in this duel Rodrigue has been fighting dirty: the cards are stacked against Chimène and her defense is, from the beginning, a defense that is a part of the system that condemns her to lose.

What distinguishes the female characters from the males in *Le Cid* is not their allegiance to a different set of values, or to an adverse ideology. Both Chimène and the Infanta wholly subscribe to the 'noble' ideals of their paternal order. In that order what separates the men from the women is the distinction between unity and division. Chimène and the Infanta can only articulate their presence, and thus their predicaments, in terms that identify them as sundered. When Chimène, at last, returns to her house, when she is free of the intruding presence of the court, the first words she utters define her as partition:

> La moitié de ma vie a mis l'autre au tombeau,
> Et m'oblige à venger, après ce coup funeste,
> Celle que je n'ai plus en celle qui me reste. (III, iii, 800–2)

Chimène is split, divided in two, and this division (between two males) is her being. Where, in this definition, is Chimène? Is she, finally, only the lesser sum of the Father–Lovers? Does she, in

other words, have a definition of herself that is not already
alienated in another's image?

This division generates the entire paradigmatic chain of signifiers
that Chimène uses to describe herself as an internalized conflict.
She is the battlefield of conflicting emotions, conflicting desires:

> C'est peu de dire aimer, Elvire, je l'adore;
> Ma passion s'oppose à mon ressentiment,
> Dedans mon ennemi je trouve mon amant;
>
> . . .
>
> Je demande sa tête, et crains de l'obtenir.
>
> (III, iii, 810–12, 825)

> Elvire, que je souffre! et que je suis à plaindre!
> Je ne sais qu'espérer et je vois tout à craindre;
> Aucun voeu ne m'échappe où j'ose consentir;
> Je ne souhaite rien sans un prompt repentir.
> A deux rivaux pour moi je fais prendre des armes:
> Le plus heureux succès me coûtera des larmes;
> Et quoi qu'en ma faveur en ordonne le sort,
> Mon père est sans vengeance ou mon amant est mort.
>
> . . .
>
> De tous les deux côtés on me donne un mari.
>
> (V, iv, 1645–52, 1659)

The Infanta, the only other litigious female character, also
articulates herself in terms of division:

> Je sens en deux parties mon esprit divisé,
> Si mon courage est haut, mon coeur est embrasé.
> Cet hymen m'est fatal, je le crains et souhaite
>
> . . .
>
> Ma gloire et mon amour ont pour moi tant d'appas,
> Que je meurs s'il s'achève ou ne s'achève pas.
>
> (I, ii, 119–21, 123–4)

This vision of women as rent is echoed by the men in their perception of them:

> Rodrigue aime Chimène et ce digne sujet
> De ses affections est le plus cher objet.
>
> (I, iii, 170–1, 1657–8 version)

In this sense, of course, Chimène and the Infanta are not really

rivals (despite what the Infanta might imply) but clones. In this schema, and on this level at least, women are united on one side of an ideological mirror, men on the other. It is this division and reflection that structures the parameters of sexuality and power in this world.[20]

Being split, Chimène is less able to accept the new order of Patriarchy that is evolving. Paradoxically, she appears, at the same time, to be the staunchest supporter of the Father. If, as we have suggested, the distinguishing mark of the male is a projection of unity that affirms while denying Death, that structures society around 'ideals' through the fetishistic compromise of castration and its sublimation as conscience (Law), and if this conscience's most imperious gesture is the recognition of its own transcendence in time, the belief in genealogy–history, then Chimène's most radically disruptive stance can be seen as a refusal of history.[21] She denies the sublimation of the self in temporality. As a woman Chimène is most clearly defined by her refusal of history, and this refusal corroborates her both as her 'father's daughter' and as the greatest enemy the new order faces.

Her grief and mourning enclose Chimène in an obsessive stance that refuses time: 'Le passé me tourmente et je crains l'avenir' (II, iii, 480). Not able to accept either a past or a future, she lives only in a present which finds her bereft, once again separated, cut off from the man whose desire defined her own and whose presence assured her of the only 'independence' (= indifference) she could maintain in the male order.

There is, therefore, operative in this play one more division, one more symmetrical split. This new division separates the 'good' children from the 'bad', the faithful sons of the new Father and the rebellious ones of the old. On the one side of the division stand Don Gomès and his supporters – Chimène and Don Sanche – on the other Don Diègue, the King's chosen representative, and his son Rodrigue. The Infanta, too, is aligned on this side of the division, completing the symmetry that opposes the nascent law of the polis (King) to the old order of chaos (Vassals).

Not only, therefore, in *Le Cid* do we have a symmetrical opposition of male–female (the generations of men, Diègue, Gomès, Rodrigue, and the women, Chimène and the Infanta) and of desire (Rodrigue–Chimène), there is also a more pervasive political opposition that informs this first antithesis and infuses it with an importance that is inseparable from the larger dynamics that underlie the more obvious 'natural' split of Chimène and Rodrigue. Just as

Don Gomès has to be eliminated, just as the bad son must be vanquished by the good because he is inimical to the State, so too must Chimène and her resistance be eliminated. She must be forced to abandon the (old) Father and to become incorporated within and to incorporate the structure of the new Father that this emerging society is articulating. It falls to Rodrigue, the icon of this society, successfully to accomplish this subjugation.

The initial act that marks Rodrigue as a 'hero', that sets him apart from mere mortals, is his killing of the (bad) father. The duel with Don Gomès is exceptional in many ways. Not only does Rodrigue's challenge of the Count uncover his inherent nobility, realizing a potential that heretofore had existed only as a 'promise':

> Ce grand coeur qui paraît aux discours que tu tiens
> Par tes yeux, chaque jour, se découvrait aux miens;
> Et croyant voir en toi l'honneur de la Castille,
> Mon âme avec plaisir te destinait ma fille   (II, ii, 419–22)

it also signals Rodrigue as a formidable opponent–warrior. More important still, the duel as a ritual putting to death of Gomès signals Rodrigue as being at once beyond the Law of the Father and its most ardent defender. Rodrigue's first venture into manhood does not free him from the confines of his own double-bind, it re-enforces his place within it.

By killing the Count Rodrigue has simply accomplished what was expected of him. He has passed from adolescence to full virility. He becomes a man. This passage is not accomplished without misgivings, nor is it unproblematic. The entire scene of the 'stances' is there to testify to this conflict about which so much has been written. I would only like to add a small coda to the 'ocean of ink' that these verses have already caused to flow.[22]

Although the killing of the Count marks Rodrigue's passage into manhood, his leaving a state of 'indeterminacy', and his taking his place in the progression of the generations, this act is just the result of a more important sacrifice that has already taken place and that the 'stances' emblematize. I am not suggesting that Rodrigue sacrifices his love. Forceful recent interpretations have clearly demonstrated that Rodrigue in choosing 'honor' is also choosing love.[23] In the code of honor–valor that informs his society Chimène could not love him, as she herself states, honorless. The real issue of the 'stances' does not lie in the manifest choice Father/Chimène, but rather in the deeper sexual-political investment that this choice camouflages.

In the scene of the 'stances' Rodrigue's position before killing the Count is symmetrical with Chimène's after the duel: he is divided. His meditation is still that of an adolescent. He jousts unevenly with an excess (of passion) that inheres in him and draws him towards that indifferent stance of division that is presented as the essence of femininity. In this monologue Rodrigue resembles – is – Chimène (still the 'sexless' brother in the symmetrical sibling couple) in that he articulates himself as the playground of contradictory forces:

> Que je sens de rudes combats!
> Contre mon propre honneur mon amour s'intéresse:
> Il faut venger un père, et perdre une maîtresse.
> L'un m'anime le coeur, l'autre retient mon bras.
>
>   · · ·
>
> Des deux côtés mon mal est infini.   (I, vi, 301–4, 307)

At the beginning Rodrigue is still torn between the conflictual demands of pleasure and social imperative in his inability to decide trenchantly (the obvious symbol of which is his refusal to assume the emblem of Paternal authority and descent – the sword, his veritable interlocutor during the entire scene). In a sense these 'stances' represent a much longer process that carries Rodrigue out of a position of bisexual ambivalence into an acceptance of the Law of the Father, into, that is, the sphere of the Integral ('je dois tout à mon père'). Rodrigue's conflict and his resolution of it, a resolution that represses pleasure, fragmentation and death, is their sublimation in an allegiance to the State. By opting for 'honor' – Father over Chimène (pleasure) – Rodrigue situates himself squarely within the Law. By opting for the Father, he opts for himself as a particularly invested sexuality within a given power schema. His allegiance to the Law assures him both of his individuality and of his place in genealogy. Having successfully conquered the divisive lure of pleasure, having sacrificed this principle, Rodrigue suppresses division and escapes from its torments ('ne soyons plus en peine').

At the same time, by opting for the Law of the Father Rodrigue situates himself as the 'good' son. He is thus structurally opposed to Gomès. Rodrigue both renounces femininity and upholds the principles of order that underpin the ideology of the new monarchical order that comes into being with him.

When, therefore, Rodrigue kills the Count he is re-enforcing a system of Patriarchy into which he, by this act, inscribes himself,

and which, in turn, defines him. At the same time, of course, Rodrigue is also attacking the 'Father', accomplishing, on quite another, but interrelated level, the Oedipal desire that is both affirmed and denied, and which, as an heroic act, places him outside the confines of society. If, as we have seen, all the men are interchangeable as 'essence', Rodrigue's removal of Gomès is tantamount to the destruction of his own father. Yet, by the political parameters of the play, by having structured Gomès as the bad retrograde father, Rodrigue's act is not a totally uncompromised infringement of a taboo. He eliminates the symbol of interdiction barring his way to sexual gratification. He eliminates the (apparent) obstacle separating him from the object of his desire. At the very moment, however, when this obstacle seems to disappear, at that moment when it actually disappears, it is incorporated into a legal–social network that is there to receive it, becoming a more diffuse, no less threatening presence.[24] The Count, dead, becomes a dangerous obstacle, which Gomès, alive, was not. Death immediately places him beyond the limits of the Law, which Rodrigue has infringed and which now defines itself as the imposition of difference, the separation of Rodrigue and Chimène into opposing (sexual) camps. What was an identical symmetrical desire is now, in each, routed through different antagonistic circuits, circuits that create a masculine/feminine opposition that appears irremediable.

This 'ritual' slaying of the Father, accomplished when Rodrigue accepts the symbol of this paternal legacy, the sword, is precisely double edged. While it frees Rodrigue from the obstacle of his own internal conflict it fixes Chimène in hers. As we saw, at the very outset of the play, Chimène's desire and her father's are the same. As long as he is alive, Chimène, because of her ambivalence, because of her 'division', can live her love as an unthreatening reflection of herself divided. The threatening aspect of sexuality is defended by the Father (= her honor). She externalizes this threat in her father who both symbolizes and yet mediates it for her. Her 'passion' appears safe because it is not opposed. When Rodrigue kills the Count, however, the mediating object is removed and immediately internalized as an exacerbation of conflict. Desire is now both stronger and more dangerous because the object of desire for both is stained with the blood of taboo. The father, dead, becomes an obstacle to passion for Chimène just at the moment when the elimination of the father establishes Rodrigue in his place. Rodrigue takes on, for Chimène, the attributes of both pleasure and Law – a combination that she cannot readily accommodate

because it effectively reduces her to nothing. She becomes a mere object. Her passion for Rodrigue now means her total negation in a system of masculine prerogative.

The duel and its outcome are only symptomatic of the reversal and strengthening of a double-bind; once Rodrigue accedes to the place of the Father he becomes the taboo object of Chimène's desire. The desire of the Father and the desire for the Father are inseparable. It is precisely this unity of Rodrigue which is imposed by the death he assumes that accentuates Chimène's split, dividing her more and more. It is through the mediation of the internalized dead Father that the sexual difference that separates the lovers in this play is defined.[25] Rodrigue, in a paradoxical reversal, forces Chimène out of an initial position of 'indifference' and into a position of 'difference', but this difference is inimical to him.

It is, therefore, from this position, from the imposition, through the mediation of the dead Father, of sexuality, that Rodrigue and Chimène confront each other as political rivals: 'Je sais qu'un père mort t'arme contre mon crime' (III, iv, 901). They have been separated by an abyss, the abyss of death, and the inherently different modes that men and women in Corneille have of confronting death.[26] It is a confrontation which confirms sexual and political difference and power distribution in the world, sundering the harmonious brother–sister couple into warring lover–rivals. It is this pairing off in opposition that forms the essential tragic knot of the play. It is this knot that has been tied by these structures and that cannot be untied until something exterior to those structures intervenes to change the sexual–political configuration that has heretofore obtained.

The central dilemma of the crucial verbal duel scene leads the two protagonists into an insoluble double-bind. Both are aware that there is no way out of their situation. The doors have been closed and they are locked into the confines of their frustrations. Venting his anger in his confrontation with his father, Rodrigue acknowledges only one way of untying this Gordian knot — death:

> Mes liens sonts trop forts pour être ainsi rompus;
> Ma foi m'engage encore si je n'espère plus;
> Et, ne pouvant quitter ni posséder Chimène,
> Le trépas que je cherche est ma plus douce peine.
>
> (II, vi, 1067–70)

Death presents itself to each as the only way out of their dilemma:

Ch. – Pour conserver ma gloire et finir mon ennui,
  Le poursuivre, le perdre, et mourir après lui.

(III, iii, 848–9)

It is only by a passage through Death that a resolution can be offered them. This resolution paradoxically makes of Death a new birth, a flight out of the confines of the taboo of the old order and into the new order of monarchical time.

Rodrigue is sent to (his) death three times by his father. The first time he is sent to the duel with Gomès:

> Venge-moi, venge-toi;
> Montre-toi digne fils d'un père tel que moi.
> Accablé de malheurs où le destin me range,
> Je vais les déplorer. Va, cours, vole et nous venge.

(I, v, 287–90)

The second time he is sent to fight the Moors:

> Dans ce malheur public mon bonheur a permis
> Que j'ai trouvé chez moi cinq cents de mes amis
>
> .   .   .
>
> Va marcher à leur tête où l'honneur te demande.

(III, vi, 1079–80, 1085)

Finally, the third time, Diègue insists that Rodrigue, fresh from his battle, must once again take up arms and duel with Sanche:

> Quoi! Sire, pour lui seul vous renversez des lois
> Qu'a vu toute la cour observer tant de fois!
> Que croira votre peuple et que dira l'envie,
> Si sous votre défense il ménage sa vie,
> Et s'en fait un prétexte à ne paraître pas
> Où tous les gens d'honneur cherchent un beau trépas?

(IV, v, 1415–20)

Each time that Rodrigue walks out on the field of honor, into Death, he returns reborn. Each time he is both nearer the father who 'sacrificed' him and farther away, on a higher, more distant plane.

Don Diègue's role in these situations is, to say the least, paradoxical. In each case, Rodrigue is his surrogate, sent forth into Death. He (Diègue), another Abraham, exposes his offspring, his future and the promise that future represents for him, to annihilation. By the same gesture Diègue, of course, exposes himself to the void of death.

57

In a sense, therefore, Diègue is in the curious position of representing the most obsessively repeated ultimatum of the play, the ultimatum of death (the 'meurs ou tue' of Doubrovsky), but, by this ultimatum of legitimizing his existence, proving that Rodrigue is his true son. At the same time that he represents the most inexorable prerogative of the Father and of the Law he also, in a perverse reversal, presides like a midwife over each rebirth of the son whose successive returns from death usher him once again into a new life. Curiously we detect that this figure most associated with the paternal imperative to renunciation is also a nurturing maternal symbol.[27] At least, Rodrigue, 'motherless', defines him as such:

> L'honneur vous en est dû; je ne pouvais pas moins,
> Etant sorti de vous et nourri par vos soins.   (III, vi, 1039–40)

Rodrigue has 'emerged' from Don Diègue and has been 'nurtured' by him. Under the repression of the Father we can perceive the no less ambivalent presence of the Mother.

Although we have been tracing the articulations of the patriarchal State in *Le Cid*, its origins, agents and dialectic, and although to do this we have been analyzing those figures of the State given to us in representation – the Fathers/Kings, men who dominate the scene, and the two women who bear the price of its repressions – it must be obvious that this overinvestment in objects of representable masculinity hides (represses) the feminine component also necessary for propagation, for genealogical descent. After *Médée* Corneille's great plays are glaringly motherless. It is as if Patriarchy not only ignores matrilineal descent, but even more radically eliminates the person (character) of the mother in a desperate attempt to place her outside the representable world, outside the 'eidos', and confuse her with the chaos of nature.

While no maternal figure is to be found in the cast of characters of *Le Cid* the play nevertheless contains an invisible presence that permeates and embraces the entire drama. This faceless, undefinable presence traces the absent body of the Mother that has been banished from representation. J. Derrida has discussed, in a different context, this ineffable maternal presence in the following terms:

For the Mother is the faceless, unfigurable figure of 'figurante'. She creates a place for all the figures by losing herself in the background like an anonymous persona. All returns to her – and, in the first place – all

addresses and destines itself to her. She survives – in the condition of remaining in the background.[28]

This 'faceless figurante' to whom all return cannot be seen in *Le Cid*, but beyond her invisibility we can detect her presence, for she can be heard. The entire play and all the characters in it, by the constant deference, the respect they show for the pervasive 'voice' of public rumor, also pay homage to the Mother.[29]

From the start of the drama to its end all of the characters evolve in a world that determines them and their predicaments, that is constantly approving or disapproving of them and to which they all bow. Nevertheless, this powerful presence remains 'nothing'. Although it cannot be touched it touches and affects them all. A voice which cannot be attributed to any 'person', which is always present as the hollow echo in another's discourse (the 'qu'en dira-t-on'), is the ethereal disembodiment of a nonperson, of an ambivalent, chaotic Other that exceeds the limits of the subject as defined by the laws of the patriarchal State. It is both inside and outside those laws. This disembodied voice is protean, necessarily taking on different timbres as it reverberates in the background of the drama. At times it serves as a projected metaphor for the State:

> Une grande princesse à ce point s'oublier
> Que d'admettre en son coeur un simple chevalier!
> Et que dirait le roi, que dirait la Castille?   (I, ii, 87–9)

> J'excuse ta chaleur à venger ton offense;
> Et l'état défendu me parle en ta défense.
> (IV, iii, 1253–4)

For the women in the play this voice assumes an admonitory tone. Always speaking in the present or the future tense, it warns them to keep their place in the social order. It reminds them of the consequences (ostracism) should they stray from the confines into which they have been placed:

> Que ne dira-t-on point si on te voit ici?
> Veux-tu qu'un médisant, pour comble à sa misère,
> L'accuse d'y souffrir l'assassin de son père?   (III, i, 768–70)

In these cases the voice is the echo of 'bad conscience', of the woman trapped in a desiring structure that is not hers and yet determines her. This is the voice that accuses Chimène of going

against 'nature', of being a traitor to her father and therefore to herself:

> Si l'on te voit sortir, mon honneur court hasard.
> La seule occasion qu'aura la médisance,
> C'est de savoir que j'ai souffert ta présence. (III, iv, 976–8)

For the women this 'voice' that is articulated in them is a constant summons to orthodoxy, a constant reminder not to infringe the limits that circumscribe and define them. The voice here represents Patriarchy's co-option of the feminine; it is the Mother who has internalized her own subservience, and who projects this servitude onto her daughters as their 'natural' condition. Here, the voice becomes the 'Mother Nature' of paternal order.

This punishing voice of the Mother can be equated to that aspect of the maternal figure that M. Klein identifies as the 'bad Mother', the Mother who intervenes to discipline and punish by reminding the daughter of her place in castration.[30] She echoes the Mother's relation to the Father. It is, however, precisely this reminder of an initial (unquestioned, because unconscious) repression that the play constantly echoes. These 'maternal', condemnatory voices are 'female' symptoms: by pointing to a future scandal they actually refer back to a past repression (to the origin of repression) in castration. It is this repression that must be constantly echoed as a reminder of the interdiction that split the sexes, that constituted the birth of sexual difference. This voice, then, inscribes in women a history of the subject as object of interdiction by re-inserting them in that history as the echo of the order that determines them.

At other moments (but often in the same mouths) the voice is heard again, not so much as the echo of a past origin but as the present matrix of generation. It is this voice that carries along and gives birth to the hero. Even before Rodrigue returns from his victory over the Moors everyone knows about the battle, talks about it. The rumor of his triumph precedes him. It is carried along by this voice. We first hear it *sotto voce*, as it were, in Chimène's anxious question to Elvire. 'Are the rumors she hears really true?' 'N'est-ce point un faux bruit?', she asks her confidante, hoping or fearing that it is. Elvire's answer is, however, unequivocal. There is good news from the front:

> Vous ne croiriez jamais comme chacun l'admire
> Et porte jusqu'au ciel d'une commune voix
> De ce jeune héros les glorieux exploits. (IV, i, 1102–4)

[Du] peuple qui partout fait sonner ses louanges
Le nomme de sa joie et l'objet et l'auteur
Son ange tutélaire et son libérateur.   (IV, i, 1114–16)

This rumor that starts as a whisper, as a confidence between the two women, gains in volume throughout the two scenes, ending in a crescendo of voices heard everywhere:

Je l'entends partout publier hautement
Aussi brave guerrier que malheureux amant.

(IV, ii, 1155–6)

By listening to this voice that cannot be stifled, by being enveloped by it and in it, we are, along with Chimène and the Infanta, present at the birth of a new, another, Rodrigue. Having been sent into Death by the Father, the hero is delivered by the praising voice of the Mother. This voice, in which his deeds resound, creates him anew as legend. This voice, in ever-increasing hosannas, makes public his new identity, and does so by repeating the mark of his different status, his new name, the 'Cid'. From the Rodrigue who left to battle the enemies and who was trapped within the double-bind of his own allegiance to the Law of the Father we are now presented with a character metamorphosed in the voice of popular adulation. The child of that adulation, Rodrigue has, by becoming the 'Cid', transcended the double-bind of history/desire. By assuming a new name conferred on him by a foreign Other, Rodrigue–the Cid partakes of both interior and exterior.[31] He is affirmed by the voices that enfold him, voices that repeat eternally the heroic deeds that are no longer condemned to the moment. The Cid transcends Death and also the necessity of history. He is constantly present, reborn in the transhistorical voice of legend:

Ce portrait vivant que je vous offre représente un héros assez reconnaissable aux lauriers dont il est couvert. Sa vie a été une suite continuelle de victoires; son corps porté dans son armée a gagné des batailles après sa mort, et son nom, au bout de six cents ans vient encore triompher en France.   (Corneille, 'Epître dédicatoire à Mme de Combalet', p. 5)

This new name, by replacing his debt to the Father, frees him from the dialectic of castration/sublimation, places him above the Law and concomitantly makes him the greatest symbol of that Law:

Ils t'ont nommé tous deux leur Cid en ma présence:
Puisque Cid en leur langue est autant que seigneur

.   .   .

Sois désormais le Cid; qu'à ce beau titre tout cède.

(IV, iii, 1222–3, 1225)

Chimène's predicament, her insistence in persecuting Rodrigue, is inextricably bound to the voices she hears and to the ways these voices entrap her further within the bind of patriarchal guilt. The force of this voice (the hollow sound of the bad Mother) determines the course of Rodrigue's and Chimène's passion. It is the echo that validates their vision of 'gloire', a vision which is diametrically opposed in its masculine and feminine interpretations. The glory of the 'brother–lover' is destined by the voice to a place in the world, to a career of arms and conquest. The sister's 'gloire' on the other hand is in her passivity, that is, in her desirability (beauty) which destines her to remain the reflection of the brother.[32] In other words, while the voice sends the son out into the world, confirming a pre-excellence of masculinity, the voice of the (bad) Mother condemns, by this same token, the women to a position of closure, to a narcissistic relation to the world. It is this 'chassé-croisé' of conflicting demands that is echoed in the transgression that constitutes Rodrigue's and Chimène's passion and which makes its resolution impossible. It is also, of course, that element that carries the desirability of the taboo, that allows the two lovers to flirt with each other and death. Each seeks the contravention of this social law:

> Crains-tu si peu le blâme, et si peu les faux bruits?
> Quand on saura mon crime et que ta flamme dure,
> Que ne publieront point l'envie et l'imposture! (III, iv, 964–6)

Here, the voice condemns its object to social death, to ostracism by its negating force, but it also serves in a masochistic dialectic of confirming an inherently retrograde narcissism of Chimène:

> Et je veux que la voix de la plus noire envie
> Elève au ciel ma gloire et plaigne mes ennuis.
>
> (III, iv, 970–1)

The voice that Chimène hears condemns her passion, but this condemnation is turned by her into a paean of glory, the paean of her own sacrifice to the Father (to her own death).

Chimène is trapped by voices that allow her no movement out of the dialectic of division in which she, as woman, is inscribed by the Law, no movement out, that is, other than the narcissistic position of self-destruction. Chimène, lost in her self-enclosure, can only look at death, at her own castration, and dwell in it. She cannot transcend it. In an attempt to reconcile her own desire to her father's, she condemns herself to the obsessive repetition of a

closure that can mean only a denial of both history and society. At the same time, this self-enclosed celebration of death is a powerful political force because it, like her father's behaviour, is tightly bound to a code of social comportment that the society of *Le Cid* is only gradually abandoning. Chimène's self-absorption refuses any ideal of change, refuses commitment to 'progress', to chronology. This refusal is tantamount to condemning her entire world to the stasis of death.

Chimène refuses to see (hear) what everyone else realizes — that the 'Cid' no longer exists within the same dynamics of history and desire as did Rodrigue. Rodrigue has been transformed, and this transformation has touched society and changed it too. The heroism of the Cid has given society the image it needed to resist backsliding into the abyss of chaos. The Infanta articulates this new status quite explicitly:

> Je n'aime plus Rodrigue.
>
> . . .
>
> Si j'aime, c'est l'auteur de tant de beaux exploits,
> C'est le valeureux Cid, le maître de deux rois.
>
> (v, iv, 1633,1635–6)

The Infanta loves the transcendent essence that has replaced Rodrigue and that she has always fantasized. She, as well as the rest of the court, recognizes in him something that both crystallizes all the values that they have internalized and that defines their world and, at the same time, something that transcends the limits of the world.

This is what Chimène, in her division, cannot accept. She remains in rebellion against the murderer of her father and thus in revolt against the State. Chimène's rebellion is always alienated by being ritualized as a passage from one father to another — from Gomès to the King ('Ton roi te veut servir de père au lieu de lui') to Don Sanche.

Chimène remains the troubling conundrum in the evolution of the society of the *Cid* because she refuses, or is incapable of, the right 'political' choice, the choice that would break her off from the old regressive order of her father and ally to the new order towards which the whole of her world tends. She remains as divided, 'indifferent', at the end of the play as the beginning, caught up in a battle for the past, for death that cannot endure:

> Et toi, puissant moteur du destin qui m'outrage,
> Termine ce combat sans aucun avantage
> Sans faire aucun des deux ni vaincu ni vainqueur.
>
> (v, iv, 1665–7)

It is perhaps in this sense that Chimène is most scandalous. It is not because she accepts the marriage to Rodrigue, but because she postpones it. The 'hyménée qui (à trois également) importe', that is the crux of the whole play because it is the symbol both of her subjugation and the promise of the continuation of society as it has been defined, is deferred. It is left in suspense. Desire is rekindled but also made to burn hotter, fanned by scandal, by blood. Much has been changed politically in the course of this play. Time has been skewed out of all verisimilitude in order to demonstrate the uncomfortable moments of the passage of history, of a new order being born and imposed by a society that still lives very much on the tremulous borders separating sublimation in chronology and the celebration of death in the evanescent present. Yet some things remain unresolved: Chimène's protest, although silenced, is still real. At the end of the play the ambiguous contradictory voices of the invisible Mother–chorus fall silent. Only one voice is heard, the King's. It is the univocal voice of newly enhanced authority. This voice proclaims the power of time, the authority of evolution, to legitimate what in the old order was outside the limits of legality:

> Le temps assez souvent a rendu légitime
> Ce qui semblait d'abord ne se pouvoir sans crime.
>
> (v, vii, 1813–14)

The last words of the King are a deferral of the paradox that neither he nor the play can resolve, but that manifests a new desire, a desire that time, a new chronology, finally put in place by the Cid, can triumph over Chimène:

> Pour vaincre un point d'honneur qui combat contre toi,
> Laisse faire le temps.   (v, vii, 1839–40)

It is not for nothing that the King has the last word in this play, that his speech is followed by silence. But how are we to interpret this ending? Is it a universal approval, assuring Chimène's eventual (historical) espousal of the Cid? Or is it not just one more question mark indicating that the battle is not over, that the Cid as transcendental masculinity, has not totally recuperated this woman, reduced her to appropriation? Perhaps the really scandalous nature of the play remains in its inability to speak, to answer the King, to agree with him. Corneille himself has warned us, in his 'Examen', that, while silence is usually a sign of consent, when the speaker is the King, silence is perhaps the only way to show one's disapproval:

Le Cid: Father/Time

Je sais bien que le silence passe d'ordinaire pour une marque de consenti-
ment; mais quand les rois parlent, c'en est une de contradiction: on ne
manque jamais de leur applaudir quand on entre dans leurs sentiments; et
le seul moyen de leur contredire avec le respect qui leur est dû, c'est de se
taire.   ('Examen', p. 13)

The enigma of *Le Cid*, its scandal, is its ultimate stillness. After the
final speech of the King silence falls with the curtain. But who can
tell what beginning or what end is contained in that hollow absence,
or what, when the voices speak again, they will say?

3

HORACE, CLASSICISM AND FEMALE TROUBLE

'Mais si près de l'hymen . . .'

Horace marks an epiphanous moment in the history of the theater. In this, Corneille's first 'tragédie régulière', Classicism, full blown and triumphant, emerges as the paragon of a new esthetic. Suddenly, a work captures and perfects those laws of harmony, symmetry and 'bienséances' that up to this point the theater had only stumbled towards blindly. The term 'tragédie régulière' that Corneille's contemporaries used to describe this new mode of representation refers both to an ethos and to an esthetic. In a first sense 'régulière' designates a work which follows the rules: those rules of unity, of imitation and verisimilitude that were first articulated (or so it was thought) by Aristotle. A regular tragedy obeys the Law. This obedience, reproduced as spectacle, continually serves as a new production of the Law's origin, the founding act of society. Secondly, 'régulière' defines the esthetic parameters of such a representation. By following the rules Classicism achieves a wholeness, an integrity of being in which the various parts of the work are subsumed in a unified, total structure. This unity stands as a condemnation of excess; it allows no overflow.

The obedience to the Law would seem, therefore, to be the structuring principle around which Corneille's Classicism elaborates the symmetry so necessary for its success. Curiously it is this 'symmetry' that Corneille in his critique of *Horace* (written twenty years later) claims is missing. The spectacle that ushers in a new epoch in the history of representation does not itself conform to that esthetic: 'C'est une croyance assez générale que cette pièce pourrait passer pour la plus belle des miennes si les derniers actes répondaient aux premiers' (*Horace*, 'Examen', p. 780).[1] The play is marred by imbalance. The last acts are out of kilter with the first. Instead of harmony there is disequilibrium. An imperfect reflection decenters the play, condemning it to the world of the asymmetrical. A hidden flaw at the origin of Classicism signals its own slippage into what it attempts to repress.

66

Corneille is quick to identify the culprit responsible for this flaw. The new Pandora who unleashes the strident notes of discord into what otherwise would be mimetic perfection is (a) woman:

Tous veulent que la mort de Camille en gâte la fin et j'en demeure d'accord, mais je ne sais si tous en savent la raison. On l'attribue à ce qu'on voit cette mort sur la scène; ce qui serait plutôt la faute de l'actrice que la mienne, parce que quand elle voit son frère mettre l'épée à la main, la frayeur si naturelle au sexe, lui doit faire prendre la fuite et recevoir le coup derrière le théâtre.   (*Horace*, 'Examen', p. 780)

The scandal is double. First, Camille's death spoils the unity of tragic action (it is considered a 'secondary' action), and secondly, to make matters worse, the actress who played Camille refused to die 'en cachette'. Rather, assuming her role, she assumes the death that is its culmination. She insists on being slain on stage before the horrified eyes of the audience. Against all 'bienséances' this woman forces the spectators to bear witness to, and thus partake in, her murder.

In his *Discours de l'utilité et des partis du poème dramatique* Corneille explicitly states that for a drama to be worthy of the title 'tragedy' it must primarily be concerned with politics. Passion can be only a secondary interest: '[La] dignité [de la tragédie] demande quelque grand intérêt d'Etat ou quelque passion plus noble et plus mâle que l'amour' (*Discours*, p. 13). Politics rather than passion will be the central concern of his plays, but 'politics' is immediately sexualized by metaphor − 'mâle'. The tragedy that is political projects an ideal of virility that is affirmed by the structures of representation. This representation is wholly inscribed within the mimesis of an order of the Integral, of the One. The circle of representation–ideology closes back on itself presenting this order as a 'natural' one, the only order possible. *Horace*, as the first regular tragedy, is above all a political act of situating the origin of the Law in the mutual imbrication of family and State (where the public supplies and replaces the private) under the totalizing gaze of a domineering master, Father/King. It is from the point of view of this totalizing masterful gaze that *Horace* elaborates the symmetry upon which its unity develops. It is an order that from the beginning is never questioned but which, in its diverse manifestations, is always a pre-condition, a naturalized state from which what it does not wish to see is already excluded.

From the beginning, then, *Horace* is invested as a representation of repression. The very first lines of the play introduce us into a universe that is split. The verses themselves are beautifully cadenced

counterpoints whose antithetical rhetoric prefigures (and normalizes) all the other divisions that inform this universe; male is opposed to female, family to State, passion to reason, Rome to Alba.

> Approuvez ma faiblesse et souffrez ma douleur;
> Elle n'est que trop juste en un si grand malheur;
> Si près de voir sur moi fondre de tels orages,
> L'ébranlement sied bien aux plus fermes courages;
> Et l'aspect le plus mâle et le moins abattu
> Ne saurait sans désordre exercer sa vertu.
> Quoique le mien s'étonne à ses rudes alarmes,
> Le trouble de mon coeur ne peut rien sur mes larmes;
> Et parmi les soupirs qu'il pousse vers les cieux
> Ma constance du moins règne encore sur mes yeux. (I, i, 1–10)

Although Sabine's speech introduces us into a world of symmetry, into a world divided between opposing, exclusive forces, her monologue also affords us another introduction. A curious intrusion, the force of her emotions, of ambiguity, gives the lie to the dominant rhetoric:

> Quand on arrête là les déplaisirs d'une âme,
> Si l'on fait moins qu'un homme on fait plus qu'une femme;
> Commander à ses pleurs en cette extrémité,
> C'est montrer pour le sexe assez de fermeté. (I, i, 11–14)

Within language, Sabine creates a space for herself that cannot quite be accommodated by the society that she articulates. A chiasmatic comparison, by crossing the two limits of her discourse (homme–femme), allows Sabine, for an instant, to fall out of representation. She situates herself in a space that is neither a man's nor a woman's but is somewhere 'in between'. It is this space 'in between' which is uninhabitable. It is a space where all are drawn and where none may reside.

In *Horace* the confines of security, of the representable, are determined essentially by the family. The State of which this play is so much the mirror is only a magnified projection of the family unit. This unit is a closed house dominated by an older male who embodies a philosophy of renunciation, a philosophy of negation and sublimation. The Father/King is identified as the cutting voice of interdiction. He is, in the final analysis, the ultimate authority, holding the power of life and death in his hands, as Vieil Horace in his anger is quick to point out:

Horace, Classicism and female trouble

J'atteste des grands dieux les suprèmes puissances,
Qu'avant ce jour fini, ces mains, ces propres mains
Laveront dans son sang la honte des Romains.

(III, vi, 1048–50)

At the same time the Father is the porte-parole of the 'Ideal', of social and political values that underpin human organization. His arbitration in all matters concerning family/State are validated as a rejection of excess – emotional, sexual, or 'passionel'. Excess is denied as a negative, anti-republican plot. It is negated most forcefully in the image of the Patriarch himself, who, paradoxically, symbolizes 'masculinity' to the highest degree precisely because he is, in a sense, no longer 'masculine'. He is unsexed. His age has de-eroticized him, allowing him to become a pure Ideal. He exists without the burden of sexuality, practically, we might say, a eunuch. He is always present to serve as a model for his sons. They, 'sexed', are much less sure of their own powers of renunciation. Still attracted to, they can be swayed by, the feminine, the feminine in them. The Father always arrives at the opportune moment to remind them of their duty to be men, a duty which can be accomplished only be fleeing the contaminating emotionality of women:

Qu'est-ceci mes enfants? écoutez-vous vos flammes?
Et perdez-vous encore le temps avec des femmes?
Prêts à verser du sang, regardez-vous des pleurs?
Fuyez, et laissez-les déplorer leurs malheurs.
Leurs plaintes ont pour vous trop d'art et de tendresse;
Elles vous feraient part enfin de leur faiblesse,
Et ce n'est qu'en fuyant qu'on pare de tels coups.

(II, vii, 679–85)

The parameters of familial organization that this particular society establishes, and that this spectacle reproduces, are based not so much on a biological distinction of sex, a distinction that only functions as an 'après-coup' justification of a political investment, but rather on how certain bodies can be counted upon to serve as political entities; that is, the capacity for renunciation and sublimation that the sexes manifest in their relation to the interdiction of the signifier (Patriarch).[2] Since these capacities are not sex-derived, but imposed on sex, since, that is, they are imposed differently by Patriarchy as it defines masculinity and femininity, their hold is not unilateral; margins of ambiguity remain possible, margins that must be watched and controlled by the State. Horace père enters the scene, walks into the tragic universe to impose/save

definition. He is there to remind the men to be men by reminding them of the ties that, binding them to sublimation, protect them from their own femininity.

This separation of the men from the women is made therefore on the level of signification. Men are men and women women, that is 'different', because of the relation each maintains to repression. In *Horace* this relation is most obvious in the way the characters relate to Death. For the men, Death, as excess, is a metaphor for an absence that is synonymous with a loss of control, a loss of self. It is a sign of their masculinity that Death surfaces in their discourse always as a metaphor. Death, like femininity, is repressed as the dispersion of individual uniqueness in bodily corruption and is acknowledged only as a form of supplementation. Death is never allowed into discourse in any way that is not already a deferral; it is always Death as 'sacrifice', as 'immolation'. Death, metaphorized, is the sublimating signifier of a political being:

> H. – Mourir pour le pays est un si digne sort,
>   Qu'on briguerait en foule une si belle mort.
>   Mais vouloir au public immoler ceux qu'on aime . . .
>
>   (II, iii, 441–3)

> Cur. – Hélas, je vois trop bien qu'il faut, quoique je fasse,
>   Mourir ou de douleur ou de la main d'Horace.
>   Je vais comme au supplice . . .   (II, iv, 535–7)

These images equate Death to a spectacular passage. In this passage no man is (really) destroyed. The passage functions as an apotheosis. A man is changed into an ideal – duty, glory, honor – which, in turn, is recuperated as the reflection of the dominant ideology of the State. In this sense Death's supplementation as metaphor is an act of sublimation that assures the ties of men to the State. We can even say that it is in the repression of Death as a physical distinction – as an end – and in its recuperation as metaphor that the State comes into existence.[3]

In the context of Cornelian tragedy the metaphorization of Death is always the representation of the masculine. It is this 'representation' that is the proof of masculinity's acceptance of 'castration' and of its capacity to sacrifice for and to ideals. Men are men because they repress the purely excessive, the physical, by never allowing it to be, without being immediately inscribed within the metaphysical. The passage into Death and the passage of Death into discourse as other validates a man's position in the family and in the State. Therefore any chance to confront Death – to confirm

the Law – that circuitously confirms virility is an honor that should be embraced with joy:

> H. – Contre qui que ce soit que mon pays m'emploie,
>   J'accepte aveuglément, cette gloire avec joie
>
> (II, iii, 491–2)

> M. – Dirai-je au dictateur dont l'ordre ici m'envoie,
>   Que vous le recevez avec si peu de joie?   (II, ii, 415–16)

This investment in metaphor is both powerful and perverse. It is the foundation of all political integrity, affirming the value of the individual only at the price of his disappearance in the ideal. Sublimation separates the masculine from the feminine by attributing to femininity chaotic disintegration which is unspeakable and relegated outside discourse.

It is precisely this leap into metaphor (into the political) that is denied the women in *Horace*. They are identified as feminine by their inability to sublimate Death.[4] For them Death is never spoken of as anything other than the physical horror of bodily rot. They cannot see (speak) beyond it:

> Cam. – La nuit a dissipé des erreurs si charmantes;
>   Mille songes affreux, mille images sanglantes,
>   Ou plutôt mille amas de carnage et d'horreur,
>   M'ont arraché ma joie et rendu ma terreur,
>   J'ai vu du sang, des morts, et n'ai rien vu de suite.
>
> (I, iii, 215–19)

> S. – Je sens mon triste coeur percé de tous les coups
>   Qui m'ôtent maintenant un frère ou un époux.
>   Quand je songe à leur mort, quoi que je me propose,
>   Je songe par quel bras, et non pour quelle cause,
>   Et ne vois les vainqueurs en leur illustre rang
>   Que pour considérer aux dépens de quel sang.
>
> (III, i, 749–54)

The exclusion of women from sublimation, their inability to understand war as anything other than a sickening carnage, doubly affects their place in society. Effectively this inability determines their powerlessness in the State, since they can never subscribe entirely to the ideology that founds the polis. At the same time their position (for the State) is always suspicious; they can never become one with it. Their inability to control through denial/repression that which exceeds the 'limits' of a subject marks them, for the masculine, as a dangerous indeterminacy. They are never quite contained, never quite 'whole', and therefore never fit exactly into

those limits that define the State. It is for this reason that marriage, the appropriation of women, their incorporation in the family plays, once again, as in *Le Cid*, such a critical, ambiguous role in *Horace*.

In the Cornelian universe a woman is given an identity, exists as a subject, only through her relation to a man. She is defined as daughter, wife or sister. It is this definition which includes her in or excludes her from a particular political entity (Rome or Alba). Women go from one camp to another, from one male to another.[5] This exchange is ritualized by marriage. If this passage is not effected smoothly, if it is not consummated, it can prove to be extremely threatening. Being left in between, in the ambiguous space, a 'no-man's land' between the two spheres of masculine definition, underlies the inherent irreducibility of women. Once this passage is made, however, once the appropriation has turned indifference into difference, women are expected to become entire, either completely Roman or Alban:

> S. – Je suis Romaine, hélas, puisque Horace est Romain;
> J'en ai reçu le titre en recevant sa main;   (I, i, 25–6)

When married, a woman is expected to participate in her husband's camp having renounced those ties to her former identity. She must repress her 'partition', the fact that she is always both, to become One. But if there is anything a woman (in Corneille) 'is', it is precisely not One. In a world of masculine prerogative, a world in which being and subjectivity are precisely the male model of the Unique, of the Integral, women who are not all, who are always double, are continually a problem.

Women, however, can never be totally reappropriated by marriage. They never hear the voice of the Law as men do, never submit entirely to it. Rather, a woman's place remains ambivalent. She acts (for the men) as a shuttle going back and forth between the camps, between the men, most herself 'in between'.[6] This position is threatening to the 'limits' of masculine representation because it always risks giving the lie to them. Perhaps it is for this reason that the women in the play are portrayed as a troubling, never controlled sensibility, whose manifestation, the image of their own plethora, is what they continually shed – their tears.

It is these tears that men must flee lest they become contaminated, lest they melt away. This fluid excess is contagious, dissolving male containment and rigidity. In the face of feminine emotion men cannot remain men. They lose their sense of self, lose their tautness:

H. – O ma femme!
>Cur. – O ma soeur!
>>Cam. – Courage, ils s'amolissent.
>>>(II, vi, 663)

If allowed to remain in the presence of excess, the men become flaccid. It is to protect their virility, to protect the State, that men must flee women and remain among themselves.

Tears are, of course, only the most obvious metaphor for feminine excess.[7] They are part of an entire representational network that subtends the essential splitting of the play into male and female worlds. Blood is a far more ambivalent manifestation of bodily excess, of liquification, shared equally but differently by both sexes. In the universe of Corneille's drama we can locate the epicenter of tragedy in the blood that courses through the text, through the veins of the characters. It is an eminently ambivalent image, an image that is both physical and metaphysical, that unites in itself all the oppositions whose maintenance is so important for the structures of the play, for the structures of Patriarchy, and confounds them all.

A chorus no longer exists in Classical theater. It would seem as if the text itself takes over the function that, in more ancient times, was entrusted to an anonymous commentator. In *Horace* the chorus is incorporated in the text. Like the Neapolitan mob crying for the 'sangue' of its saint, the text echoes the word 'blood' and its derivatives throughout the play, calls for its own release in sacrifice. Defying the repression it is subject to, 'blood' resurfaces constantly in the course of the tragedy, creating an acoustic network that underlines and prepares the eruption of the tragic in this universe of containment. It is precisely the polysemic ambiguity of the word that enables it to reappear and to function as a signifier of both masculinity and femininity.

For the man, blood retains (as with death) an inherently metaphysical status. It represents genealogy, family and history. As part of a metaphoric axis, it has an essentially vertical imbrication in the text, uniting lower to higher, men to family, and family to State. In masculine terms blood binds men together in collectivity. A son receives his 'blood' from his father who remains its true proprietor. The father can reclaim it whenever he wishes.[8] The sign of being a perfect son/citizen is the willingness to return your blood to its origin: 'Disposez de mon sang,' Horace tells his father, 'les lois vous en font maître.' By this same process of idealization this

blood which belongs to the father is also the property of the State, the 'Fatherland'. The State can also demand its sacrifice:

> Sire, on se défend mal contre l'avis d'un roi;
> Quand aux yeux de son prince il paraît condamnable,
> C'est crime envers lui se vouloir excuser.
> Notre sang est son bien, il en peut disposer.   (v, iii, 1538–41)

Just as men sublimate Death so too must they retain blood which, contained, makes them men. Their blood is never lost, but circulates in metaphor from generation to generation and from individual to State. As opposed to females, men do not lose blood. They do not bleed. When they shed blood, they do so in another place outside the polis, between the two political constructions that define them, in the space of 'indifference'. The eruption of blood in the world of men is co-eval with the appearance of another order of representation, or rather of an order that exceeds representation.

For the women, on the contrary, blood represents an essential co-mingling that excludes metaphysical 'distinction'. It is in their own bodies that bloods come together – to form a new, yet indistinct co-mixture. While men see the erection of oppositions, the women can only see a displacement along a horizontal (metonymic) axis.[9] This co-mingling of blood in a feminine perspective abolishes, rather than maintains, separation as a political necessity.

> S. – Ingrate, souviens-toi que du sang de ses rois
> Tu tiens ton nom, tes murs et tes premières lois.
> Albe est ton origine; arrête et considère
> Que tu portes le fer dans le sein de ta mère.   (I, i, 53–6)

On the one hand women are shuttles, going back and forth between the two cities, the two poles of masculine symmetry. On the other hand, they create, within their own bodies, by the mixing of blood, the new ties that, unrecuperated in Patriarchy, would remain essentially indistinguishable, neither one nor the other but both. The oppositions that so rigidly structure the tragic universe are always ambivalent for them. They are imposed by a power structure that purposely and forcefully ignores them. All the women know what the men allow in their discourse *in extremis* – 'Nous ne sommes qu'un sang et qu'un peuple en deux villes' (I, iii, 291) and that a distinction between a brother's blood and a husband's is impossible:

Je verrai les lauriers d'un frère ou d'un mari
Fumer encore d'un sang que j'aurai tant chéri.

(II, vi, 649–50)

It is this 'indifference' that is intolerable to masculinity. It must
be split into two. The origin of this indifference, its 'matrix', is
somewhere 'in between' the poles of genealogy. This oscillation
confounds the males. What the men dislike and distrust in
themselves, and what inheres in them and must be destroyed, is
their own indifferent origin. In essence this means that they wish
to destroy (repress, negate) women who create them and from
whose embrace they cannot escape. Women are the mediators,
creating a threatening vortex of masculine co-mingling. In this
(fantasmatic) scenario femininity must be paradoxically both
denied and affirmed; denied because it is an indifference that
signifies too close a male sexual bonding to be tolerable, affirmed
precisely to stand in for this homosexual co-mingling. Women, in
this appropriation, protect men from their own mutual desire.
They represent a reflection of difference as a mirror which can
repeat male desire while refracting it.[10]

Although Camille's and Sabine's situations appear at first to be
different only in degree, they are, for the reality of the tragedy,
radically separate. From the outside, to the observer in her en-
tourage, Camille's misfortune is perceived to be less absolute
because, unlike Sabine, she is not married. Camille can, she is told,
simply renege on her commitment to Curiace, sever her ties to the
enemy and find an appropriate partner in the Roman camp. By so
doing she would be free of the torments of ambivalence which con-
found her and Sabine:

Elle [S.] est pourtant plus à plaindre que vous.
On peut changer d'amant mais non changer d'époux.
Oubliez Curiace et recevez Valère:
Vous ne tremblerez plus pour le parti contraire.
Vous serez toute notre et votre esprit remis
N'aura plus rien à perdre au camp des ennemis. (I, ii, 145–50)

By sacrificing her 'lover' she can stop oscillating ('trembler') and
become whole ('toute'). Julie's solution, which is, at one time or
another, the solution of all the members of her family, is the correct, political one. This is, of course, exactly what Camille refuses:

Donnez-moi des conseils que soient plus légitimes.
Et plaignez mes malheurs sans m'ordonner des crimes.

(II, ii, 151–2)

Instead of opting for a solution that would release her from the bonds of an untenable position, Camille steadfastly clings to her ambivalence. She refuses to become 'toute', that is to become virilized, but remains ambivalent – 'pas-toute'.

Although this refusal to abdicate to political expedience has traditionally been interpreted as Camille's (romantic) defense of love over 'raison d'Etat', has, in other words, been seen as an 'unambiguous' affirmation of love, I would like to suggest that Camille's obstinacy in opting for love is actually the only chance she has to maintain her ambivalence, her place 'in between'. What Camille opts for, and what makes her difficult, is her 'love' rather than her lover. It allows her to assume an excess that is denied and to assume her being as a space of mediation, an essential 'blank' in representation, a 'no-man's land' of indeterminacy.

From the very beginning of the play, Camille explicitly states that she will never marry Curiace:

> Cher amant, n'attends plus d'être un jour mon époux;
> Jamais, jamais ce nom ne sera pour un homme
> Qui soit le vainqueur ou l'esclave de Rome.   (I, ii, 230–2)

We would do well to listen to what she says: 'jamais, jamais'. It is clear that Curiace is important to Camille because he is (in the chronology of their love) absent. This absence allows her – unique among her sex – to remain in an intermediary position, neither (yet) Alban, no longer (entirely) Roman. She continues to toe a precarious line that remains close to appropriation, but does not succumb to it: 'Mais si près de l'hymen' (III, iv, 886). Curiace is allowed to come close to the 'hymen' but is also kept from it. Camille retains her indeterminacy by exposing it, but never letting it be breached.

Camille is obviously the character most concerned with her 'hymen'. In rebuffing Sabine's contention that she rather than Camille is actually more pitiful, Camille tells her that, on the contrary, marriage resolves the problem of a woman's dual loyalty by placing her, squarely, in the family (house) of her husband:

> L'hymen qui nous attache en une autre famille
> Nous détache de celle où l'on a vécu fille.   (III, iv, 883–4)

As the rhetoric of her statement reveals, however, this appropriation is never a totally untainted transferral. We can see that while here Camille is talking about the political consequence of marriage ('hymen' as a metaphor for marriage), her use of words reveals consequences that are far more important for the tragedy. If we

take 'hymen' in its metonymic rather than in its metaphoric sense, the word functions as a signifier for the woman herself. Just as the woman's place is most properly her own, 'in between', so too is the 'hymen', that diaphanous membrane. It is the most invested avatar of feminine ambivalence — separating inside from outside, virgin from wife, socialized from non-socialized, appropriated from free.

If we understand Camille's statement purely as a metaphor we are following a (masculine) slippage that reflects the political significance of marriage, and elides the violent gesture that this appropriation implies. Camille tells us, however, that marriage serves a dual function; it 'attaches' and 'detaches' the women. It seems clear, however, that the affirmation/denial which is at work in the prefixes ('at–dé') really suppresses another reading which defies their either/or rhetoric. Marriage, that is the hymen's appropriation by the male, his piercing of it, is paid for in blood. The hymen both 'at-taches', and 'dé-taches', but what it seems most significantly to do is 'tacher' (that is, to stain). The man is tainted by his appropriation of female indifference. Man, in marriage, destroys femininity as ambivalence, placing the woman 'inside' his structures of representation. This act, however, can never be contained. It provokes, at the very instant that the hymen, as 'difference', is breached, a new violence, the flowing of blood. It is this staining which, eventually, leads all the characters from the world of the self-contained, mutually opposed units, into the terror of the 'Other'.[11]

Unlike Sabine, who is married, and who is, therefore, despite her constant emotional turmoil, politically 'fixed', Camille is free-floating. She drifts in a nether space outside the symmetrical structures that define her society. Her indifference discovers the 'mauvaise foi', the self-inflicted blindness, that is necessary for the power of the Father to exist and to be re-presented. She becomes the perfect 'paria', uniquely qualified to serve as a principle victim of Patriarchy's revenge, the perfect sacrificial lamb.

There is, therefore, an original tension which Camille inscribes within the structures of the drama. For the women (and for those 'feminized' males — i.e. Curiace), there is a malaise at not being able to define themselves. They never successfully 'cross over' the space of indeterminacy, but remain inside it, filling it up, being both at once. This inexpugnable ambivalence is expressed as oscillation, of being continually tossed back and forth, from Rome to Alba, from husband to brother, from family to State:

> Je suis Romaine, hélas, puisque Horace est Romain:
> J'en ai reçu le titre on recevant sa main;

Mais ce noeud me tiendrait en esclave enchaînée,
S'il m'empêchait de voir en quels lieux je suis née.
Albe, où j'ai commencé de respirer le jour,
Albe, mon cher pays et mon premier amour,
Lorsque, entre nous et toi, je vois la guerre ouverte,
Je crains notre victoire autant que votre perte.   (I, i, 25–32)

These oppositions that so rigidly structure the tragic universe, that fix its parameters, are ideological rather than empirical. Outside discourse there is no difference. Rome and Alba are different only insofar as they articulate masculinity's fear of feminine indifference. The confrontation of the two City-States is the opposition of the mirror, a confrontation with the same. There is no 'real' difference:

Nous sommes vos voisins, nos filles sont vos femmes,
Et l'hymen nous a joints par tant et tant de noeuds,
Qu'il est peu de nos fils qui ne soient vos neveux;
Nous ne sommes qu'un sang et qu'un peuple en deux villes.

(I, iii, 288–91)

It is these bonds, the bonds of marriage, of the mixing of blood, that must be denied in the ideology of difference because it is essentially too homoerotic a mimesis. The two camps are involved in a symmetrical stand-off to determine which of the two will succumb to the other, which one will be the master and which the slave, which the male and which the female:

Mais aujourd'hui qu'il faut que l'une ou l'autre tombe,
Qu'Albe devienne esclave ou que Rome succombe,
Et qu'après la bataille il ne demeure plus
Ni d'obstacle aux vainqueurs ni d'espoir aux vaincus. (I, i, 79–82)

In a curious tragic fashion, masculinity's repression of difference leads the men (and the State that they represent) to the point where what they fear is precisely what is left them. Their fear of their own femininity, of their own succumbing to the female in them, with all the ambivalent desire that represents, leads them out of the polis into the space of Death. It is here, in between the two camps, in this locus that is beyond representation, that the males must meet their own tragic heroic destiny. For it is only here that one can, by completely severing all those ties that both structure repression and deny that structure, become a hero – a hero in Freud's sense – that is, someone who places himself outside all the boundaries of community, outside the limits of family and outside the confines of sexuality that they articulate.[12]

This is what Horace, and he alone, says he is willing to do:

> Combattre un ennemi pour le salut de tous,
> Et contre un inconnu s'exposer seul aux coups,
> D'une simple vertu c'est l'effet ordinaire,
> Mille déjà l'ont fait, mille pourraient le faire;
> Mourir pour le pays est un si digne sort,
> Qu'on briguerait en foule une si belle mort.
> Mais vouloir au public immoler ce qu'on aime,
> S'attacher au combat contre un autre soi-même,
> Attaquer un parti qui prend pour défenseur
> Le frère d'une femme et l'amant d'une soeur,
> Et rompant tous ces noeuds, s'armer pour la patrie
> Contre un sang qu'on voudrait racheter de sa vie;
> Une telle vertu n'appartenait qu'à nous.   (II, iii, 437–449)

Horace recuperates Death in the mirror world of masculine reflection. The sacrifice to the Father/State is the sacrifice of a self caught in the web of sentiment/blood, those vestiges of femininity. In this, the purest form of sublimation, Horace is united with his Ideal. He becomes one with it. By choosing to sacrifice his familial ties, by opting for his own immolation, Horace is freeing himself from contamination and attempting to exist solely in the realm of the integral. Horace wishes to stand beyond those ties, to stand alone, and no longer be defined by the tissue of society. He can exist only insofar as he is willing to deny that existence, to face Death, pass through it and emerge on its far side united with the Father. He desires to be transformed into the ultimate avatar of the Law.

When Horace steps out onto the field of honor, he steps out of representation. Act III, the culminating act in which the duel to the death between the Horatii and the Curiaces, between Rome and Alba, is decided, is singularly devoid of any masculine presence. Corneille describes Act III as the most 'artificieux' of this theater.[13] I suggest we take him at his word; Act III is perhaps the most artful, but also the most artificial construction of Classical theater. It is the dividing line of the play separating the first and second acts from those two maverick acts that, we remember, cause the play's structure to fall out of symmetry. We should perhaps look to Act III therefore, that 'mirror' act, in which the first and last acts reflect and refract each other, for the reason for this distortion.

In the symmetrical division of the play Act III serves as an absent center. It, too, is a locus of indifference. In this hierarchy of

symmetry, Act III is an act of absence and presence. It is, in a sense, the 'hymen' of the tragedy. It will come as no surprise that this act is entirely given over to women. It is they who represent for us, who stand in and inform the spectators of the Death that is occurring simultaneously in 'another place', on another stage, in front of other spectators. The only male allowed in this act is Vieil Horace, and he is allowed into this act precisely because here he is not a 'male' at all. Eunuch-like, he guards the women. They have been entrusted to him by the young warriors who fear the contamination of their excessive sensitivity:

> Mon père, retenez des femmes qui s'emportent,
> Et de grâce empêchez surtout qu'elles ne sortent.
> Leur amour importune viendrait avec éclat
> Par des cris et des pleurs troubler notre combat;
>
> (II, viii, 695–8)

As the women's act, Act III is marked by oscillation. The entire movement of the drama, its artfulness, its tension and suspense, is created by the pendulum-like swing between life and death, between hope and despair, between Rome and Alba. This oscillation, an essential and pivotal indeterminacy, gives the act its power over us. It is precisely this fluctuation that projects the act as the veil, the ambiguous diaphanous re-presentation of the feminine, the hidden invisible mirror of the tragedy.

In the 1641 edition of the play, the frontispiece clearly situates the duel of Act III as the pivotal moment of the tragedy. The engraving on the title page shows on the right and left margins the two warring States lined up, facing each other. In the space between them, two Horatii lie dead. Horace thrusts his sword through Curiace while the latter's two brothers rush to his aid. The engraving clearly indicates that this duel is the political apogee of the play. While the women are out of sight, imprisoned in their place (their private apartments, the space of family, of copulation, of appropriation), while they are prisoners of that space –

> Et ne savez-vous point que de cette maison
> Pour Camille et pour moi l'on fait une prison?
>
> (III, ii, 773–4)

the men are out of the field of honor, in front of the two armies, deciding the fate of nations, the fate of families, and the destiny of the prisoners.

It is strange, therefore, that this central action of the play is available to us only as an act of supplementation. The death of the

men is allowed into the space of the tragedy 'in drag', in the mouth and in the person of the women. In this fashion, Death, disguised, is sublimated in rhetoric: it has here become a metaphor. In this act, and perhaps here we can underline the second sense of 'art-ificieux' – artificial – the women are effectively made to take on the representation of masculinity. In a perverse fashion, Death, assigned to and associated with the women, is like them trapped in their place. It is repressed (as spectacle) and domesticated in an ordering discourse that will not, cannot, tolerate it as spectacle. The death of the five warriors takes place while we watch the women, their counterparts, in a sexual/political symmetry. As re-counted by and to them, the execution of the five men makes the women responsible for, a party to, the masculine sublimation of Death. In this act the women are transformed. They are virilized because their presence serves as the metaphor for Death. They are there because they replace Death, they say it, but it is controlled, impersonal, contained. In this act women reflect a masculine order.

It is an order that balances and articulates, on the one hand, the cadences of Classical form and, on the other, the structures of Classical ideology. It is, however, a repression whose force is so great, and the structure it elaborates so taut, that they break under their own tension. The Death that the women represent is not so easily contained. It is there, waiting for them in Act IV, and in that other space, in that space that defies representation, in which, un-seen, Horace is covering himself with blood.

It is here, upon this other stage of representation, its underside whose sight is denied us, that Horace discovers the 'partage des femmes',[14] the immersion into the reality of the excessive, into the blood that cannot be contained. His baptism is shattering. Here, like the women, he crosses over. Outside the space of representa-tion, Horace crosses the line, and becomes, in the heat of battle, in the violence of dispersion, fragmented and, in a sense, feminized.

It is from this experience that defies spectacle that Horace returns. He is shaken, contaminated by his passage. The duel with the Curiaces was only the first step in a process of descending hor-ror; having confronted and eliminated his spectral other in the do-main of the political, Horace is now exposed to the confrontation with himself, with his ultimate symmetrical reflection. The con-frontation of Camille and Horace which is pre-structured by the entire tragic universe of the play and which reproduces, on the individual level, the most acute example of symmetrical opposition,

results, in the final analysis, from a tension that is too great to hold and that explodes the constraining apparatus of the Law.

Although marked as different, Camille and Horace (like Rome and Alba) are more significantly identical. Their identity is proclaimed, at the same time as it is denied, by their father:

> Faites-vous voir sa soeur, et qu'en un même flanc
> Le ciel vous a tous deux formés d'un même sang.

(IV, iii, 1193–4)

'Même flanc', 'même sang' – an identical origin, an identical essence defines them. Nothing (radically) distinguishes Camille from Horace except for the 'defiling bar of the signifier' that traverses their bodies, defining their relation to Death and sublimation.[15] It is the signifier that confers/confirms sexuality. It is their allegiance to subordination, to this difference of signifier which is essentially a political order, that structures their final confrontation. It is a confrontation that is played out under the equivocal sign of identity and difference, of masculine and feminine, of origin and end – of blood.

When Horace returns from his meeting with Death he re-enters the world of representation as confusion: he identifies himself as a metaphor – 'Rome' – but his fragmentation articulates his being as a metonymical displacement; he is scattered bodily parts – 'cette bouche', 'ce bras', etc. When he talks he no longer speaks in his name, an identity that has been singularly disrupted, but in the name of Rome.[16] In an attempt to re-structure his hold on the world Horace can grasp himself only as fused to the Ideal to which he has sacrificed. Yet, he is fragmented by it. Camille's response to his fusion (Horace–Rome), her invective against her brother, is all the more radical because it perversely echoes Horace's own (pre-duel) rhetoric. In his advice to her upon departing, Horace had effectively told her to 'unsex' herself, to accept sublimation:

> Armez-vous de constance, et montrez-vous ma soeur;
> Et si par mon trépas il retourne vainqueur,
> Ne le recevez point en meurtrier d'un frère,
> Mais en homme d'honneur qui fait ce qu'il doit faire
>
> .   .   .
>
> Mais si ce fer aussi tranche sa destinée,
> Faites à ma victoire un pareil traitement,
> Ne me reprochez point la mort de votre amant.

(II, iv, 517–20, 524–6)

According to this ethic, which he claims as his own, the more ties one is capable of repressing, the greater the glory that accrues in the service of sublimation (the State). In her speech Camille goes even further than this. She calls for the destruction not only of the self, but also of those intermeshing structures that define the self, the family and the State. This destruction is presented as a suicide. The State is destroyed by disintegrating, falling into parts. It tears itself apart with its own hands:

> Qu'elle-même sur soi renverse ses murailles,
> Et de ses propres mains déchire ses entrailles!
>
> (IV, v, 1311–12)

By lashing out at Horace, Camille turns Horace's principles against him, against herself, as she is imbricated in those structures, and finally against those most elemental ties, the knot of sexual interdiction.

Camille's revolt is scandalous because she rebels not just against her fate, not just against the destruction of her 'love', but against the structures of society that situate her by denying her a 'specificity' other than that contained within society's limits. She articulates her desire not to be incorporated into this structure as a fall away from the Law (Father):

> Dégénerons, mon coeur, d'un si vertueux père;
> Soyons indigne soeur d'un si généreux frère.
>
> (IV, iv, 1239–40)

Her revolt is a rejection of the masculine as it is inscribed within, and inscribes her within, the limits of familial/political authority. Rejecting the father/brother she rejects her role and her pleasure as they are defined for her by those relations. Camille, freed from her lover, still must protect herself from the other males who surround her and seek to appropriate her. Her rebellion is marked as an assumption of a self that is not a reflection of the masculine but of a different term which has no place in the symmetrical construction of Patriarchy. Her request for a place apart, for a place which is neither in the One nor the Other ('Ne cherche plus ta soeur où tu l'avais laissée') in the reflection of masculinity, causes an anxiety to well forth in that symmetry that can only be tested by the confrontation of the ultimate symmetrical dyad left, the perfect resemblance of the male/female mirroring that she forms with her (br)other.

By the violence of her speech, Camille's pleasure in her curse reaches an orgasmic ecstasy that fleetingly places her outside those

limits which define her. For a brief moment she allows herself the thrill of tottering on the brink of the unrepresentable. She calls for the spilling of familial blood by masochistically exposing herself to appropriation by Horace. She offers herself, her hymen, to her brother. Camille allows herself to be pierced by her brother, as a way out of his schema of desire, by destroying the sublimation that subtends that desire, by destroying the taboo that founds society, by making him take her. This moment of possession, of blood-letting, is, for her, a moment of total destruction and of supreme pleasure:

> Voir le dernier Romain à son dernier soupir
> Moi seule en être la cause et mourir de plaisir!
>
> (IV, v, 1317–18)

Camille, who has prevented her marriage throughout the play, who has retained her 'hymen' beyond the reach of the males, and who has thus remained outside (or on the margins of) their world of 'either/or' in her own place, forces her brother to ravish her. But this 'ravishment' allows her the only, the greatest pleasure, that is not within the House of the Father, that cannot be recuperated by male Law. Camille's taunting speech establishes her marriage/death as outside the order of Patriarchy.

Her moment of paroxysmic pleasure/death is the epiphanous moment of Corneille's tragedy which decenters the structures that have heretofore been elaborated and accepted as constituting the symmetrical parameters of the dramatic universe. Camille, by enunciating her desire, breaks out, for an instant, of the bonds of patriarchy, bonds determined by blood and State, and gives the lie to the ideology that underlies their representation. By so doing she drags Horace with her into the world of 'indistinction' that has been kept at bay by those bonds. Horace falls into the world of 'incest', into the world of parricide, the chaotic world of uncontrollable passion. He is tainted by this other world of female indifference. He is branded by the feminine even as he attempts to destroy its hold on him. His crime, a crime of passion, implicates him in Camille's desire. He becomes the instrument of her revenge, and is made to be the vehicle that undermines the laws of community, family and Patriarchy that he represents. By being contaminated by the excess he claims to despise he becomes an outcast. His immolation of Camille makes him stand, in the eyes of all, in that place of difference that must be veiled. It is from this place that he must be rescued, recuperated, if society as it is presented and affirmed in Cornelian tragedy is to survive.

The eruption of the tragic, the return and triumph of Death in the last scenes of Act IV, rends so totally the symmetrical structure of the dramatic universe, creates an abyss so total, an echo so deafening, that the play dedicates an entire act to its recuperation. This act re-structures the laws of patriarchal symmetry through the communal absolution of the stains of female blood. It would not be an exaggeration to say that the entire movement of the tragic has been one of a progressive descent; we move from the level of abstraction − a conflict of the States − to the level of the familial and finally to that of two individuals, to the tragic epiphany. In the same sense the way out of the tragic follows the same path, but in reverse: from the individual to the familial, which are both subsumed in the political.

While Act IV had witnessed the eruption of the chaotic and the violent, of emotions and of the feminine, Act V is entirely given over to discursive reason. It is an act which from the start has been criticized for its static, declamatory nature.[17] While it is not my intention here to defend this act on dramatic grounds, to excuse its stasis, is is my intention simply to indicate why and how this act is both necessary and 'vraisemblable' to the underlying ideology of the play.

A spoken denegation follows immediately upon the tragic murder and sets the tone for its exorcism. Horace's first words after killing his sister are to claim that his murder was an act of justice. More importantly, he denies those ties of blood that he rent. He denies the parricidal fury of his act by negating consanguinity:

> Ne me dis point qu'elle est et mon sang et ma soeur.
> Mon père ne peut plus l'avouer pour sa fille:
> Qui maudit son pays renonce à sa famille.   (IV, vi, 1326–8)

Here the State is invoked to nullify the family. Camille is dismissed as a 'monstre'. She is branded as not human, not familial. She is an outsider to culture. Camille is marked as a negativity. This verbal mark inscribes her recuperation into a rhetoric that represses her by controverting her being.

This denial is most effectively continued and perfected in the renunciation of her father. His words, solemnly ushering in Act V, reiterate a condemnation, a total rejection of Camille as human: 'Retirons nos regards de cet objet funeste' (V, i, 1403). Camille in death is an 'object', a thing denied the attributes of sex and of family. A stasis is imposed upon her that she had continually refused.

She is pushed outside the parameters of 'community'.[18] It is as an aberration that she takes her place in her father's discourse. Camille is not pitied; rather, he tells us, it is the men, Horace and himself, who deserve the greatest sympathy:

> Je ne plains point Camille: elle était criminelle;
> Je me tiens plus à plaindre, et je te plains plus qu'elle:
> Moi, d'avoir mis au jour un coeur si peu romain;
> Toi d'avoir par sa mort déshonoré ta main.   (v, i, 1411–14)

The remainder of the tragedy represents the attempts of masculinity to re-establish its shaken supremacy, to suppress and deny the difference of women which erupted in the sacrifice of Act IV. It is, perhaps, for this reason that Act V must bring into the play Tulle, that 'pater ex machina' who appears to double the familial Patriarch. Tulle, King of the Romans, enters this act ostensibly to thank the Horatii for saving his crown, for adding to it new dominions, for, in other words, marking a new origin of Roman hegemony. Tulle comes to acknowledge Horace's act as the founding of a new State, a new Law.

The initial act of foundation, the origin, is, however, tainted – reminding us in verse of that other original sin, the mythological parricide that presided over the founding of Old Rome. In order for it to be acceptable it must be absolved (repressed). Just as the power shifts in this act from the father to the King, the point of origin of the new State shifts from the violence of blood (the Horatii) to the sublimation of violence in the judgment (discourse) of the new Law. The act of enunciating a judgment consolidates the King's power. It symbolically marks as a political act the 'new beginning' of the State; a new beginning that is new repression.

What is said in accusation and defense of Horace is less important than the mode in which it is debated, the very fact that it is enunciated and that this speaking of guilt is, in fact, its excusal. As has often been noted, the declamatory mode of this act smacks of the law court. The whole last act is the Law that, speaking, constitutes itself. What we have is a symmetrical triangular structuration in which first the two young males, Valère and Horace, parry, then the word is passed to the head of the family, Vieil Horace. Finally it is assumed by the King, whose verdict ends the play.

The entire act is, therefore, an incantation of the male voice, a rising crescendo of that which had defined masculinity, a logical, paternal, structuring of desire in discourse and the final apotheosis of this discourse as Law. What the Law celebrates is the erection

of the order of the 'Integral', the One. In the person of the King Rome now stands alone. It is not surprising that this new King and this new Law are co-terminous and that their own apogee is reached precisely at the end of this 'trial,' which excuses an 'original' sin for political reasons, which sweeps away the blood and violence of femininity in the symmetrical structure of its own discourse. It also and more radically reaffirms an entire system of masculine pre-rogative based on the idea of integrity. In announcing his judgment we cannot but be struck by the ironic note it sounds, how under the guise of sympathy, of tenderness, the play ends with the final disposal of Camille by the Father. For this woman whose feminini-ty was defined by her refusal to be either Roman or Alban, her desire to remain indifferent, is, in the final speech of Tulle, relegated to the world of the One. What her family and a war could not do while she was alive, the State in the person of Tulle will do to her dead:

> Je la plains; et pour rendre à son sort rigoureux
> Ce que peut souhaiter son esprit amoureux,
> Puis qu'en un même jour, l'ardeur d'un même zèle
> Achève le destin de son amant et d'elle,
> Je veux qu'un même jour, témoin de leurs deux morts,
> En un même tombeau voir enfermer leurs corps.
>
> (v, iii, 1777–82)

The circle is completed. A new re-iterated 'same' is constituted, echoed in the repeated 'même' of the closing lines. The tragedy of origins and difference, of symmetry and State, ends in the establishment of a new, triumphant order of the same. Camille is put where she did not want to be, in the same place/grave as Curiace. The two are made One. We can only think that this 'ap-peasement' of Camille's spirit is an ironic foundation of a Law which inscribes as its first act, as its origin, the repression that will return to haunt it.*

4

CINNA: EMPTY MIRRORS

'Ah! souffrez que tout mort/Je vive encore en vous.'

Perhaps no other of Corneille's major tragedies was greeted with such unanimous praise as *Cinna*. In his famous letter to Corneille, Guez de Balzac expressed what was surely the general admiration of his contemporaries: 'Votre *Cinna* guérit les malades, il fait que les paralytiques battent des mains, il rend la parole à un muet . . . La belle chose.'[1] Corneille, in his 'Examen' of the play, accepts this praise and admits that *Cinna* is the most universally admired of his works: 'Ce poème a tant d'illustres suffrages qui lui donnent le premier rang parmi les miens' (p. 152).[2] He offers, as a possible reason for the play's popularity, a technical explanation. *Cinna* is successful principally because the laws of verisimilitude are made to function so well that form and content are intimately fused, creating a gleaming, shining mirage of theatrical splendor:

Cette approbation si forte et si générale vient sans doute de ce que le vraisemblable s'y trouve si heureusement conservé aux endroits où la verité lui manque qu'il n'a jamais besoin de recourir au nécessaire. Rien n'y contredit l'histoire bien que beaucoup de choses y soient ajoutées: rien n'y est violenté par les incommodités de la représentation, ni par l'unité du jour, ni par celle de lieu.   ('Examen', p. 150)

The play's perfection mirrors, as it manifests, Classicism's precepts. Paradoxically, it is because of its shining surface that *Cinna* has, of all Corneille's plays, been used as a mirror reflecting its own contradictory readings.

Since the end of the eighteenth century *Cinna* has been seen as an essentially political tragedy. Whether or not Napoleon was a good judge of the theater, and whether or not he was correct in interpreting Auguste's inviting Cinna to be his 'friend' as 'la feinte d'un tyran', his judgment is emblematic of the trend that interprets *Cinna* as a study in totalitarianism.[3]

Curiously, for Corneille's contemporaries the political import of the play was its least compelling aspect. For them the heart of

Cinna: empty mirrors

Cinna was passion. They were moved by the love of Cinna and Emilie and by the threats to that love:

En voyant jouer *Cinna*, on se récrie beaucoup plus sur toutes les choses passionées qu'il dit à Emilie et sur toutes celles qu'elle lui répond que sur la clémence d'Auguste, à laquelle on songe peu et dont aucun des spectateurs n'a jamais pensé faire l'éloge en sortant de la comédie.
(Le prince de Conti, 'Traité de la comédie et des spectacles', 1667)[4]

The play's title, *Cinna, ou la clémence d'Auguste*, seems to reflect, in its own ambivalence, these contradictory visions of the play: either 'Cinna', that is the story of a love affair set against the backdrop of the intrigues of imperial Rome, or 'Auguste', the mise-en-scène of the Machiavellian workings of tyranny.

That these two visions of the tragedy are not mutually exclusive, that they are, in fact, reflected in the copula ('ou') that joins them, should not surprise anyone familiar with the typical imbrication of Cornelian dramaturgy. Neither in his theoretical writings nor in his previous practice has Corneille allowed the political to be separated from the passional, nor for the passions to exist outside the limits of the polis.

What is new in *Cinna*, and what is perhaps so unsettling, is the greater subtlety Corneille brings to this, his second 'Roman' tragedy. When we consider, for instance, that *Cinna* was composed at the same time as *Horace*, that both plays were worked on simultaneously, it does seem shocking that the two plays project a glaringly different representation of the tragic. Compared to *Horace*'s white-hot fury, with its descent into the abyssal sacrifice of familial blood, *Cinna* appears as a strikingly 'pallid' tragedy. For the first time in Corneille's dramatic oeuvre we are spectators at a tragedy that appears to skirt around the 'tragic'; there is no blood shed in this play, and no expiatory victim dies so that a new State may rise from this immolation.

It would, however, be an error to judge the tragic of *Cinna* on this basis. For here, in the most conflictual of plays, we witness Corneille's audacious redefinition of tragedy. *Cinna* presents an insidiously clever articulation of a new tragic vortex. It is a vortex of rhetorical illusion which draws into its own center, in ever-descending 'spirals of power and pleasure',[5] the diverse demands of sexuality and politics. It produces a violence so great, yet so subtle, mutilation so total, that death can be omitted without in any way diminishing the shattering effect the play exercises on its audience. In *Cinna*, Cornelian tragedy truly becomes 'cosa mentale'.

Although never actualized in the tragedy, violence pervades it throughout. The entire drama is bathed in an atmosphere of paroxysm as pervasive as it is impalpable. All the characters of *Cinna* are the products of a fiercely traumatic history. They have been radically sundered from a past which in their fantasies and rhetoric is reconstituted as a moment of utopian plenitude; *then* they were linked to a genealogy that defined them socially, politically and economically. In their articulation this past is metaphorized as 'Republican' Rome. Although forever inaccessible to them, this metaphor survives in the form of fragmented memories, fantasies and desires. It is the repetition of the past in their rhetoric that constantly serves as a reflection of their present. In this discourse past and present are joined by the strange mirror of their own words:

> Quand je regarde Auguste au milieu de sa gloire,
> Et que vous reprochez à ma triste mémoire
> Que par sa propre main mon père massacré
> Du trône où je le vois fait le premier degré:
> Quand vous me présentez cette sanglante image,
> La cause de ma haine, et l'effet de sa rage,
> Je m'abandonne toute à vos ardents transports,
> Et crois pour une mort, lui devoir mille morts.   (I, i, 9–16)

The intrusion of this rhetorical history with its violence and its refusal to let the past remain other has a fragmenting effect on the present. The characters are continually buffeted between two unattainable fantasies, the past of Republican Rome and their own future vengeance. The mediation joining the two is a rhetorical mirror of nightmares, turmoil and disorder:

> Je les peins dans le meurtre à l'envi triomphants,
> Rome entière noyée au sang de ses enfants:
> Les uns assassinés dans les places publiques,
> Les autres dans le sein de leurs dieux domestiques:
> Le méchant par le prix au crime encouragé,
> Le mari par sa femme en son lit égorgé;
> Le fils tout dégouttant du meurtre de son père,
> Et sa tête à sa main demandant son salaire.   (I, iii, 195–202)

An interruption inheres in each of the characters as an original and essential loss. The point of rupture which they all carry with them turns them not only against each other but also against themselves. No one in this play can speak, can find the words that express, or that are adequate to, his own truth, a truth that if it were told would, once and for all, make them whole. Their own

uncertainty as to who they are, coupled with the uncertainty of their present position (perpetrators or victims of an assassination) makes them all speak in 'demi-mots'. Secrecy and silence define their rhetorical relation to each other in the present. All the characters exist with only a tremulous hold on this present. Nevertheless they try to master it even while it fades away from them, becomes mixed with yesterday. In *Cinna* everyone is constantly looking backward. Seeking a grounding, they all gaze into the distant mirror of history. All they can glimpse are fragmentary images of another life and of other possibilities, glimpses that are as fascinating as they are elusive. In this play history splits the characters, establishing the initial and antithetical standoff that we have already noticed in the drama's title, and that is repeated on all levels of the play. It is the one essential and symmetrical opposition that defines the initial political and sexual structures of *Cinna*. The present of the tragedy, the actual moment of representation, is but the rhetorical mirror that bridges the gap between the past and the future, those 'other scenes' that are actually more important, but also absent, for the characters.

For being a forceful and consummate recreation of a particular moment of Roman history, *Cinna* is, nevertheless, carried along and informed by one of the most persistent and transhistorical of myths. *Cinna* plays out the tragedy of Roman politics, the evolution of a new form of society, while floating upon the same troubling waters where Narcissus attempted to capture his own image. From these waters Death seductively gazes back at the characters with strangely compelling eyes. To their amazement, these eyes turn out to be their own. This mythic subtext defines the limits of a certain ideology where power is distributed along the axes of sexuality and politics, axes which, as we know, are themselves mirror reflections of each other.[6]

The play opens with a fierce declaration of separation. Emilie's tirade clearly divides the world of the drama into two opposing camps: hers, the world of Cinna, of the conspirators and of a certain ideal of republican 'freedom', and Auguste's, the world of corruption, of tyranny and of degeneration. Nevertheless it becomes apparent that this vehement division is more rhetorical than real. Actually the common ground that unites them in their opposition, the inescapable necessity for their opposition to exist, is more important than any of their particular differences.[7] Emilie's first speech is, in this respect, revelatory. Despite the 'hysterical' tone of her monologue, despite, that is, the upswelling of diverse and con-

tradictory memories whose emotional charge is so strong as to risk suffocating her:

> Impatients désirs d'une illustre vengeance
> Dont la mort de mon père a formé la naissance,
> Enfants impétueux de mon ressentiment,
> Que ma douleur séduite embrasse aveuglément,
> Vous prenez sur mon âme un trop puissant empire;
> Durant quelques moments souffrez que je respire   (I, i, 1–6)

we detect, underlying the cataclysmic rhetoric of desire and destruction, a more stable, repetitive structure, a structure that recuperates her hysteria in a pattern of cyclical return: mort, naissance–enfants.

There is a contradiction that is operative between, on the one hand, a rhetoric of revenge that sees itself as totalizing and unique:

> Puisque de trois tyrans c'est le seul qui nous reste,
> Et que, juste une fois, il s'est privé d'appui,
> Perdant, pour régner seul, deux méchants que lui:
> Lui mort, nous n'avons point de vengeur ni de maître
>
> (I, iii, 222–5)

and, on the other hand, an ideology of history which functions as a fatalistic repetition.

Like Emilie each of the main characters of the play is given a monologue where s/he attempts to explain his/her present by the past. Perhaps nowhere in Cornelian theater does the weight of history lie so heavily upon the actions, ambitions and desires of his characters. History, as it is described in *Cinna*, is a fatal cycle which unfolds in the narratives of each of the characters and which seems to entrap them in a constant impasse. The present is immediately engulfed as a simulacrum of the past. No differentiation is possible. The present can only repeat, in an endless cycle, the 'same' thing as the past. One cannot get out of history. Origin and end continually reflect one another and in this reflection no idea of progress, no ideal of individual subjectivity, is possible. Livie, the porte-parole of a 'new' order, repeats this stultifying message to Auguste when she tries to persuade him to do something different, to break the mimetic bind:

> Votre sévérité, sans produire aucun fruit,
> Seigneur, jusqu'à present a fait beaucoup de bruit;
> Par les peines d'un autre aucun ne s'intimide:
> Salvidien à bas a soulevé Lépide;

Cinna: empty mirrors

Murène a succédé, Cepion l'a suivi:
Le jour à tous les deux dans les tourments ravi
N'a point mêlé de crainte à la fureur d'Egnace,
Dont Cinna maintenant ose prendre la place. (IV, iii, 1199–206)

Auguste, however, does not hear or believe her. He has said the very same things to himself; all of their history is an endless succession of death and revenge, retribution and more revenge:

Et puis ose accuser le destin d'injustice
Quand tu vois que les tiens s'arment pour ton supplice!
Et que par ton exemple à ta perte guidés,
Ils violent des droits que tu n'as pas gardés!
Leur trahison est juste, et le ciel l'autorise:
Quitte ta dignité comme tu l'as acquise;
Rends un sang infidèle à l'infidélité,
Et souffre des ingrats après l'avoir été. (IV, ii, 1141–8)

In the world where past and present are fused together everyone sees himself as the replica of another. Auguste is constantly trying to establish his own identity, to find the role he can most comfortably play by fluctuating between the images of two 'Fathers', César and Sylla:

Sylla m'a précédé dans ce pouvoir suprême:
Le grand César mon père en a joui de même;
D'un oeil si différent tous deux l'ont regardé,
Que l'un s'en est démis, et l'autre l'a gardé;
Mais l'un, cruel, barbare, est mort aimé tranquille,
Comme un bon citoyen dans le sein de sa ville;
L'autre tout débonnaire, au milieu du sénat,
A vu trancher ses jours par un assassinat.
Les exemples récents suffiraient pour m'instruire.

(II, i, 377–85)

Auguste's anxiety is the direct response to the contradictory nature of his models. Their contradiction corresponds to a deeper opposition in his own nature between the lust for power and the desire for 'repos'. History does not offer an adequate (that is, an integral) model to guide him.

Cinna, too, is constantly looking into the past for a correct image of himself, a precedent that will assure him of the role he would play. Is he a mere parricide or rather a savior of Roman freedom?

93

Demain, j'attends la haine ou la faveur des hommes,
Le nom de parricide, ou de libérateur,
César celui de prince ou d'usurpateur.   (I, iii, 250–2)

To encourage him, Emilie compares him and his act to Brutus and Cassius, models of Roman virtue, once again locking him into an endless chase for a stable, fixed origin–reflection:

> Regarde le malheur de Brute et de Cassie;
> La splendeur de leurs noms en est-elle obscurie?
>
> (I, iii, 265–6)

As for Emilie herself, her own desire for vengeance finds its justification by modeling her hatred and treachery on the tyrant she wishes to destroy:

> A. – O ma fille! Est-ce là le prix de mes bienfaits?
> E. – Ceux de mon père en vous firent mêmes effets.
> A. – Songe avec quel amour j'élevai ta jeunesse.
> E. – Il éleva la vôtre avec même tendresse;
> Il fut vôtre tuteur, et vous son assassin:
> Et vous m'avez au crime enseigné le chemin.
>
> (V, ii, 1595–1600)

History telescopes the past and the present in a mise-en-abîme of repetition. In this world no real 'individuality' is possible. Every character is joined to a past and to the others along fragmented links of difference and similarity. Any image of the self is immediately deflected back into the past to a spectral other (model, example) and outward into the future. One defines oneself by opposition to another, but this opposition turns out to be a collaboration. All victimization – and Cinna, Emilie and Maxime see themselves as victims – needs a projected master, just as much as the master needs his victims. There is a connivance at work here in which the 'narrative' of history negates any individuality and where the desire for narrative coherence also diffuses the present 'subject' along a fragmenting network of fantasies.

At the beginning of *Cinna* we are, therefore, confronted with a rather strange phenomenon. On the one hand, all of the characters are disseminated along axes of history and desire that fragment them and, on the other hand, when they attempt to articulate a fixed position for themselves, this position is always determined as the negative reflection of itself. The major narcissistic element of the play, its emphasis on doubling, of seeing oneself as at once other and same, is therefore integrally related to a certain dynamic of

power in which positions of force are mutually interwoven and interdependent. At the beginning of the play Auguste may be Emperor, but he is not yet Sovereign.[8] Despite what he may think and what he may say, he is still as much tied to and defined in his place by the hatred and jealousy of his subjects as they are obliged to constitute themselves in a group whose only real cohesiveness is their opposition to him. These groups can only look across an abyss at each other and see in that other the negative reflection of themselves.[9]

The relation of desire and ambition that unites Emilie and Cinna is most forcefully articulated in their contradictions, the bonds of mutual dependence that unite all of the play's characters. Of all the ill-fated couples that populate the Cornelian universes Cinna and Emilie are the most unsettling. Very soon in the play, certainly before the first act is finished, we begin to have an uncomfortable, almost embarrassed premonition that theirs is an aberrant interdependence. There is something troubling in the 'passion' that unites these two young lovers. In *Le Cid*, despite the intrusion of an impossible political reality, we never doubt that Chimène and Rodrigue are drawn to each other passionately, or that in *Polyeucte* Pauline and Polyeucte are, in one respect at least, the prey to their love. In *Cinna*, however, we are never really convinced that Cinna and Emilie are first and foremost 'lovers'. We are aware of a split that divides them, creating a scission between what they desire and what they say they want.[10] For the first time in Corneille's theater, words, those carriers of his celebrated clarity, reveal the unfathomable depths that separate the private world of individual psyches and the domain of public interrelations.[11] It is this split that blinds the characters to their own motivations and that leads them, despite themselves, into the center of the tragic. The passion that seemed of such compelling interest to Corneille's contemporaries strikes us, in its expression, more by what it hides than by what it can ever reveal.

While in his previous plays the obstacle separating the lovers emerges during the course of the tragedy as part of the dramatic plot, the obstacle to Cinna's and Emilie's love pre-exists the play. It is part of history. Something happened in another place, at another time, and this history forms the extreme outer limits marking the possibility of the passion they share. Both are orphans of the storm, both products of the civil wars that have deprived them of social and genealogical continuity. By the same gesture this rift that marks the end of a moment of plenitude reconstitutes itself in

95

them as a nostalgia for an origin. Paradoxically the origin they find, the origin that joins them together, that is at the beginning of their love, is precisely a depossession of the self, a fragmentation – the murder of Emilie's father:

> Quand vous me présentez cette sanglante image,
> Le cause de ma haine, et l'effet de sa rage,
> Je m'abandonne toute à vos ardents transports,
> Et crois, pour une mort, lui devoir mille morts.
> Au milieu toutefois d'une fureur si juste,
> J'aime encore plus Cinna que je ne hais Auguste.
>
> (I, i, 13–18)

In the beginning was an image, a bloody spectacle of dismemberment that perversely can be used both to separate and to join. This image–vision is a composite representation; it portrays not only the slaying of the father, but links the murdered father, his murderer and her lover. For Emilie, at least, the obsessive scene that marks her entry into the world of passion and into the world of politics is a primal vision of blood and of carnage, an ambiguous mirror where the massacred innocent reflects the coupling of killer and lover. In her obsession, Emilie can only oscillate between these two poles. Just as it is impossible for Emilie to separate in her fantasy/discourse her father from Auguste, so too does this fantasy render Auguste indistinguishable from Cinna. The one is inextricably interwoven in the image of the other:

> Au milieu toutefois d'une fureur si juste,
> J'aime encore plus Cinna que je ne hais Auguste,
> Et je sens refroidir ce bouillant mouvement
> Quant il faut, pour le suivre, exposer mon amant.
>
> (I, i, 17–20)

The verse imbricates Cinna and Auguste in a comparative stance that excludes the possibility of the one existing outside a relation to the other. At the same time the rhyme 'Auguste–juste', floating free from its textual anchorage, has a disconcerting echo that will reverberate throughout the play.

In her speech Emilie re-articulates, although quite at odds with the intention of her message, the same triangular relation that joins the males together in the Cornelian universe. It is the same chain that we saw so clearly operative in *Le Cid*. It is a chain of masculine order that excludes her even as she articulates it. In this masculine genealogy that Emilie gives voice to, Emilie structures the triumvirate of three generations (her father–Auguste–Cinna) in a

genealogical descent that comes into existence not from a birth (the implied presence of the female) but through Death (the imposition of the Law). Death is the negative matrix of this chain. It is also the representative of the feminine that exists outside this descent but which articulates it. Emilie, in the structures of this universe, can exist, can have power, only by situating herself in the place of the dead.

All of the men are aware that their relation to Emilie must necessarily pass through Death:

> A. – Pour épouse, Cinna, je vous donne Aemilie;
> Vous savez qu'elle tient la place de Julie,
> Et que si nos malheurs, et la nécessité
> M'ont fait traité son père avec sévérité,
> Mon épargne depuis en sa faveur ouverte
> Doit avoir adouci l'aigreur de cette perte.   (II, i, 637–42)

> C. – Ah! souffrez que tout mort je vive encore en vous;
>
> .   .   .
>
> Rien n'est pour vous à craindre: aucun de nos amis
> Ne sait ni vos desseins, ni ce qui m'est promis;
> Et leur parlant tantôt des misères romaines,
> Je leur ai tu la mort qui fait naître nos haines.
> (I, iv, 336, 339–42)

Emilie, much like Antigone, is a chthonian presence.[12] She is the guardian of the dead, and through her Death enters into the present of the play. In a sense Emilie is the goddess of the underworld and the waters of the Styx reflect the distance men must traverse to attain her. Men look into her eyes, see reflected back at them an image of another glory, of another time, which remains constantly at an asymptotic distance from their own reality. To approach Emilie, possess her, they must first attempt to cross that distance. This quest implies the necessity of a violent passage through the disintegration of death. Emilie is the prize that is reserved for the suitor who can successfully accomplish the impossible feat of situating himself in the place of the dead Father. This is her ultimatum, not only to Cinna, but to all the men, that resonates obsessively throughout the play:

> Quoi que j'aime Cinna, quoi que mon coeur l'adore,
> S'il me veut posséder, Auguste doit périr;
> Sa tête est le seul prix dont il peut m'acquérir.   (I, ii, 54–6)

This same 'fiat' is repeated to her other would-be suitor, Maxime:

> Tu m'oses aimer, et tu n'oses mourir!
> Tu prétends un peu trop, mais quoi que tu prétendes,
> Rends-toi digne du moins de ce que tu demandes;
> Cesse de fuir en lâche un glorieux trépas,
> Ou de m'offrir un coeur que tu fais voir si bas.
>
> (IV, v, 1352–6)

In order to be good enough to ask for her hand, Emilie's suitors must first bloody their own. What is more, this blood must be Auguste's – the blood of her 'new' father. What Emilie is looking for in her ideal man, what she most desires, is a hero who can come to her from death, who can kill her father and take his place. In the blurring of the opposition dead father–Auguste, of the image that is at the origin of her passion, only Auguste is in the oscillating role of being both father and murderer, of being, that is, both the object of Emilie's taboo and, co-terminously, the object of her desire. The only man capable of fulfilling Emilie's desire for a mate has already done so, and this act has immediately established him as the object of her hatred and, perhaps more important still, as the object of an unspeakable lust.

It is this unresolvable conflict between unavowable desires that places Emilie in the position of destroyer-avenger in the couple she forms with Cinna. For in the symmetry that joins them together in their own double-bind Emilie can only represent the destructive force of Death that traps in a fascinatingly sadistic stance her specular other, Cinna, in his role of sexual and political thraldom.

When, in his letter to Corneille, Guez de Balzac described Emilie as 'la belle, la raisonnable, la sainte et l'adorable Furie', he undoubtedly meant to compliment her.[13] Nevertheless, his description points to a more archaic metaphor that underpins and defines Emilie's relation to Cinna. Although Emilie thinks of herself as an avenger, as the appointed retaliator for Auguste's crimes, she has chosen to accomplish this revenge by delegation. Revenge for Emilie must pass through a man, and because of this mediation the man becomes at the same time avenger and victim. Cinna's life is the price Emilie must pay for her vendetta:

> Pensez mieux, Aemilie, à quoi vous l'exposez,
> Combien à cet écueil se sont déjà brisés;
> Ne vous aveuglez point quand sa mort est visible.
>
> (I, ii, 115–17)

From the beginning of the play to the last act, Cinna and Emilie

are united by the structures that define their relation (structures of mirroring, of sexual and political interdependence) into an interlocking dependence where 'love' becomes a rhetorical codeword for a more insidious exercise of power that is a most political enterprise. On a very basic level Emilie confuses avenging her father's death with defending Roman republicanism. Her father and the Rome of the past become for her one and the same cause:

> Joignons à la douceur de venger nos parents
> La gloire qu'on remporte à punir les tyrans,
> Et faisons publier par toute l'Italie:
> 'La liberté de Rome est l'oeuvre d'Aemilie.' (I, ii, 107–10)

In order to justify her revenge, Emilie must recreate her father as the paragon of an ideological imperative. She must inscribe the Father within an entire political order which has vanished with him, leaving her bereft. Like her brother/lover, Cinna, Emilie is a 'free-floating' subject in search of a past, an anchoring that would define her and free her of her guilt/desire. What she must do in order to be free, in order to be free of the taint of being a *proscrit*'s daughter, on outlaw, is to re-structure in her mind a true genealogy which is based on a 'status-quo ante'. Under the guise of a return to an ideal of Roman liberty, Emilie is actually like Cinna, looking for her own grounding and refusing to recognize that the remnants of the past are irreconcilable with a new, emerging order. Despite her claims to republicanism, Emilie in her quest for her own past/position is actually reactionary.[14] What is more, by the obsessive totalitarian forms this quest takes, a quest that is grounded in immolation, she becomes a real 'Fury'.[15] In order to survive she must kill. It is in this sense, rather than just as a coy epithet, that we must understand Cinna's definition of her as both 'inhumaine' and actually more tyrannical than Auguste. Emilie becomes the most notable example of Corneille's recalcitrant female 'Furies', irreducible to laws of community and exchange. She manipulates these laws in such a way as to pose herself as an object of desire so that while she tantalizes she also destroys.

In Emilie's mind, or at least in her rhetoric, there is both a link-ing and a confusion of the men in her life, metaphoric substitutes for the power structures that define and alienate her. The un-breakable chain that she articulates links her father to Auguste and Auguste to Cinna through the mediation of sacrifice. Each male is but a substitute for another and each can replace the other. Just as

Auguste, in a perverse way, now stands in the place of her father, Cinna can be substituted for Auguste:

> Quoi qu'il en soit, qu'Auguste ou Cinna périsse,
> Aux mânes paternels je dois ce sacrifice.   (I, ii, 133–4)

When Emilie declares that either Auguste or Cinna must perish she clearly recognizes that one of them can be saved. Surprisingly that 'one', that 'empty slot', can be Auguste. What is important is that one of them must be sacrificed to 'her father's ghost', to his 'image', that is to the memory–fantasy of the Father that is Emilie's projection. The sacrifice that Emilie requires is not to the Father, but rather to her desire for the Father.

Throughout the play Emilie adamantly refuses any alteration in the political structure of her world which would allow Cinna to live. In the couple she forms with him the 'political structure' is emblematized by a rhetorical one. The pact that joins them, that seals their agreement, is a verbal one: Cinna is bound to Emilie by a 'promise':

> Cinna me l'a promis en recevant ma foi   (I, ii, 135)

> Mais je dépends de vous, ô serment téméraire!
> O haine d'Aemilie! ô souvenir d'un père!   (III, iii, 893–4)

It is a promise which is inviolable. It locks both of them into their mutual dependence because it is a contract, where the physical is most highly invested in the political, where desire takes the form of a new law, justifying it and at the same time controlling, limiting and vitiating it.

Although Emilie appears to waver during the course of the play, although she seems torn between 'love' and 'honor', to repeat the old dichotomy, this wavering is actually an oscillation between two extremes of a structure that never varies. This oscillation most clearly defines Emilie as the object of Cinna's desire because it cloaks her in a form of closure representing a totality that is both reassuring and unattainable. Cinna is attracted to Emilie precisely because of her self-contained, narcissistic relation to the world.[16]

In fact, Emilie never wavers. The last time she and Cinna confront each other she repeats her ultimatum exactly as she had previously defined it. Despite the change in Auguste, Emilie refuses to change. The transformation of Auguste, as Cinna has interpreted it, necessarily involves their joint future. Emilie, fixed in the past, remains totally unconcerned by this future. Emilie and Cinna are locked into a battle to the death. Each, in Act III, after accus-

ing the other of betraying their 'love', renounces the other, or at least breaks the bonds that allied them to each other, in order to exist as an independent unit in relation to Auguste. At the same time, and by this same gesture, each claims that their relation spells his/her demise:

> E. – Vis pour ton cher tyran, tandis que je meurs tienne:
>   Mes jours avec les siens se vont précipiter,
>   Puisque ta lâcheté n'ose me mériter.
>   Viens me voir dans son sang et le mien baignée.
>
> (III, iv, 1038–41)

> C. – Vous le voulez, j'y cours, ma parole est donnée;
>   Mais ma main aussitôt contre mon sein tournée,
>   Aux mânes d'un tel prince immolant votre amant,
>   A mon crime forcé joindra mon châtiment. (III, iv, 1061–4)

After Cinna's departure Emilie re-iterates her conditions to Fulvie, conditions which are disguised as a 'choice':

> Qu'il achève et dégage sa foi,
> Et qu'il choisisse après de la mort ou de moi.
>
> (III, v, 1075–6)

The choice is, however, purely rhetorical. Death is, in the structures that define Cinna's and Emilie's passion, the only prize awaiting Cinna. Emilie's possession and Death's embrace are one. It is an embrace in which Emilie hopes to find her father and Cinna the mirage of his own identity.

It is only by accepting Emilie–Death, by accepting a position of passivity in relation to Emilie, that Cinna can find worth as a loved object. He is loved not because of his power, but because of his lack. Cinna and Emilie trace the Classically symmetrical outline of all sado-masochistic relations. Emilie can 'love' Cinna only in the place where he suffers (dies) and Cinna can 'love' Emilie only where he is sacrificed.[17] It is in that 'space', the space of immolation, that Emilie and Cinna are obliged to live and to love as they play out in their own relation the entire political and historical aporia they have inherited. The 'love' of Cinna and Emilie is political in the sense that it and they float upon the murky waters of the past, of their memories and desires. It is, however, precisely because this love is in the past, intimately connected to a vanished retrograde political system, that it is impossible. Paradoxically, Cinna and Emilie, in their anachronistic, narcissistic desire for the past, in the way their desire structures their self-destructive

manipulations, are the most modern of Cornelian couples. The relations of sexuality and power that they articulate inscribe them as the most obvious precursors of a long tradition of contentious lovers. Although constantly looking into the past they point the way to the future. From their position in ancient Rome they prefigure Valmont and Merteuil in eighteenth-century Paris and the even more dangerous liaisons found in the anonymous dungeons of the Sadian underground.

In his relation to Emilie, Cinna is the negative, absent cipher. It is not surprising therefore that as he makes his entrance in the play which bears his name, his first words are a negation:

> Jamais contre un tyran entreprise conçue
> Ne permit d'espérer une si belle issue;
> Jamais de telle ardeur on n'en jura la mort,
> Et jamais conjurés ne furent mieux d'accord.
>
> (I, iii, 145–8)

According to Corneille, *Cinna* is the most rhetorically successful of his major tragedies. In his 'Examen' Corneille stresses both the perfection of his verse and the rhetorical ornaments that adorn them. In this play the choice of words is never innocent; their use as both offensive and defensive weapons can lead the speaker to death. Cinna's thrice-repeated 'jamais' cannot therefore be seen as just as ingenuous happenstance. Rather, Cinna is, more than any other of the major characters, most inscribed by rhetoric. His use of words forcefully indicates not only his position in the fragmented history he attempts to dominate, but also the impossibility for him to exist outside the abyss of language.

While constantly attempting to attain a self definition that would be integral, Cinna exists only as a creation of others. He oscillates between the conflictual, but often overlapping, desire of his mistress and his lord. As an initial representation, his 'jamais' forcefully indicates his negativity/passivity. His past has been destroyed and anything that would attach him to a particular 'gens' wiped out. All that remains of his identity, as Auguste tells him, is his resentment:

> Tu vois le jour, Cinna; mais ceux dont tu le tiens
> Furent les ennemis de mon père et les miens:
> Au milieu de leur camp tu reçus la naissance;
> Et lorsque après leur mort tu vins en ma puissance,
> Leur haine enracinée au milieu de ton sein

Cinna: empty mirrors

T'avait mis contre moi les armes à la main;
Tu fus mon ennemi même avant que de naître.

(v, i, 1435–41)

With great insight Auguste details for him his complete rupture with the past. His future, however, is even more unpredictable. The plot of which he is the leader may or may not succeed. The entire dramatic tension of the play is based precisely on this uncertainty. Cinna's present, like him, is torn between these two unstable, unfathomable extremes. Floating between the mists of the past and the future, Cinna's present oscillates between Emilie and Auguste as he attempts to define himself in relation to these two poles that fix the parameters of any possible self-representation.

Serge Doubrovsky has called our attention to the split that has occurred in this Cornelian hero especially when he is compared to either Rodrigue or Horace: 'là où Horace agissait, Cinna parle. De sa conspiration, il fait un magnifique tableau, un chef d'oeuvre de rhétorique, mais le récit épique que Rodrigue faisait après sa victoire, Cinna le fait avant.'[18]

The importance that Corneille gives this hero, whose heroism is nothing but a show, would appear strange unless we understand that the tragedy of Cinna is precisely the tragedy of words. Words, always inadequate to the reality they are supposed to represent, are the tremulous, often deceptive, links between the suffering of the individual psyche and the articulation of this suffering in the world of others. In this conspiratorial drama, words are the most untrustworthy of arms and at the same time they are the only weapon the characters have in their murderous duels.

The Cornelian universe has traditionally been seen as the realm of (verbal) light. Cinna is the most corrosive example of the obscurity that is so often the product of this clarity. Not only does Cinna constantly find himself alienated from his interlocutors, he is alienated within his own discourse. Cinna never is what he claims to be, nor can he ever be what others say he is.

In his perception of the couple he forms with Emilie, Cinna's role follows a neat division that reaffirms traditional masculine and feminine separation. He is more 'active' in the political sense of existing in the world, in the public domain, while Emilie, sequestered in the private space of the palace, is more 'passive'. Emilie's involvement in the conspiracy, her actual direction of it, is unknown. To the world Emilie remains secluded, cloistered within the chambers of Auguste's palace. Her only movements are back and forth from her own rooms to Livie's. Her life is a simulacrum of

feminine reserve, decorum and passivity. We are told that Emilie was chosen by Auguste as a 'replacement' for Julie, his biological daughter. Julie, because of her inordinate lust, diffused a sexual contagion that, spreading from the women's quarters to the entire palace and from there to Rome, threatened the stable order of Patriarchy. She, therefore, has to be removed and sent off into solitary exile at the far reaches of the empire. Emilie has been adopted as a far more acceptable female presence. She can, Auguste thinks, be a daughter and not pose any danger to the Father.

Cinna, on the other hand, as is 'normal' for a man, comes and goes, crossing the threshold separating private from public with ease. He is out in the world where he accomplishes his political and passional projects. Cinna assumes a certain place in the world either as the leader of the plotters, or as the friend–advisor of the emperor. To the observer, at least, Cinna and Emilie appear to conform to a symmetrical essentialization of opposites in the normal heterosexual couple. Yet the chiasmus between seeming and being, between activity and passivity, between fragmentation and unity, lies just beneath the surface and erupts in the rhetoric that Cinna uses to define his politics as a representation of himself.

Cinna's first speech is one of the most accomplished 'tours de force' in Corneille's repertoire. Corneille signals it out as a particularly well-polished exercise of oratory: 'c'est pour quoi, quelque longue que soit cette narration, sans interruption aucune, elle n'ennuie point. Les ornements de rhétorique dont j'ai tâché de l'enrichir ne la font pas condamner de trop d'artifice, et la diversité de ses figures ne fait point regretter le temps que j'y perds' ('Examen', p. 151). Hypotyposis is the dominant strategy of this rhetorical display. In order to inspire his co-conspirators, to fire their zeal, Cinna must make as vivid as possible the injustices and horrors of the past:

> Là, par un long récit de toutes les misères
> Que durant notre enfance ont enduré nos pères,
> Renouvellant leur haine avec leur souvenir,
> Je redouble en leurs coeurs l'ardeur de le punir.
> Je leur fais des tableaux . . .   (I, iii, 173–7)

Cinna's speech paints scenes that recreate the chaos of civil war. The underlying metaphor with which he constructs his paintings equates civil war to a body turned against itself, its unity rent. The tableaux that he paints present this body politic as a sundered,

fragmented and chaotic dispersion. Natural order has been over-
turned by Auguste. All semblance of stability has become an aberrant monstrosity of a world turned topsy-turvy:

> Je leur fais des tableaux de ces tristes batailles
> Où Rome par ses mains déchirait ses entrailles,
> Où l'aigle abattait l'aigle, et de chaque côté
> Nos légions s'armaient contre leur liberté
>
> .   .   .
>
> Je les peins dans le meurtre à l'envi triomphants,
> Rome entière noyée au sang de ses enfants:
> Les uns assassinés dans les places publiques,
> Les autres dans le sein de leurs dieux domestiques.
>
> (I, iii, 177–80, 195–8)

In his speech, Cinna constantly returns to pictorial/visual
imagery:[19]

> Mais je ne trouve point de couleurs assez noires   (I, iii, 173)

> Sans pouvoir exprimer par tant d'horribles traits
> Qu'un crayon imparfait de leur sanglante paix.
>
> (I, iii, 203–4)

History, as Cinna's desire creates it, is one large canvas which,
despite its fragmentary nature, can like a painting be possessed in
its immediacy. It is no longer something distant, inchoate and
unfathomable, but present, alive and ordered.

Cinna concludes his speech with an appeal to action, an appeal
which also is formulated in visual terms:

> Ainsi d'un coup mortel la victime frappée
> Fera voir si je suis du sang du grand Pompée;
> Faites voir, après moi, si vous vous souvenez
> Des illustres aïeux de qui vous êtes nés.   (I, iii, 237–40)

but here these terms activate a strategic reversal. Seeing has become
showing, passivity has evolved to activity. Tomorrow, Cinna says,
he will show who he really is. History, as he has just constructed
it, will be vindicated. In the beginning of his speech history was a
painting, an object offered to vision; at the end painting (showing
yourself) becomes history. Cinna will finally be part of the canvas
of history and that canvas will, tautologically, serve as his defining
mirror. He will be part of the portrait to be painted. It will define
him, let him 'be'.

This rhetoric has at least two consequences for Cinna. The first is that he will be able to trace his own self portrait which will contain in the figures it sketches a ratification of his past ('sang du grand Pompée') that lends credence to the present, justifying it. But, and this is more important still, his portrait remains necessarily unfinished. Only 'tomorrow' can complete it and this future is highly problematic; unity once again is a future deferral. No one knows, least of all Cinna, what tomorrow will bring. The split between rhetoric and reality re-opens the abyss that Cinna attempts to disguise. It plunges him, again, into the horrors of undecidability:

> Demain j'attends la haine ou la faveur des hommes,
> Le nom de parricide ou de libérateur.   (I, iii, 250–1)

For the moment, for the time of representation, Cinna and his portrait remain incomplete. He is only a desire, a desire, made rhetoric, for a control that is total and totalizing. Cinna tries to paint the world, organize reality into narrative that includes him and which he dominates.

Nevertheless, Cinna is torn apart by conflicting desires that are presented as the intrusion of the political into the passional. These desires problematize his relation to Emilie. His rapport with Auguste is no less ambivalent for the same reasons reversed: here, the sexual appears as an obstacle to the political. What is clear, however, in both of these cases is that it is Cinna who remains the desiring subject in the triangular configuration he forms with the other two. Auguste becomes the obstacle to his love for Emilie; Emilie blocks his rapport with Auguste. These two 'obstacles' alone are interchangeable. While Emilie and Auguste can, at one level at least, substitute for each other, Cinna remains unique in that he is always a slave to each. He always desires their impossible reconciliation. His subjection to his fragmentation makes him both a slave of love and a slave to political totalitarianism.

All Cinna's objects of desire become tyrannical. Auguste is the obvious 'political' dictator, while Emilie is the more subtle executioner of love:

> Eh bien! vous le voulez, il faut vous satisfaire,
> Il faut affranchir Rome, il faut venger un père,
> Il faut sur un tyran porter de justes coups;
> Mais apprenez qu'Auguste est moins tyran que vous.
> S'il nous ôte à son gré nos biens, nos jours, nos femmes,
> Il n'a point jusqu'ici tyrannisé nos âmes.   (III, iv, 1049–54)

Cinna: empty mirrors

The surest sign of a universe on the brink of chaos is to be found in Cinna's articulation of tyranny. What Cinna reveals in his invective is the truth of his own enslavement and of Rome's degeneration: Emilie is more tyrannical than Auguste. She, rather than the Emperor, has the sovereign gift of exercising her dominion from the inside. She captures and controls men's 'souls'; Auguste, despite the trappings of his office, despite the military and political power he wields, has still not succeeded in doing this.

Once we understand the destructive death-dealing nature of the love that unites Cinna and Emilie, it becomes apparent that the passionate subplot of the text reveals this love as an 'unnatural' political investment. It is not the product of a world terrorized by a tyrant, but rather the result of a world that has no leader and that needs one. Despite the representation of the conspirators as an anti-monarchical force which deserves our credibility (at least when its ideas find expression in the mouth of Maxime), in reality the entire dynamics of political and sexual imbrication in the play is there to prepare the eventual adoration of the Emperor as the only hope leading society out of a state of perversion and into a structure of ordered, harmonious symmetry, a symmetry constructed around the figure of the Monarch. Auguste must evolve in the play to occupy Emilie's place. He must do this to harness the chaotic forces of fragmentation, of an unnatural dissymmetry where an entire generation of young Romans is being led astray. Auguste must move into the central position of this world so that from this center he can check the disintegration of Roman society, restructure the political/sexual forces of this world and thereby save Cinna and Emilie from themselves.

In spite, therefore, of what appears to be a blatant contradiction, what seems really to be at stake in *Cinna* is not so much a duel between 'love' and 'duty', between freedom and tyranny, as the secret workings of a desire to be tyrannized, to submit to and worship one's subjection to a tyrannical king if this tyrant can protect society from a more insidious, more corrosive and more unspeakable subjection that unmans it. *Cinna* actually plays out for us the messianic endeavor to recreate from chaos a monolithic order that saves Patriarchy from its immersion in forces that (almost) destroy it.

Despite his rhetoric Auguste, when he first comes on stage, is not what he says he is. He, like Cinna, like Maxime, deludes himself with his own words. He defines reality in one way, but reality escapes his rhetorical grasp and taunts him.

> Cet empire absolu sur la terre et sur l'onde,
> Ce pouvoir souverain que j'ai sur tout le monde,
> Cette grandeur sans borne et cet illustre rang . . .

(II, i, 357–9)

Although Auguste begins by articulating himself as Sovereign, he immediately introduces into the verbal edifice he is constructing a flaw which undermines his hold on the world and threatens to bring the entire structure down on his head:

> J'ai souhaité l'empire, et j'y suis parvenu:
> Mais en le souhaitant, je ne l'ai pas connu.   (II, i, 371–2)

There is a fine line that Auguste draws between desire ('souhait') and possession ('connu'), but this line opens up the abyssal space of desire in which he is lost. Auguste is still a desiring subject, the Don Juan of Roman politics, never able to exist in and for himself because his idea of self is always present in another place, in another victory, in another murder. Caught at the aporia of his own desire, Auguste is divided. He is constantly separated, never coincident with that fleeting image of himself as Sovereign. He intuits this coincidence as attainable only in death:

> Et comme nostre esprit, jusqu'au dernier soupir
> Toujours vers quelque objet pousse quelque désir . . .

(II, i, 367–8)

It is because of his internal division, because he can never make need and desire coincide, that Auguste vacillates between two extreme political versions of his own vision of his life. Should he remain in power, carry on as Emperor with all the dangers and dissatisfactions this entails, with Death as its ultimate signifier:

> D'effroyables soucis, d'éternelles alarmes,
> Mille ennemis secrets, la mort à tout propos (II, i, 374–5)

or should he abandon all he has earned and opt for a retirement where he hopes to find peace and tranquillity ('le repos')?

Much has been said about Auguste's desire for 'repos'. Most commentators see this as a thematic metaphor either for a stoical acceptance of life, or for a desire for death. Rather than see it as a thematic metaphor I suggest that Auguste's 'repos' be seen as a spatial one. It seems that in this play where so much importance is given to metaphors of 'place', where the only chink in the play's perfection is its possible infringement of the law of unity of place (see Corneille, 'Examen', p. 150), the idea of coming into, of finding

one's own place in a chaotic world is essential. The 'repos' that Auguste seeks is perhaps less a state of mind than a state of presence in the world. He uses the word as an inherently spatial metaphor where he objectifies himself, becoming rather like a statue, a self-contained presence which is delimited as much by the space that surrounds it as it is by the space that it itself delimits.

When Auguste poses his dilemma as an opposition between activity and passivity he is actually articulating the underlying problematic of *Cinna*: how does one become Sovereign, how can this sovereignty be represented, and how, by this representation, is sovereignty recognized and affirmed by other? How, Auguste asks, can he move politically (but politics draws with it all the passional structures of the play) from the position of a strongman who is condemned to being just another link in a perpetually evolving, and changeless, chain to being beyond change, beyond Death, beyond desire, to being Sovereign? How can he be loved because of the security others feel in his presence when paradoxically this security comes precisely from their sacrificed independence? How can he become the universal object of desire so thoroughly integrated in his subjects that he subverts their own desire entirely? How, finally, can Auguste find his 'repos' which is not at all the negation of Empire, but its supreme avatar?[20]

Although in the famous 'political' scene of Act II Auguste, Cinna and Maxime all seem caught up in a dilemma that is essentially one of reconciling irreconcilable alternatives, either retaining power or opting for retirement, the assumption of power that the tragedy as a whole traces is a much more difficult and much more subtle apotheosis. Auguste does not so much want one or the other of the two alternatives as he wants to be the representation of the one in the other.

In order to reign and be free of the risks of mutability, Auguste must be perceived by his subjects as both incarnating their past and transcending it. He is in the extremely paradoxical position of having to die, of having to go through the dispersion of death and of continuing to speak to his subjects in the present from the place of their (dead) fathers. He must remain in the present as an immanent revelation that the past has been subsumed and that a radically new order has begun.

This impossible reconciliation of opposites is made possible in *Cinna* by Auguste's having, alone of all the characters, an immediate double. Although, as we have seen, all the characters in this tragedy are divided against themselves, and although all,

because of this split between their desires and their rhetoric, delude themselves, Auguste alone is given a way out of this world of fragmentation. He is the only character presented as his own other – Octave/Auguste.

'Octave' is what the conspirators call Auguste as an insult underlining the savage tyranny they denounce. 'Octave' is what Auguste calls himself in the moments of his most intense anguish, moments of deeply felt emotional shock which instantly strip away all the imperial trappings of Auguste. 'Octave' is presented as the most profound subjectivity of Auguste. He is the repressed other who returns to haunt Auguste, who returns to remind him of the sham of his new persona, and of the original primal sins that gave birth to Auguste:

> Rentre en toi-même, Octave, et cesse de te plaindre
> Quoi! tu veux qu'on t'épargne et n'as rien épargné!
>
> (IV, ii, 1130–31)

Octave and Auguste co-exist, and yet remain strangely separated. Octave is the past, the paroxysm of the civil wars, the moment of the frenzied fratricidal holocaust:

> Songe aux fleuves de sang où ton bras s'est baigné,
> De combien ont rougi les champs de Macédoine,
> Combien en a versé la défaite d'Antoine,
> Combien celle de Sexte, et revois tout d'un temps
> Pérouse au sien noyée et tous ses habitants   (IV, ii, 1132–6)

and finally Octave is lost in the last act of fury, a parricidal slaying, where he plunges into his own dispersion in the killing of his (surrogate) Father:

> Remets dans ton esprit après tant de carnages,
> De tes proscriptions les sanglantes images,
> Où toi-même des tiens devenu le bourreau,
> Au sein de ton tuteur enfonças le couteau. (IV, ii, 1137–40)

Here, Auguste–Octave's vision rejoins Emilie's, making them coincide in a common image that serves as the origin of a new order, and that splits them, making them continually alienated from an identity (a common origin) they can never capture.

It is only through this alienation, through a disappearance in the cauldron of sacrifice, that Auguste emerges, that an Emperor is born who is exonerated of the stains that marked a new beginning for Rome:

> Tous ces crimes d'Etat qu'on fait pour la couronne,
> Le ciel nous en absout alors qu'il nous la donne,

Cinna: empty mirrors

Et dans le sacré rang où sa faveur l'a mis,
Le passé devient juste, et l'avenir permis.   (IV, ii, 1609–12)

Yet, until Auguste assumes this difference and forces others to recognize it, until others accept Auguste, he can never be free of Octave. This recognition is absent as *Cinna* begins but is accomplished in the actual unfolding of the drama, in the unfolding of the familial drama in which Emilie, Cinna and Auguste are implicated. For monarchy, divine and absolute, to triumph the initial violence that is its origin must be accepted by those who were (are) its most eminent victims.

When Auguste learns of the plot to assassinate him, when he is told that his most cherished confidant is its ringleader, he reacts less like a hardened politico than as a spurned lover. So astounded is he by what appears to be a purely irrational deception that, like a lover trying to find excuses for a betrayal, he attempts to rationalize a passionate rejection. He establishes a list of all those reasons why Cinna should be grateful and faithful to him, why, in other words, Cinna should love him. He ignores the central underlying passional explanation that defies all logic and which he chooses strategically not to see. From the beginning, as he himself admits, Cinna was inscribed as his born enemy;

Leur haine enracinée au milieu de ton sein
T'avait mis contre moi les armes à la main;
Tu fus mon ennemi même avant que de naître.

(V, i, 1439–41)

In spite of this, Auguste, who would appear to have an ardent masochistic desire for paternity, adopts Cinna. He spares his life, restores his inheritance ('Je te restituai d'abord ton patrimoine') and establishes himself as a new Father. This paternity is both the most narcissistic and the most dangerous act of Auguste. It is an attempt to make Cinna, who is, he tells him, a nothing, a blank, a mere reflection of himself:

Ma faveur fait ta gloire, et ton pouvoir en vient;
Elle seule t'éleve, et seule te soutient;
C'est elle qu'on adore, et non pas ta personne:
Tu n'as crédit ni rang qu'autant qu'elle t'en donne.

(V, i, 1527–30)

When Auguste gazes into Cinna's eyes he wants to see only himself.

This desire for paternity defying all political logic makes Auguste look for his children among the victims of his rise to power. In the same way he has, as we have seen, chosen Emilie to replace his own unnatural daughter:

Corneille, Classicism and the ruses of symmetry

> Pour ses débordements j'en ai chassé Julie,
> Mon amour en sa place fait choix d'Aemilie
>
> . . .
>
> O ma fille! Est-ce là le prix de mes bienfaits?
>
> (v, ii, 1589–90, 1595)

Auguste's 'love' has created this odd brother–sister couple and has placed them as the reflection of the image he wants of himself as a benevolent Patriarch. Projecting on them a narcissistic fix, Auguste and they are trapped in a reciprocal relation of power and passion where, just as they mirror his projection, he mirrors their own ambivalent passion, a passion that joins them all in a dangerous game of mutual destruction.

The symmetries that *Cinna* establishes lock all the characters into an insoluble dilemma. In the initial distribution of power, Auguste is opposed to the parricidal couple Emilie–Cinna who in turn are turned against each other. Power and control keep them all locked into a profoundly frozen bind that cannot be overcome, unless a radical re-alignment undoes the positions of this initial imbrication. In this play no one can move without causing a symmetrical displacement of the others. Everyone moves together. They dance around the stage, locked into the ambivalent and antithetical attraction–repulsion which is the very articulation of the power structure they all worship and reject. There can be no change introduced into this world that is anything other than a revolutionary difference, that re-aligns the positions of all the characters in relation to each other.[21]

Despite all the verbal jousting of this most rhetorical of tragedies, it is precisely the conspiracy of silence that underpins the entire edifice of political and sexual manipulations, enclosing all of the characters equally. What remains unsaid, unspeakable, most forcefully constrains the characters to stances that paralyze them. The paradoxical levels of discourse that each of the characters articulates to himself and to each other mutually cancel out any liberating–individuating act. Everyone is trapped in the torpor of silence. It is this silence that serves to instill mistrust among all the conspirators. No one is ever sure of what motivates the others: there is always an abyss between what one says and what one might be thinking, plotting:

> Pensez-vous avoir lu jusqu'au fond de son âme?
> Sous la cause publique il vous cachait sa flamme,
> Et peut cacher encor sous cette passion

Les détestables feux de son ambition.
Peut-être qu'il prétend, après la mort d'Octave,
Au lieu d'affranchir Rome, en faire son esclave,
Qu'il vous compte déjà pour un de ses sujets,
Ou que sur votre perte il fonde ses projets. (III, i, 749–56)

In the 'huis clos' of *Cinna* the only openness is the empty space of silence, the invisible prison entrapping all the characters in what becomes the veritable locus of the tragic. The limits of this tragic space are exploded in Act V by the successive confessions that, coming one upon the other, break down the walls erected by silence, and by so doing allow for a new alignment of power. It is this new alignment which in the end assures the triumph of Auguste's totalitarianism. In Act V for the first time the characters finally speak their truth. They finally bridge the abyss of appearance that sunders them in two, and allow their desire and their rhetoric to coincide.

Confession is a highly invested ritual.[22] The confession of the conspirators paradoxically both frees them from their subservience to Octave and eventually binds them more firmly to Auguste. The initial consequence of each confession is to liberate the confessee from his debt to the Emperor by reaffirming an allegiance to the past: 'Seigneur,' Cinna tells him, 'je suis Romain, et du sang de Pompée.' Breaking with his entire recent history of false (adopted) lineage, Cinna re-establishes his link with a genealogy that had been proscribed. Cinna's past is his only real freedom, and this freedom, articulated, is Death:

Je sais ce que j'ai fait, et ce qu'il vous faut faire.
Vous devez un exemple à la postérité,
Et mon trépas importe à votre sûreté. (v, i, 1554–6)

In their confessions the characters at last become integral − but this integrity exists only as the mirror of Death. Emilie's confession also becomes a coincidence of liberty and annihilation:

Punissez donc, seigneur, ces criminels appas
Qui de vos favoris font d'illustres ingrats;
Tranchez mes tristes jours pour assurer les vôtres.
(v, ii, 1619–21)

Finally, Maxime, the most abject of the conspirators, confesses his betrayal and also, confessing, seeks his execution:

De tous vos ennemis connaissez mieux le pire:
Si vous régnez encore, seigneur, si vous vivez,

> C'est ma jalouse rage à qui vous le devez.
>
> . . .
>
> souffrez que je meure aux yeux de ces amants.
>
> (v, iii, 1670–2, 1688)

By finally speaking their desire, their truth, they condemn themselves. The world where they live cannot tolerate a discourse from which silence and secrecy vanish because such a discourse countermands the very laws of its existence. In *Cinna* truth when it is finally spoken frees the characters, but it also kills them.

And yet, no one dies in *Cinna*. A tragedy of blood lust, of ritual retribution is avoided. At the climactic moment of confession, at the moment of the most intense pleasure that the conspirators experience in the freedom of speaking, each is transformed. The confession breaks the parameters of the power structure that heretofore pertained, and, undoing the Gordian knot, breaks open an entire network of pleasure and power that condemned them to fragmentation.

The act of confession is an inherently solitary pleasure, performed for another, for a real or imaginary interlocutor, but experienced paradoxically as a narcissistic affirmation of the self, as a breaking of the bonds that united the self to others. Secrecy had bound all the characters together in a network of power that was actually impotence. Confession separates and isolates the participants from each other (each confession = death = individuality). Cinna and Emilie through their own avowals revert to positions that are mutually exclusive. Each depicts the glory, the right to an ultimate, superior truth, that would affirm the hegemony of his/her own self. From the union of love, they arrive at the isolation of truth:

> E. – Cinna, qu'oses-tu dire? est-ce là me chérir,
> Que de m'ôter l'honneur quand il me faut mourir?
> C. – Mourez, mais en mourant ne souillez pas ma gloire.
> E. – La mienne se flétrit, si César te veut croire.
> C. – Et la mienne se perd, si vous tirez à vous
> Toute celle que suit de si généreux coups. (v, ii, 1639–44)

The truth they proclaim pits them against each other, and effectively undoes the illusion of power of their sado-masochistic tropism. They have undone themselves as a threat to Auguste. In their squabbling they can define themselves now only as a negativity, as the death that they cannot give themselves, but which must come, they declare, from Auguste.[23] It is this request for death,

tacitly recognizing Auguste's supreme and ultimate power to pardon or to kill, that elevates him as it debases them.

Death is precisely what Auguste, rejecting Octave, refuses them. His 'clemency' is perhaps an ultimate ruse. By not giving in to their desire that he be Octave, that is, cruel and death-dealing, by saying 'no' to their truth, by refusing them the power of martyrdom, Auguste effectively becomes the Sovereign they feared he was all along.[24] By his 'grace' Auguste situates himself at last in a sphere that exists as totally independent of another's desire. Auguste, by negating his own ambivalence, by effectively denying the Octave in him, seals himself off. By this gesture he becomes, in his splendid, isolated integrity, the impossible reflection of all self-containment – the model and reflection of all desire for his subjects.

By not giving in, by not being Octave, Auguste undoes the oscillation that had obtained in him. By negating any dependence to the Other he becomes 'le maître de l'univers' that he claimed to be. Auguste becomes in this ultimate apotheosis the narcissistic mirror by and through which all other desire is now reflected. By placing himself above the demand of the plotters he has established a new system of power: instead of a system of circular exchange that had united all of them along a horizontal axis (Auguste = Cinna = Emilie = Maxime = Auguste =) we now have a vertical structure where all meaning flows down from Auguste, become godlike.

At the start of the play, Auguste was merely 'le maître des corps'. At the end of the play he has found 'l'art d'être maître des coeurs'. This move, the most totalitarian of gestures, is presented, paradoxically, as the most progressive. Auguste breaks out of the system of repetition that had condemned Rome to constantly replay her internal strife in dissension and fragmentation. He has constituted a new order of history where all is sacrificed to the Monarch, and where the supreme pleasure of the citizen is to die so that the Law may live:

> Puisse le grand moteur des belles destinées,
> Pour prolonger vos jours, retrancher nos années.
>
> (v, iii, 1749–50)

Livie's speech at the end of the play confirms Auguste's new position as existing outside time (out of the cycle of time), and therefore outside the world of ambivalence, of human mutability:

> Oyez ce que les dieux vous font savoir par moi;
> De votre heureux destin c'est l'immuable loi.

115

Après cette action vous n'avez rien à craindre
On portera le joug désormais sans se plaindre.

(v, iii, 1755–8)

Contrary to other initial acts of foundation, which have traditionally been a transgression of the body, a murder, the action that established this new political order is a birth. By his gift of life Auguste has successfully replaced the (dead) fathers and become their substitute. Each plotter owes his existence anew, again, to Auguste and can be defined only by this debt to him. Their allegiance from now on is not to the past but to Auguste, who has created himself as both their past and their future. This debt makes them entire, stable and strong:

Souffrez que ma vertu dans mon coeur rappelée
Vous consacre une foi lâchement violée,
Mais si ferme à présent, si loin de chanceler,
Que la chute du ciel ne pourrait l'ébranler. (v, iii, 1745–8)

Auguste's final gesture is perhaps his most insidious. His pardon spares their lives, but it also gives the conspirators back to each other. After they have revealed their inherent and insurmountable incompatibility they are all trapped in a system of competition for the Father's approval. It is a system, however, from which the Father, become divine, has removed himself. No longer within their system, but its essential absent cause and mover, Auguste is assured of total control.

The end of the play sees, then, a complete reversal which affirms a political system that was only shakily in place at the tragedy's start. It also, significantly, fuses this new political edifice to a new concept of history, a history that now flows from Auguste, that progresses to a future that is no longer a mere repetition of the past.[25] For a tragedy, the play ends quite joyously. We witness the institution of official well-being, the happiness of a monarch who has achieved the voluntary sacrifice of republican values (individual freedom):

Vos royales vertus lui vont trop enseigner
Que son bonheur consiste à vous faire régner:
D'une si longue erreur pleinement affranchie,
Elle n'a plus de voeux que pour la monarchie,
Vous prépare déjà des temples, des autels,
Et le ciel une place entre les immortels. (v, iii, 1767–72)

From his place among the immortals, outside time and history,

outside desire, Auguste can contemplate all of his former enemies who now, vying with each other, outdo each other in sacrificing to their new divinity:

> Rome, avec une joie et sensible et profonde,
> Se démet en vos mains de l'empire du monde;
> Vos royales vertus lui vont trop enseigner
> Que son bonheur consiste à vous faire régner.

(v, iii, 1765–8)

Is it not the ultimate ruse of a tyrant to make one's subjects happy, to give them a sense of their subjectivity as inseparable from the repressions of his Law, and to have them articulate this repression as their supreme pleasure?

5

POLYEUCTE: SEEING IS BELIEVING

'Je vois, je sais, je crois.'

Polyeucte, although a 'tragédie chrétienne', is firmly grounded in political history. The drama that is centered in the immolation of Polyeucte is strategically situated at a moment of historical passage. *Polyeucte* lies on the threshold of a new world order. As the play begins, at the far corners of the Empire, in Armenia, the Christians are an ever more present menace to the internal stability of the Roman world. On the borders of that world, the Persians, although contained for the moment, are a threat to its geographic integrity. Clearly, the atmosphere in which *Polyeucte* evolves is one of malaise, of instability. When the curtain goes up on the first scene of this drama, the 'throne and the altar' are in danger.

The moment of passage from one order to another is a sacred one; it is a moment of agony, the agony of an entire system of legal, social and sexual codes, and of the birth pains of a new society. It is this trembling that we are called upon to witness. It is the terror and anticipation of our participation that accounts for *Polyeucte*'s hold on us. In this, Corneille's most complex tragedy, the lines that separate life and death are confused and inverted. At its religious core, the tragedy engages theater in its very nature as a form of representation. The borders separating seeming and being shift. Concurrently those other borders, the divisions that society imposes between its members, division of sex and of power, are engaged in their own dislocation. The distinctions that make representation possible are blurred, and in this blurring a new order which is rooted in the world and yet not of it comes into being. In this new society the Classical subject that has so laboriously tended toward stability is paradoxically exalted at the same time that its existence is put into question.

It is clear that the questioning which causes the Cornelian world to tremble revolves around the conundrum of sexual desire, that is, the relation the individual, as a desiring, sexed subject, must main-

tain with his fellows and the State. In this, *Polyeucte* continues and refines the predominant problematic that has already played so large a role in Cornelian dramaturgy. In fact, for those who consider *Polyeucte* Corneille's masterpiece, the play fulfills the promise that the preceding tragedies only approximated.

Despite, however, its involvement in a problematic that remains essentially identical in all the great tragedies, *Polyeucte* also differs radically from its predecessors. The difference, a mere turn of the dramatic situation, may seem slight and yet it is of enough significance to catapult the Classical edifice into disarray. For however different the plays that preceded *Polyeucte* were from each other, they had in common a central, underlying tension that, in all, served as the impetus to tragic action. The desire that propelled the protagonists toward each other, the sexual attraction of 'two halves' seeking their complement in a symmetrical union, was forever exacerbated in its own frustration.[1] In them, the marriage that engages the sexuality of Corneille's protagonists in an elaborate socio-political network is always forestalled. The appropriation of the symbol of feminine difference is never given to representation; it is left intact, evanescent and undefinable. Desire and dramatic tension are maintained.

Polyeucte fundamentally alters this situation. It is the only major tragedy to be situated on the other side of what was posited as the limit of representation, on the other side of an impossible divide. For the first time in Classical tragedy we are given this appropriation as a 'fait accompli'. With this already-there of marriage we are also given the satisfaction, the sexual satisfaction of the hero:

> Mais vous ne savez pas ce que c'est qu'une femme;
> Vous ignorez quels droits elle a sur toute l'âme
> Quand après un long temps qu'elle a su nous charmer,
> Les flambeaux de l'hymen viennent de s'allumer.   (I, i, 9–12)

> Polyeucte, un seigneur des premiers d'Arménie,
> Goûte de son hymen la douceur infinie.   (II, i, 417–18)

The hymen disappears, consumed in the pleasure of the hero. The pleasure of this appropriation is not, however, without profoundly unsettling consequences. These consequences are only hinted at in the malevolent echoes of metaphor, in the litotic designations of pleasure: 'flambeaux', 'allumer', 'goûter'. Although surely describing the passion of the lover, the words also reverberate, in their own excess, with the loss of control they signal,

with images of hecatombs of flames, of the destruction of Empires (the burning of Troy), and of the devouring, destructive aspects of all passion.

As we begin our reading of *Polyeucte* we must, therefore, engage the following questions: if, in the preceding plays, the appropriation of the hymen, ardently desired and just as ardently refused, could serve as the central absence around which whirled the tragic storm − if, in other words, the 'hymen–hyménée' was the talisman of the tragic − should we not expect that in *Polyeucte*, where this taboo has been infringed, that some cataclysm must mark this transgression? Must we not look to the sexual in order to understand both the breakdown of a culture that is undone in its own predicates and the coming into being of another order, the order of the divine?

By the appropriation that *Polyeucte* posits, by the acting out of sexual desire, the tragedy figures the moment of passage, the 'hymen' of history, in which it evolves. Situated at a crossroads, *Polyeucte* plays out Classicism's investments in subjectivity against the background of the collapse of the Roman Empire with the death of innumerable hordes of pagan deities and the birth of a new unknown order, the order of the One, in whose embrace Polyeucte is both lost and found. It is as a crucible, a crucible that confounds as it inverts Classicism's investments in a certain sexual symmetry, that *Polyeucte*'s scandal mesmerizes us.

Even before it was given a public production, *Polyeucte* was uneasily situated at the crux of a theoretical debate. For over a hundred years theoreticians and practitioners of the theater had been arguing the appropriateness of using the stage to represent sacred history. Almost all the ecclesiastical orators of the seventeenth century opposed the theater's use of Christian mysteries.[2] In choosing to stage Polyeucte's martyrdom, Corneille clearly situated himself on the antagonistic side of this debate, aligning himself with such notable figures as Grotius, Buchanan and Heinsius.[3]

Corneille's defense of his choice of subject matter is interesting to us not so much because of what he says but of how he says it. The rhetorical structures of his apology are intimately linked to the textual strategies of his tragedy. The same oppositions, the limits of representation, that we find operative in *Polyeucte* are operative in its defense.

Dramatic illusion is, Corneille tells us, the 'plus beau secret de la poésie' ('Abrégé des martyrs de St Polyeucte', p. 209). In front

of this secret, a 'mystery', two reactions are possible. On the one hand there is the passive participation, by the spectator, in the mystery: 'Les uns se laissent si bien persuader à cet enchaînement qu'aussitôt qu'ils ont remarqué quelques événements véritables, ils s'imaginent la même chose des motifs qui les font naître et les circonstances qui les accompagnent' ('Abrégé', p. 211). These credulous spectators are the dupes of the theater. They are illuded by their own ignorance and are possessed by the artifact they are viewing. The other group of spectators, rather than being seduced by the illusion, rejects it out of hand: 'Quand nous traitons quelque histoire écartée dont ils ne trouvent rien dans leur souvenir ils l'attribuent tout entier à l'effort de notre imagination, et la prennent pour une aventure de roman' ('Abrégé', pp. 210–11).

Corneille divides the theater-going public, a world which he says is made up of a 'diversité des esprits', into two: the credulous and the incredulous. If we extend his analogy further, credulous and incredulous are but two antithetical reactions to a same 'stimulus' (the 'mystery'): passivity (one group is possessed by the illusion) and activity (the other refuses it). In any case neither of these reactions is fully adequate to the mystery; something always escapes: 'L'un et l'autre de ces effets serait dangereux en cette rencontre' ('Abrégé', p. 211).

Rather than as a fixed opposition, it would seem more plausible to see these positions for what they are, equal and reversible manifestations of an undefinable phenomenon – the 'secret' that is available to us only as one or the other reaction, both and still more. The two reactions are simply reverse images of each other. What causes half of the spectators to react actively and the other half passively is part of the 'mystery', the result of their investments in a signifying system. (Here, the more or less 'knowledge' one brings to the theater, the greater or lesser participation in a cultural order.)

It would be only a slight exaggeration to equate Corneille's division of the theater-going public with the sexual divisions of his dramatic universe: its division into the camps of masculinity and femininity that are always operative in the tragedies presented to this audience.

The paradox of poetry's ambivalent effect on an audience is linked in its articulation to the problematic of sexual desire that is at the crux of Polyeucte's drama. This problematic is always an enigma, a mystery. At the heart of *Polyeucte* is the essential question of individual consciousness – How does the human subject,

sexually defined by those systems into which s/he is born, work out of those very systems that, by defining him in the world of the living, also condemn him, simultaneously, to death? Those systems (economic, social, political, familial) that define the individual confine him. This confinement is felt as an exile in a world of fragmentation, isolation and desire. The religious cry that echoes throughout *Polyeucte*, the unanswerable question, asks how it is possible to exist in the world, when this very existence inexorably contains within its own definition its own disappearance.[4]

What is presented as the Christian tragedy of *Polyeucte*, what Corneille intends to show us about God, is, nevertheless, and perhaps in spite of its Christian metaphors, a play that reflects the more general human predicament. It talks to us about the horror that reigns in the soul of man when, for reasons that escape our quotidian existence, we realize that the image we embrace in the depth of the night is only a mirror reflection of ourself, the hollow return of our own emptiness. In this dark night of the soul this searing realization tears us from the illusions of representation and forces the desiring subject out of the embrace of the 'same' and into union with the Other. In this union, sexuality (division as representation) is abandoned but, at the same time, the subject as he is defined/defines himself ceases to exist.

Like all the major tragedies, *Polyeucte* begins on a note of conflict. Here, however, the focus of discord has shifted. Instead of a woman sundered by the alienating demands of a male-dominated universe (cf. *Le Cid*, *Horace*, *Cinna*), *Polyeucte* presents us with a divided hero. Polyeucte is torn between two irreconcilable claims on him: the exigency of spiritual salvation and the imperious demands of sexual gratification; between Christianity and Pauline. The new creed that Polyeucte ardently desires to embrace is just as ardently held beyond his grasp by his own sexual pleasure. Christianity, as it is represented by Néarque, takes on the coloration of an exclusively male community, or at least of a community which must, in essence, oppose the contamination of heterosexual indulgence. In *Polyeucte* Christianity denies division in the neophyte's total submission to God who:

> Veut le premier amour et les premiers honneurs.
> Comme rien n'est égal à sa grandeur suprême,
> Il faut ne rien aimer qu'après lui, qu'en lui même,
> Négliger, pour lui plaire, et femme, et biens, et rang,
> Exposer pour sa gloire et verser tout son sang.　　(I, i, 72–6)

The God we are presented with here is manifestly an imperious Father who, in his totalizing/totalitarian stance, completes all those unfinished, because mortal, portraits of the ideal Patriarch Corneille has sketched in his previous work. At the same time this 'ur' father serves as the mirror for his subjected sons. He is the symbol of the integrity that may be theirs but which paradoxically only total submission to him can achieve. In *Polyeucte* it is this imperious Other, the final avatar of the Ideal, that controls the sublimation of the son. If we follow Néarque's rhetoric, in order to be a Christian one must imitate God's 'integrity' ('Il est toujours tout juste et tout bon') by a total consecration of one's being. This consecration is possible only to those who are already in a state of grace:

> Et Dieu, qui tient votre âme et vos jours dans sa main,
> Promet-il à vous voeux de le pouvoir demain?
> Il est toujours tout juste et tout bon; mais sa grâce
> Ne descend pas toujours avec même efficace.   (I, i, 27–30)

As the play begins, Polyeucte is precisely not in this state. Néarque chides him for procrastinating. He calls to him from the camp of the 'pure', untainted males, of those 'sexless' males who ignore women ('Vous ne savez pas ce que c'est qu'une femme'). Néarque, already a priest, accuses Polyeucte of being seduced by his sexuality, a seduction that renders him effeminate:

> Quoi, vous vous arrêtez aux songes d'une femme!
> De si faibles sujets troublent cette grande âme!
> Et ce coeur tant de fois dans la guerre éprouvé
> S'alarme d'un péril qu'une femme a rêvé!   (I, i, 1–4)

Néarque's opening diatribe equates women with dreams (illusions) and eventually both to the devil. At the same time this equation is opposed to another in which masculinity is equated to 'reality' ('Ce coeur . . . dans la guerre éprouvé') and to God.

Polyeucte's rather disarming response, àlready quoted:

> Mais vous ne savez pas ce que c'est qu'une femme;
> Vous ignorez quels droits elle a sur toute l'âme
> Quand après un longtemps qu'elle a su nous charmer,
> Les flambeaux de l'hymen viennent de s'allumer   (I, i, 9–12)

only corroborates Néarque's fears. Polyeucte is in the most dangerous position for a Cornelian hero. He is in the throes of sexual pleasure and this pleasure has contaminated him. This con-

tamination turns him away from his true calling as a man — the ability and the desire to sublimate — and traps him within the unfamiliar and dangerous world of the feminine. Pleasure does what Death ('la guerre') could not; it sunders men from their hold on ideality and turns them away from their political investments and toward their own anarchic satisfaction.

In *Polyeucte*, therefore, marriage is presented as a destitution. It perverts Polyeucte, making him incapable of that leap into pure Ideality, into total union with the Father:

> Mais que vous êtes loin de cette ardeur parfaite
> Qui vous est nécessaire et que je vous souhaite!   (I, i, 77–8)

Instead of being possessed by God, Polyeucte is possessed by Pauline:

> Pauline, sans raison dans la douleur plongée,
> Craint, et croit déjà voir ma mort qu'elle a songée;
> Elle oppose ses pleurs aux desseins que je fais,
> Et tâche à m'empêcher de sortir du palais.
> Je méprise sa crainte, je cède à ses larmes;
> Elle me fait pitié sans me donner d'alarmes;
> Et mon coeur attendri sans être intimidé,
> N'ose déplaire aux yeux dont il est possédé.   (I, i, 13–20)

In this most visionary of tragedies all the devices of the theater are put into play to subvert the illusoriness that is at its heart and at the heart of the world. This world is just another stage, where we are called upon as spectators to share in a Divine vision, to share, in other words, the point of view of God. By our position of spectator we are in the position of the divine, ubiquitous gaze. It is therefore natural that the underlying metaphoric network that supports as it confounds the structural divisions of the play should be visual. We are the witnesses (= martyrs) of the martyrdom that is played out in our field of vision.

Jean Starobinski has written eloquently on the inherent ambivalence of the eye for Corneille's theater.[5] No other organ is as privileged as the eye for expressing antitheses and for collapsing such oppositions into each other, negating them. All of the sexual and political structures that are set in place as the play begins and that are, in the course of its development, inverted and finally collapsed into each other are grafted onto the more pervasive visual imagery that divides the universe of *Polyeucte* into a constantly shifting play of mirrors. It is a play where we as audience are spec-

tators and also actors, in a play of seeing, being seen and showing. At first these divisions are easily dichotomized into a general split between textual allusions to voyeurism or to exhibitionism. This basic opposition sustains certain of the more obvious antitheses that inform *Polyeucte*. Yet this opposition is inherently untenable because eminently reversible.[6] The two poles of the opposition are not in an immutably rigid stand-off, but exist in oscillation; each is involved continually in the other, becomes the other. The emphasis on visual metaphors affords us an insight into the final bankruptcy of any system that would maintain untenable oppositions, false symmetries that are invested as 'natural' in the face of their own obvious mutability. It is in the disruption of these oppositions, their negation in an all-embracing vision, that the world of *Polyeucte* becomes transfixed and transformed.

Polyeucte begins his journey to martyrdom enfolded by Pauline's gaze. Her vision traps him and in this visual field he is undone. As her gaze encompasses Polyeucte it also splits him ('Je méprise . . . je cède') and blinds him. His 'oeil d'époux', his attachment and deference to his pleasure in Pauline, effectively keeps him away from baptism which alone provides a truly clear-sighted perception of reality. It:

> lave nos forfaits dans une eau salutaire,
> Et qui, purgeant l'âme et désillant nos yeux,
> Nous rend le premier droit que nous avions aux cieux.
>
> (I, i, 46–8)

Trapped by Pauline's vision (her dream/gaze), Polyeucte is kept in a state of servitude, of damnation, is not allowed the keys to the Kingdom. And yet, is not Polyeucte's imprisonment in Pauline's vision precisely the human predicament?[7] We are all looked at, transfixed in the gaze of the Other. The problem, the essential tragic problem, for Polyeucte as well as for Pauline is not that they are both encompassed by a totalizing, all-seeing, unseen eye that is their own consciousness of themselves, but rather that in their mutual reflection, in their way of looking at each other, they can never see the other. In *Polyeucte* the tragic predicament, the impossibility of human sexual love, could be described as a visual dysfunction — 'Jamais tu ne me regardes là où je te vois (et) inversement ce que je regarde n'est jamais ce que je veux voir.'[8]

Polyeucte's description of himself as psychologically torn apart reflects, in a strange reversal, Pauline's vision of him in her dream.

In this, her inner sighting of Polyeucte, he is torn apart physically in a vision of death and dismemberment. Pauline's view of Polyeucte strategically places him at the center of her inner stage, the sacrificial victim of her desire, of her nightmare. Pauline's dream serves as a frame inside which the dramatic evolution of *Polyeucte* takes place. It is the most successful emblem of the political, religious and sexual tensions that exist in the universe of the play, as it is also the most successful instance of the paradox of representation itself. As the play evolves, exactly according to the scenario announced in and precipitated by the dream, the vision slowly divests itself of its role of frame and invests itself as reality. As *Polyeucte* works itself out, Pauline's initial vision of Polyeucte dissolves into his (and her) reality. With this fading the illusions of the unconscious become the reality of spiritual salvation, while the reality that framed the unconscious gradually disintegrates before our eyes.

I have argued in another context for our having to understand Pauline's dream as not just an ancillary invention of the dramatic plot, but as essential for understanding the ambivalent role played by Pauline's desire in Polyeucte's martyrdom.[9] It is my contention that the dream that weighs so heavily on the conscience of Pauline and that casts its shadow over the first act of the tragedy is an expression of Pauline's sexual ambivalence. Pauline is torn between an investment in a system that excludes her, a system that makes her only an object of masculine rivalry and exchange, an investment she calls her duty ('devoir'), and a pleasure that is denied her and which she denies herself. What I would like to insist upon here is that the power of Pauline's vision is a fragmenting, murderous one. When Pauline looks at Polyeucte, when she sees him in her dream, she sees him bloodied, sacrificed:

> J'ai vu mon père même, un poignard à la main,
> Entrer le bras levé pour lui percer le sein:
> Là ma douleur trop forte a brouillé ses images;
> Le sang de Polyeucte a satisfait leurs rages.   (I, iii, 239–42)

Pauline sees Polyeucte murdered by an inchoate mob. A new Penthesilea, another Agave, she assists, absent, at the dismemberment of the male she both loves and hates.[10] Her vision of his sacrifice is so troubling ('j'ai frémi, mon âme s'est troublée') because simultaneously Pauline glimpses a prospect of sexual pleasure that she had renounced: the bloodied vision of the dead

126

husband is inseparable from the glorious vision of the taboo lover, Sévère:

> Il semblait triomphant, et tel que sur son char
> Victorieux dans Rome entre notre César.   (I, iii, 227–8)

Pleasure is possible only in another place, another metaphor. Through the slippage of the connotations of 'devoir' Polyeucte is confused, by Pauline, with the Father, Félix, and Sévère, replacing Polyeucte, is replaced by César. Pauline is clearly in a strange, inadmissible relation of desire–pleasure–suffering with the Father. This interdiction weighs so strongly on her that Pauline can pleasure only in visions. In a society which has successfully eliminated feminine pleasure from the realm of the representable, which has totally recuperated women's desire in the schema of the male, Pauline's subservience to that desire can surface only in her dreams as a sado-masochistic scenario of guilt and revenge.[11]

Pauline is certainly the most perfect example of self-sacrifice to the Law of the Father in Corneille's theater. More than any other of the heroines of Cornelian tragedy, she seems most totally subjected to and proud of her self-negation in the Father's Law:

> Il possédait mon coeur, mes désirs, ma pensée:
> Je ne lui cachais point combien j'étais blessée;
> Nous soupirions ensemble et pleurions nos malheurs;
> Mais au lieu d'espérance, il n'avait que des pleurs;
> Et malgré des soupirs si doux, si favorables,
> Mon père et mon devoir étaient inexorables.   (I, iii, 197–202)

> Je découvrais en vous d'assez illustres marques
> Pour vous préférer même aux plus heureux monarques:
> Mais puisque mon devoir m'imposait d'autres lois,
> De quelque amant pour moi que mon père eût fait choix,
> Quand à ce grand pouvoir que la valeur vous donne
> Vous auriez ajouté l'éclat d'une couronne,
> Quand je vous aurais vu, quand je l'aurais haï,
> J'en aurais soupiré, mais j'aurais obéi.   (II, ii, 469–76)

Is it not Pauline's sacrifice, her acceptance of her debt, of her capitulation to her role and definition of herself in the world of the Father, that makes her, in our 'view' the most enigmatic, the most touching of Corneille's heroines, the most feminine? For centuries critics have waxed poetic in their praise of Pauline's 'je ne sais quoi', her moving triumph over her own feelings, her self-

effacement, which has appeared as the highest, most complete example of femininity in Corneille's theater. What they have ignored is the other side of that coin, the price of repression, the fierce, sadistic desires that swell up and pleasure in fantasies of masculine rivalry where alone, the focal point of all male eyes, Pauline pleasures as the men cut themselves up for her, as they annihilate themselves, as she has been annihilated. And all this right in front of her eyes:

> Que de soucis flottants, que de confus nuages
> Présentent à mes yeux d'inconstantes images!
>
> . . .
>
> Mon esprit, embrassant tout ce qu'il s'imagine,
> Voit tantôt mon bonheur, et tantôt ma ruine,
> Et suit leur vaine idée avec si peu d'effet
> Qu'il ne peut espérer ni craindre tout à fait.
> Sévère incessamment brouille ma fantaisie:
> J'espère en sa vertu, je crains sa jalousie;
> Et je n'ose penser que d'un oeil bien égal
> Polyeucte en ces lieux puisse voir son rival.
> Comme entre deux rivaux la haine est naturelle,
> L'entrevue aisément se termine en querelle.
>
> (III, i, 721–2, 729–38)

Pauline's pleasure is possible only in a visionary, that is a fantasmatic, stance. In this stance, however, something very strange is at work, stranger than the subject of her gaze, stranger even than her pleasure in the vision of her own destruction. In the first instance, it would seem that Pauline is the 'voyante' of the play. Hers would be a position that is by nature ambivalent. It is on the one hand passive, in the sense that a voyante does not participate in the spectacle she sees: in the spectacle of Polyeucte's death the mob is the active pole of Pauline's vision. On the other hand her vision also performs actively to frame and direct the spectator's perception of the tragedy. It is Pauline's vision that directs the gaze of the world, both in and out of the represented universe. The audience is represented/supplied in the play by Pauline; passive, our gaze is superimposed on hers. She is our visual surrogate.

Pauline's vision/dream is equated by Néarque to the world of false illusions, a world which should not be troubling to a man. On the other hand, he quickly associates dreams and women with the satanic:

Polyeucte: seeing is believing

> Ainsi du genre humain l'ennemi vous abuse:
> Ce qu'il ne peut de force, il l'entreprend de ruse.
>
> . . .
>
> Et ce songe rempli de noires visions
> N'est que le coup d'essai de ses illusions   (I, i, 53–4, 59–60)

and Satan as we should all know is certainly a formidable opponent to any Christian.

In the first act the play of seeing/being seen is a highly ambivalent signifier. It at once situates Pauline voyante as both a passive force and as participating in phallic pleasure; the pleasure of framing, of organizing, of cutting off and determining meaning, even if this meaning, her own desire, remains ambivalent.[12] In this way, as the director of our seeing, as the agent of her vision, Pauline penetrates Polyeucte, exposing and opening him up to our gaze, unsexing him. In his mutilation she turns him into the divided indecisive male he describes himself to be. The force of Pauline's vision, the power of her eyes, reflects Polyeucte's sexual thraldom. Néarque is quite right, Pauline is satanic. She is a monster whose gaze turns Polyeucte away from himself. A new Medusa, her eyes are an abyss of pleasure which Polyeucte, if he is to be saved, must escape:

> N. – Fuyez un ennemi qui sait votre défaut,
>   Qui le trouve aisément, qui blesse par la vue,
>   Et dont le coup mortel vous plaît quand il vous tue.
>
> (I, i, 104–6)

> P. – Fuyons, puisqu'il le faut.   (I, ii, 107)

Polyeucte, like all Cornelian heroes, must flee the eyes of his mistress/wife lest he be totally undone, lest he retain nothing of a manhood gained with such sacrifice:

> Adieu: vos pleurs sur moi prennent trop de puissance;
> Je sens déjà mon coeur prêt à se révolter,
> Et ce n'est qu'en fuyant que j'y puis résister.   (I, ii, 122–4)

When Polyeucte walks off stage, he walks out of Pauline's vision (and out of our view), out of the prison of her eyes, and into God's embrace.

Should he tarry in front of her, they would remain locked forever in a visual double-bind that reflects their own loss in the sexual couple they form. Although Polyeucte claims, as we have seen, to be a satisfied bridegroom, Pauline's reserve indicates a refusal of sexual gratification:

> Mon abord en ces lieux
> Me fit voir Polyeucte, et je plus à ses yeux;
> Et comme il est ici le chef de la noblesse,
> Mon père fut ravi qu'il me prît pour maîtresse,
> Et par son alliance il se crut assuré
> D'être plus redoutable et plus considéré;
> Il approuva sa flamme, et conclut l'hyménée:
> Et moi, comme à son lit je me vis destinée,
> Je donnai par devoir à son affection
> Tout ce que l'autre avait par inclination. (I, iii, 207–16)

In a strange reversal, what Polyeucte receives in Pauline's bed is her duty. Her desire is elsewhere. There is a bizarre interchange of husband and father in Pauline's discourse. It is obvious that they are linked together, made equivalent terms for what Pauline articulates as her 'devoir'. Here, as in all Cornelian tragedy, 'devoir' is always synonymous with the acceptance by the female characters of their impossible debt to the Father, of their acceptance of themselves as the lack that the Father must successfully deny as he erects the Law of the Integral. It would seem that in the case of Pauline and Félix (Polyeucte) this sacrifice to 'devoir' is exacerbated precisely because in *Polyeucte* not only is Félix a metaphoric agent of the Law, he is, in a very real sense, the actual agent of imperial authority. Nowhere else in Corneille's dramatic oeuvre is this link so tightly articulated.[13] It is precisely this articulation that circumscribes Pauline in a circle of authority and negation. It is this confusion between Pauline's sacrifice to the Ideal Father of Rome and to her own father who is never adequate to the Ideal he is made to represent, who is its contradiction, that makes her anxiety all the greater. As Félix shows himself to be nothing more than a cowardly courtier trapped by his own illusions, trapped by his own myopic view of the world, Pauline finds herself trapped in a system of contradictory referents in which she no longer has any grounding.

The interreaction of the visual metaphors and the inherent sado-masochistic sexuality that dominates in *Polyeucte* is never more apparent than in the oscillation that occurs as Pauline moves from seeing Polyeucte to being seen by Sévère. Polyeucte, married to Pauline, does not see her because for him there is nothing to see. Pauline is his: the 'hymen' he has breached instantly changes Pauline from an object of contemplation to an invisible extension of Polyeucte's pleasure. In this passage from virgin to wife, Pauline disappears:

Tu vois, ma Stratonice, en quel siècle nous sommes,
Voilà notre pouvoir sur les esprits des hommes;
Voilà ce qui nous reste, et l'ordinaire effet
De l'amour qu'on nous offre, et des voeux qu'on nous fait.
Tant qu'ils ne sont qu'amants nous sommes souveraines,
Et jusqu'à la conquête ils nous traitent de reines;
Mais après l'hyménée ils sont rois à leur tour.   (I, iii, 129–35)

For Sévère, however, Pauline, though married, still shines with
the splendor of a virgin, shines as that tantalizing enigma of his
own desire. Pauline remains for him intact, a perfect object offered
to his devouring contemplation:

Ah! quelle comble de joie!
Cette chère beauté consent que je la voie!
Mais ai-je sur son âme encore quelque pouvoir?
Quel trouble, quel transport lui cause ma venue?
Puis-je tout espérer de cette heureuse vue?   (II, i, 373–7)

The entire dialogue between Sévère and his confidant, Fabian,
turns upon the desire of Sévère to 'see' Pauline. In his case the
scopic metaphor is only a veiled disguise for a desire to possess her
(il veut la voir/l'avoir). Physical possession is enhanced, pre-
figured, rendered more tantalizing and, ultimately, more frustra-
ting by Sévère's 'viewing' Pauline. As the scene progresses the 'seeing' of Pauline eventually reveals its hidden unspeakable link with
the ultimate erotic encounter, with Death: 'Je ne veux que la voir,
soupirer et mourir.' In one way or another, having or not having
Pauline, the sexuality of all the males in the play, the sexuality of
which she is the center, the focal-vanishing point, leads them all to
their death.

This change, this turn of meaning that has carried Sévère from
the hope of sexual pleasure to the despair of death, passes through
his own masochistic vision of Pauline's possession by another:

Faibles soulagements d'un malheur sans remède!
Pauline, je verrai qu'un autre vous possède.   (II, i, 421–2)

At no time in *Polyeucte* can the pleasure of seeing be separated
from the pleasure/pain of the subject's own annihilation. While
what is given in the vision always seems to indicate a totality of
apprehension (a jubilation in that totality), in actuality it points to
the abyss of repression—fragmentation that lies beyond the image
production, that is on the other side of the mirror. In this way there
is no 'vision' possible of the loved object that is not a sign of

frustration, that does not signal the lack, the division, in the viewing subject. The vision instantly reveals the initial fall away from wholeness. Instead of a sovereign unity we have a constant mise-en-abîme of difference, the impossibility ever to inter-relate, ever actually to form an integral subject. The vision of the other, instead of suturing the wound of difference, opens the subject up to his own fragmentation within a vision/discourse that appears as his salvation.

Throughout Act II Sévère constantly appeals to visual imagery to reveal his desire for Pauline. The vision is always an illusion, is never there. Sévère is never permitted to see Pauline. The Pauline whom he sees remains always unattainable. When Sévère looks at Pauline, Pauline shows herself to him as a tantalizing prohibited metaphor of interdiction. Sévère looks at her ('Fabian je la vois . . .') and sees her 'vertu':

> De grâce montrez moins à mes sens désolés
> La grandeur de ma perte et ce que vous valez;
> Et cachant par pitié cette vertu si rare
> Qui redouble mes feux lorsqu'elle nous sépare.
>
> (II, ii, 527–30)

We must listen carefully to the echoes of this highly invested word as it reverberates in *Polyeucte*. If we remember not only the original Latin meaning of 'virtus' where we hear the 'vir', but also, more close to Corneille, the Machiavellian connotation, her 'vertu' is clearly a signifier for Pauline's virility. It is the metaphor for her own penetrating, controlling gaze, it stands in for her (supposed) lack and completes her, makes her 'integral' and allows her a place in the polis. Pauline's 'vertu', which she invokes throughout the play, has a talismanic quality: it causes men both to desire her and yet to retreat from her. It increases their flame while it keeps them from her.

Pauline's 'vertu' functions as an ambivalent enticement. By being virtuous Pauline offers herself as a re-assuring reflection of male desire for the same, a desire for an unfragmented intact body, a woman who is also a man. At the same time this very 'vertu' which Pauline invokes, especially in its metaphoric association with 'gloire' and 'devoir' (terms that, while not identical, are inseparable), effectively protects her against any masculine attempt to recuperate her. Pauline's 'vertu' is her 'hymen' that is, a new investment of difference which men desire but which she cannot or will not give them lest she lose it, lest she deprive herself of their

desire for her, deprive herself of the only power she can ever have in a world where illusion supplies difference.

Whenever Sévère confronts Pauline, whenever he looks at her, he sees her 'vertu', which jumps up in front of her, which she brandishes as a protective shield between herself and her desire. What Sévère sees in this reflection of Pauline's potency is an image of himself. When we understand the inherent ambivalence of the chain 'vertu–gloire–devoir' as it encircles and imprisons Pauline, but also as it reconstitutes her for herself as intact, always a virgin, we can begin to understand how this new 'hymen' is the link that joins the two aspects of *Polyeucte*'s plot, aspects that have traditionally been seen as irreconcilable. On the one hand we have the Christian tragedy – the martyrdom of Polyeucte and the coming into being of a new, Christian order – and on the other the 'romance', the love story between Pauline and Sévère, which figures the old Roman universe. What most intrigued theater audiences in the seventeenth and eighteenth centuries was not so much the tragedy of Polyeucte's immolation as the impossible love of Sévère for Pauline. This antithetical splitting of the drama into two mutually exclusive subplots cannot any more hold here than it could in *Cinna*. The love that unites Sévère and Pauline is inextricably bound to the frustration in the love of Pauline and Polyeucte. Both loves are doomed because both are caught in a representational fallacy that seeks in the other a complement for the self.

Sévère enters the tragedy with a long history both as a character and as a topos. The love he bears Pauline is noble, virile, respectful and, alas, empty. Sévère is the most 'chivalrous' of seventeenth-century lovers: he is an extension into the world of Classicism of the love that flourished in the twelfth century, at the very dawn of the West's idealization of passion. Sévère has been admired and pitied as a Classical update of the chivalrous knight errant.

And err he does indeed. For Pauline, Sévère journeys from beyond the confines of the world, returning from the dead to surprise her: 'Sévère n'est point mort.' His journey back from Death has transformed Sévère. From the poor but noble Roman knight he was when first they loved, he returns rich in power and prestige:

> Et soudain l'empereur transporté de plaisir,
> Offre au Perse son frère et cent chefs à choisir.
> Ainsi revient au camp le valeureux Sévère
> De sa haute vertu recevoir le salaire;
> La faveur de Décie en fut le digne prix.   (I, iii, 303–7)

Corneille, Classicism and the ruses of symmetry

Despite the changes in his fortune, despite the even more radical change in his life, Sévère's amorous fate never varies. From the beginning his love was and remains doomed. It was and remains reduced to the claustrophobic confines of Pauline's 'devoir'. Pauline tells Stratonice that before his miraculous change of fortune she could not, would not, marry him. Now, of course, despite her love (or because of it), she repeats the same refusal:

> Mais ce même devoir qui le vainquit dans Rome,
> Et qui me range ici dessous les lois d'un homme,
> Repousse encore si loin l'effort de tant d'appas,
> Qu'il déchire mon âme et ne l'ébranle pas;
> C'est cette vertu même, à nos désirs cruelle,
> Que vous louiez alors en blasphémant contre elle;
> Plaignez-vous en encor; mais louez sa rigueur
> Qui triomphe à la fois de vous et de mon coeur,
> Et voyez qu'un devoir moins ferme et moins sincère
> N'aurait pas mérité l'amour du grand Sévère. (II, ii, 513–22)

Sévére is enthralled by Pauline's rigorous virtue, her firm 'devoir'. He idolizes them:

> Pour moi, si mes destins, un peu plus tôt propices,
> Eussent de votre hymen honoré mes services,
> Je n'aurais adoré que l'éclat de vos yeux,
> J'en aurais fait mes rois, j'en aurais fait mes dieux.
>
> (IV, v, 1327–30)

As the perfect chivalrous knight, Sévère can appropriate as his 'devise' the words Polyeucte uses to express his desire for God – 'le désir s'accroît quand l'effet se recule'. The closer the lovers get to each other, the greater the obstacle they place between themselves. That obstacle figures almost as a separate reality, a fetish they both worship and that is there to be adored and never possessed.

For Sévère, the very condition of his love for Pauline is its impossibility. That impossibility is marked by his inability to appropriate Pauline, an inability that is not exterior to them but produced by them.[14] Pauline does not want Sévère to have her. She is afraid of his embrace, of the annihilating force of her own desire. If ever realized, her ôwn construction of herself, her new untouchable virginity, her negative empowering of herself in the world of Patriarchy, would disappear. It is exactly the impossibility of their relation that predicates their desire while rendering it always foreclosed. Pauline must remain an 'object', must remain enfolded in her own negation:

Polyeucte: seeing is believing

O devoir qui me perd et qui me désespère!
Adieu, trop vertueux object et trop charmant.

(II, ii, 570–1)

In the very same way, but in reverse fashion (negative symmetry), it is the impossibility of love, of the relation that binds
Pauline to Polyeucte, that turns Polyeucte away from her and
toward God. Polyeucte's conversion to Christianity is predicated
on his forsaking the illusions of the world that his marriage to
Pauline symbolized. The state of grace attained by Polyeucte
through baptism dissolves the marriage ties and breaks the hold
that his sexual pleasure has on him. Pauline is correct when, in her
rage and frustration, she clearly indicates that what Polyeucte turns
away from is her loss, her sexual sacrifice to him; the 'disgust' he
had temporarily overcome has welled up anew in him:

C'est donc là le dégoût qu'apporte l'hyménée?
Je te suis odieuse après m'être donnée!   (IV, iii, 1251–2)

Once again the symbolic status of the hymen returns as the
epicenter in which all the political, social and sexual values of
Pauline's and Polyeucte's society are reflected, magnified and
condemned.

A wealth of anthropological as well as psychoanalytic writings
has suggested to us that the ritual of marriage, that is, the public
ceremony that surrounds the appropriation of the hymen, is always
an ambiguously violent rite from which neither partner leaves
unscathed. The essential violence of its physicality, which no
ritualization ever completely recuperates, spills out into the domain
of the metaphysical, tainting both participants with an existential
anguish that binds them together and establishes this bond as a
hostile play of mastery and submission.[15]

As a husband Polyeucte enters a different sphere of sexuality
that changes him. When he enters the space of the hymen, Polyeucte abandons an essentially homo-sexual universe. He moves
from the camp defined by exclusively masculine parameters to a
more ambivalent co-mingling. The baptism for which Néarque so
zealously argues is to be the first step of Polyeucte's journey back
from dissolution to Integrity. It is truly an exorcism: his body must
be rid of an evil spirit that possesses it. It must be rid of the pleasure
of Pauline.

This voyage to God is a journey back to a masculine ideal, back
to the embrace of the same. This essential homoerotic desire is
always sublimated in the metaphysical where it appears as an

'Ideal' from which the mediation of the feminine has been excluded. At the same time the words that are used to describe this journey back to God clearly indicate that it is a sexual one also. Polyeucte's conversion to Christianity is described as a 'seduction':

> P. – Quoi! Néarque en est donc?
> S. –   Néarque l'a séduit;
> De leur vieille amitié c'est là l'indigne fruit.

(III, ii, 807–8)

Néarque, the symbol of misogyny, turns Polyeucte away from his wife, away from heterosexual pleasure, and makes him his own in Christ. There cannot be any misunderstanding of the nature of the words used to describe Néarque's seduction of Polyeucte, 'séduire', 'indigne fruit'. They clearly denote a sexuality which, though not literal, is powerfully actual in the drama.

Néarque is, of course, only an instrument of God's and Polyeucte's will. He is the new mediator, a stepping stone leading Polyeucte to the altar of his real marriage with God. Néarque is a surrogate bridegroom who guides Polyeucte to his own sacrifice. Polyeucte's passage to God, his offering of himself to God, is a mystic reversal. In this passage, Polyeucte sacrifices Pauline, symbol of his heterosexuality. This sacrifice is his hymenal passage, his return to the Father which, like all marriage, must be marked by the spilling of blood – Polyeucte's immolation.

For Pauline, on the other hand, the marriage, the sacrifice of the hymen, acts as a dam, stopping her within a metaphorical appropriation that defines her at the very moment that this definition alienates her. Like all of Corneille's heroines Pauline is split. She is torn between the roles of daughter, wife and mistress. What this means for Pauline and for the men who surround her is that she is encodable only as a negative cipher; she is allowed subjectivity only as that subjectivity can function as an object of masculine desire and representation. This helps us to understand the essential visual split that we have been examining in the play. Pauline sees, is the framing reference that directs our gaze at the male participants in her drama, because only men are given to vision. As a metaphor for the Paternal order, carriers of the penis/logos, only the men are *there*, only they have something that is representable. Pauline, as the only woman, the woman who is always other, has no-thing, offers nothing to sight.[16] As woman, Pauline is essentially a blank in representation, or rather she is an empty space that is constantly filled by male projection, male definitions. She

136

becomes a metaphor ('wife', 'daughter', 'mistress') of a relation to her men, of their system of appropriation that exceeds their own field of vision.

As a desiring entity, as a subjectivity, Pauline is always scattered in the metaphors of the Other, always a changing reflection of masculine appropriations/definitions. Lost in these diffractions, Pauline is passed from one male to the next, from Félix to Polyeucte and from Polyeucte to Sévère. In order for her to 'be' she must be in relation to a man. She must be married. At one time or another in the tragedy all the men who surround her suggest marriage (to Sévère) as her only option. Pauline must never be allowed out of the system that represents her.

What, of course, they do not realize is that Pauline cannot allow herself to fall out of her 'devoir', out of her metaphorical representation of her place in Patriarchy. She must protect herself against her own dispersion because her return to a chaotic non-differentiation would annihilate not only Pauline but the entire edifice of Roman Patriarchy that is crumbling around her. Pauline's monolithic devotion to Polyeucte is her attempt to shore up an order that alienates her but in which, paradoxically, she receives the only definition that valorizes her.

Pauline's marriage to Polyeucte has little to do with Pauline's desire for him. She has accepted him in her bed out of filial duty. Pauline sacrifices her desire to duty, gives herself, her hymen, to an image of Paternal Law. The consequences of her sacrifice, her failed attempt to harmonize herself as object of Polyeucte as subject, has consequences that are as far-reaching for her as for Polyeucte.

Even in its most intimate details the marriage ceremony is always a public spectacle. It is a voyeuristic exercise in which is invested the presuppositions of Patriarchy. The 'hyménée' is both a metaphor for this act of appropriation, the appropriation and disappearance of the feminine into a social, sexual and political code that subtends and validates Patriarchy, and a metonymical reduction of difference, the reduction of femininity to a transparent membrane. In the 'hymen–hyménée', there is a blurring of metonymy and metaphor, a blurring of the physical and the metaphysical. In this confusion something is lost, but also gained. From his 'capture' of the symbol of feminine otherness the man comes to possess a vessel in which he can reproduce, unsullied, his own image. The woman is given an image that at last fixes her own dispersion, stops her own indecidability in the space of the Other. Both are always an

illusion. It is an illusion that no one, however, caught within the ideological parameters of this code can ever admit to seeing. Seeing the illusion threatens the destruction of the entire network that has been erected around this absent center.

In the actual deflowering of the woman, the symbolically invested taking of the hymen, the controlling of sexuality, what is functioning is the Law of the Father, the ideal of all Patriarchy, as it is invested in the containment of another it fears. In this sense, the man to whom is entrusted the task of defloration is always a surrogate for the entire patriarchal order; the husband is always also the Father. (We have seen that this is the essential slippage, the confusion in Pauline's desire/dream where Polyeucte and Félix are joined and conflated in Pauline's unconscious.) The husband is put in the place of the Father, is always a substitute for his Law. When the bridegroom penetrates the 'hymen' he always does so, for the social order and for the woman, as the Father.[17]

Defloration is a highly invested erotic encounter between the woman and her husband-as-Father. Its erotic nature is always a shattering experience. It exposes and brings to the surface incestuous drives that can never be dealt with adequately, that can never be allowed to surface except as masochistic displacements. The shock to her ego is so great, the narcissistic wound so ugly, that the only recuperation possible is a leap into the protective stance of total acceptance of the husband become the mirror of her own inadmissible desire. He becomes the mask behind which hides the Father and his desire.[18]

So, while the ritual 'hyménée' seems to bring Polyeucte into the world of division, of femininity, for Pauline it seems to fix not her 'being', but her image of being, in the realm of the Integral. The integrity of the husband (Pauline's 'devoir') becomes for her her own sign of meaning and eventually of salvation. This is how we must understand her monolithic devotion. Pauline is devoted not to Polyeucte, but to her 'devoir', to Polyeucte as 'devoir', to Polyeucte as representing and effacing the Father: 'Je l'aimai par devoir, ce devoir dure encore' (III, ii, 90).

Since this integrity of being is only an image, only a simulacrum for Pauline, a simulacrum that her own desire constantly threatens to fragment, Pauline must guard herself from that desire, must prevent it from coming to the surface, from being seen, being reflected to her in the eyes of Sévère. In the world of the Patriarch, Pauline exists as the object of the regard of those men to whom she is attached and can see herself only as she is reflected in their eyes.

What she does see is unsettling because just as she serves to reflect their activity they reflect her (passive) desire. This is why Pauline wishes no longer to 'see' Sévère. In his presence Pauline looks into his eyes and sees the ambivalent reflection of her own desire and fears:

> Moi! moi! que je revoie un si puissant vainqueur,
> Et m'expose à des yeux qui me percent le coeur!
> Mon père, je suis femme, et je sais ma faiblesse
>
> . . .
>
> Je ne le verrai point.   (I, iv, 339–41, 345)

In order not to betray her 'devoir' and reveal her desire to the world, Pauline flees its gaze. She entreats Sévère to stop 'seeing' her: 'Conservez-m'en la gloire, et cessez de me voir' (II, ii, 540) and refuses to expose herself anew to his sight: 'Et moi, dont votre vue augmente le supplice/Je l'éviterai' (II, ii, 561–2).

Like Polyeucte, Pauline hopes that by flight she can be freed from a penetrating, revealing gaze. Both partners are locked into their roles, roles of representation within Patriarchy, which are intolerable to them. Pauline marks Polyeucte as her one and only, her mirror, spouse and Father. Polyeucte becomes the metaphor for Pauline's virtue. He is her investment as phallus, exactly the way she is for Sévère. It is precisely because Pauline is invested in Polyeucte that she can never love Sévère. At the same time, it is because Pauline has made Polyeucte her one and only that she has also prepared her way, opened up the possibility of transcending that physical investment for a mystical union with the Ideal Polyeucte becomes in his own immolation.[19] It is because of her 'virtue' that Pauline is already on the way to becoming Christian:

> Seigneur, de vos bontés il faut que je l'obtienne;
> Elle a trop de vertus pour n'être pas chrétienne.
>
> (IV, iii, 1267–8)

No sooner has Pauline firmly ensconced herself within the universe of patriarchal Law than she is abandoned by the two corepresentatives of this Law. Both her husband and her father, in the politico-religious conflict that separates them, disassociate themselves from each other, sundering the unity they had represented, confounding Pauline not only with the illusions, with the sham of the system into which she has bought, but with its entire dislocation.

Pauline articulates Félix's and Polyeucte's relation to her as the

extreme metaphoric limits – nature and love (culture) – that define her world, the limits that enable her to represent herself within that world:

> Qui de vous deux aujourd'hui m'assassine?
> Sont-ce tous deux ensemble, ou chacun à son tour?
> Ne pourrai-je fléchir la nature ou l'amour?
> Et n'obtiendrai-je rien d'un époux ni d'un père?
>
> (v, iii, 1580–3)

Husband/father, love/nature form a closed network inside which Pauline articulates herself and inside which her desire is both posited and denied. This closure of the world, the seamless locus inside which Pauline is given the only security and power she can have, this tautological turning in and naturalization of the universe in which husbands are fathers and love an extension of nature, doubles back on itself in the perfect totalitarian structure Pauline needs and desires. When neither her husband nor her father, trapped as they are in the dynamics of masculine rivalry that defines their relation to that closure, can recuperate her loss, Pauline is left to drift without any anchorage on the troubled waters she fears.

In a dizzying chassé-croisé Pauline is left at the crossroads of seeming–being, in the interstice of reality and illusion, of loss and salvation. When Polyeucte returns from his baptism, he returns as an integral being. Having renounced the pagan gods, symbols of his fragmentation and loss ('vos dieux frivoles/Immuables et sourds, impuissants, mutilés'), he renounces his own division. The division that sundered him internally is now projected out onto the world. Polyeucte's conversion has made him entire. Once Polyeucte has begun his walk to God he can see the world that he has left divided in Manichean terms between truth and evil. As he struggles to tighten his hold on his new-found faith Polyeucte can see Pauline only as a member of one of two groups, either a friend of God, or an enemy:

> Madame, quel dessein vous fait me demander?
> Est-ce pour me combattre, ou pour me seconder?
> Cet effort généreux de votre amour parfait
> Vient-il à mon secours, vient-il à ma défaite?
> Apportez-vous ici la haine ou l'amitié
> Comme mon ennemie, ou ma chère moitié? (iv, iii, 1161–6)

Polyeucte's conversion re-articulates the essential problem for Pauline as woman: she, like Camille, must be one or the other, she

must choose one camp or the other. There is no staying in between, no indifference possible. Only now the camps have been realigned. All the notions of divisions and articulations that have heretofore pertained are changed.

For both Polyeucte and Pauline 'baptism' is an eye-opening experience. Polyeucte, upon his return, has a burning inner vision that he must realize in the world. Freed from the fragmenting vision of Pauline, Polyeucte must make a spectacle of an inner truth that, offered to the world, gives the lie to its illusions:

> Allons, mon cher Néarque, allons aux yeux des hommes
> Braver l'idolâtrie, et montrer qui nous sommes.   (II, vi, 645–6)

Polyeucte offers his entire being to the world. He becomes the center of that world by fixing all eyes on himself. He affirms his role as the 'focal' point of an ideological conflict:

> J'ai profané leur temple, et brisé leurs autels
> Je le ferais encor si j'avais à le faire
> Même aux yeux de Félix, même aux yeux de Sévère,
> Même aux yeux du sénat, aux yeux de l'Empereur.
> (v, iii, 1670–3)

Polyeucte appeals to the gaze of the entire political structure that he taunts. He places himself at the center of that gaze as a vision of its own failure. In this fashion we might say that Polyeucte, by situating himself as the focal point in which two conflicting political ideologies are confounded, is also the vanishing point where the human disappears into the divine. Polyeucte, an overinvested spectacle, reproduces himself (in his vanishing act) as the 'join', the point of passage, the sacrificial symbol that makes the transition from one order to the other possible.

Polyeucte's sacrifice of himself, his own disappearance in the vision he offers his fellows, is the ultimate triumph of ideality over materiality, of metaphor over metonymy, in the Cornelian canon. Polyeucte's death is immediately affirmed as a transcendental experience. By negating Death Polyeucte reveals himself to be the ultimate hero. In his martyrdom he effectively destroys Death, that extreme limit from which the representatives of the old order recoil in horror:

> Quand il verra punir qui l'a séduit.
> Au spectacle sanglant d'un ami qu'il faut suivre,
> La crainte de mourir et le désir de vivre
> Ressaisissent une âme avec tant de pouvoir,
> Que qui voit le trépas cesse de le vouloir.   (III, iii, 880–4)

Seeing death, Polyeucte is not affected by its horrors because he sees through it, sees it as (true) life:

> Les bontés de mon Dieu sont bien plus à chérir:
> Il m'ôte des périls que j'aurais pu courir,
> Et sans me laisser lieu de tourner en arrière,
> Sa faveur me couronne en entrant dans la carrière;
> Du premier coup de vent il me conduit au port,
> Et, sortant du baptême, il m'envoie à la mort:
> Si vous pouviez comprendre, et le peu qu'est la vie,
> Et de quelles douceurs cette mort est suivie! (IV, iii, 1225–32)

Polyeucte goes to his martyrdom with all eyes on him. In a curious reversal, however, this death which is the tragic epicenter of the drama, the political, religious and sexual crux of the play, is denied the spectator. Polyeucte's martyrdom is not given to our vision. It is kept out of sight by the 'bienséances', by religious and esthetic 'délicatesse'.

What we do see, however, is Pauline. She is the center of our gaze and, in this sense, she stands in for, represents, Polyeucte. Pauline has witnessed her husband's immolation and this spectacle transforms her. Polyeucte's martyrdom realizes Pauline's desire/ dream. Her illusion has become reality.

The effect of this 'working out' is both exhilarating and shattering. Polyeucte's execution is the acting out of Pauline's ambivalent subservience to Patriarchy, to her own renunciation. This 'acting out' is a violent disruption of the limits that have defined the possibilities of Pauline's self-representation. Pauline returns from the other scene, the scene of death, with its mark on her. She re-appears bearing the sign of Death, the symbol of the old system's undoing, inscribed on herself; she is bathed in Polyeucte's blood:

> Mon époux en mourant m'a laissé ses lumières;
> Son sang, dont tes bourreaux viennent de me couvrir
> M'a désillé les yeux, et me les vient d'ouvrir.
> Je vois, je sais, je crois, je suis désabusée. (V, v, 1724–7)

Polyeucte's death has awakened Pauline from the nightmare of reality. By her immersion in the blood she called forth, Pauline is disabused. This immersion has destroyed the old Father – the power of Roman paganism – who had proved himself to be a mystification and freed her from her subservience to him. Now Pauline, transfixed in the vision of the new Ideal, can at last show herself. Pauline, freed by Polyeucte, is no longer only a 'voyante', but can be her own spectacle, a spectacle that is a rebellion:

Polyeucte: seeing is believing

Polyeucte m'appelle à cet heureux trépas:
Mène, mène-moi voir tes dieux que je déteste;
Ils n'en ont brisé qu'un, je briserai le reste.
On m'y verra braver tout ce que vous craignez,
Les foudres impuissants qu'en leurs mains vous peignez,
Et, saintement rebelle aux lois de la naissance
Une fois envers toi manquer d'obéissance.   (v, vi, 1733–9)

For all the restraint imposed upon it by Classical bienséances, Pauline's renunciation of Rome is one of the most heated examples of female passion in Corneille. Pauline's baptism in Polyeucte's blood is an 'ecstasy' in the full sense of that word: in the image of her husband's immolation, Pauline is shaken out of her own place in patriarchal representation. She 'stands out' of the system that defines her in the excess of her own pleasure. This pleasure reveals (as it does for Emilie, for Camille) the destructive Medea that is hidden in all of Corneille's heroines, the parricidal, anti-political force that, in moments of utter dispossession, moments in which the hidden flaws in the totality of patriarchal order are revealed, comes rushing forth in a stream of orgasmic invective.

This glimpse we have had of female pleasure is perhaps our only glimpse, in this play, of its absent unrepresentable underpinning, of the undefinable otherness that defines the new system – of God.[20] Pauline's revolt would be too dangerous for Classicism to tolerate, too great a crack in the edifice of control it elaborates, if it were not recuperated at the very moment it is revealed. From ecstasy Pauline returns converted. A movement out is blocked by a turning back (con-verso).

By the very fact that Pauline is the center of 'our' vision, is the object defined by the gaze of the spectators, which in this visionary play is also the all-seeing, all-informing gaze of Totality, of God–Monarch, Pauline's revolt is still contained. We, the audience, are the gaze that enfolds Pauline, entraps her as spectacle. She remains inscribed within a system of representation against which she may rebel, but that controls her revolt in a way it did not for Polyeucte. Pauline, in her fury, has abandoned the Father for an image of her husband that is never given to vision, that is always a mystery, always Pauline's inner vision, for us. By this vision Pauline constituted Polyeucte as the model, the Ideal, of her own mystery, of her own mysticism.

Pauline's spectacle supplies this model's absence as it becomes one with God. For this reason Félix's conversion, following on his daughter's excessive outburst, is miraculous in more ways than

143

one, reaffirming not only the spiritual order but the temporal order as well. When Félix is filled with grace, when the scales fall from his eyes, he realizes the sham that was his life as a Roman courtier. He recaptures Pauline:

> Qu'heureusement enfin je retrouve mon père!
> Cet heureux changement rend mon bonheur parfait.
>
> (v, vi, 1784–5)

Félix's transition from the old order to the new is a beatific one for Pauline. His crossing over from paganism to Christianity reaffirms the survival and continuity in Christianity of Roman Patriarchy. While both Polyeucte's fate and Pauline's ecstasy threatened the foundations of society, threatened both the throne and the altar, Félix's conversion shores them up, makes them stronger than ever by uniting them, making them One, the reflection of his new God.

The triumph of Christianity that the play announces assures the co-existence of religious and temporal power in God's representative on Earth, Félix (King–Emperor). Rather than being dismissed and executed as a seditious rebel, Félix is confirmed in his authority by Sévère:

> Gardez votre pouvoir, reprenez-en la marque,
> Servez bien votre Dieu, servez votre monarque.
>
> (v, vi, 1803–4)

Invested as the representative of the new Law, Félix proclaims its universality:

> Allons à nos martyrs donner la sépulture,
> Baiser leurs corps sacrés, les mettre en digne lieu,
> Et faire retentir partout le nom de Dieu.   (v, v, 1812–14)

It is as the servants of this new God that Félix and Pauline remain behind. Just as Polyeucte disappears into God, Félix reappears as his surrogate – the new husband(–father) in the couple he forms with Pauline. Conversion has joined father and daughter together in Christ. This joining, the grace that they have received, frees them of their desire, frees them from the taint, the taboo, of incest. Their vision of glory has purified them, returned them to each other in a Christian, virginal embrace. They can go forth freed of their materiality, their sexuality, and bear witness – see the truth and show it to others.

This new 'couple', the last emblem of Classicism's investment in sexual symmetry, can only show what can never be seen. Cornelian

Classicism's highest triumph brings together in this perfection the two halves upon which all its harmony is based while showing that these halves are forever inaccessible to each other.[21] They are only a vision, a mystery, a mystification. In its greatest creation, Classicism only repeats and offers to our vision the impossible conditions for its own subverted dream.

6

NICOMÈDE, RODOGUNE, SURÉNA: MONSTERS, MELANCHOLY AND THE END OF THE ANCIEN RÉGIME

'Un pas hors du devoir peut nous mener bien loin.'

With *Polyeucte*'s epiphany Classicism is transformed into a vision of divine transcendence. This vision is both a mystery and, of course, a mystification. In *Polyeucte* sexuality and politics, individual desire and 'raison d'Etat' continue their spiraling ascension. In the culminating apotheosis they leave the realm of history, the frame which has enclosed all the great tragedies, and, breaking free of the mimetic bind, find their ultimate resolution in the silence and repose of the empyrean. In his most perfect tragedy Corneille presents the problematic that has defined the Classical subject with an acuity that effectively signals its end: *Polyeucte* closes the Classical universe upon its own transcendence. The polis of Cornelian dramaturgy is transformed into the Heavenly City of Absolutism. In this transcendence the essential predicates upon which Classical perfection rests are shown to be inconsistent with themselves. Their inconsistency is, nevertheless, obfuscated by the dazzling light of spiritual metamorphosis.

After *Polyeucte* something changes in Cornelian dramaturgy. Although Corneille's theatrical career lasted well into the century, never again does he create a tragedy of the overwhelming power and grace of the four canonical plays. The scope of this book does not allow an extended exploration of the greater part of the Cornelian opus. Nevertheless, I would like to offer, as a speculative conclusion, first some words on two plays – *Nicomède* and *Rodogune* – which strike me as particularly emblematic of the shift in the Cornelian world after *Polyeucte* and then on *Suréna*, Corneille's last tragedy. These first two 'transitional' tragedies intrigue me not least because of the uncanny way they reflect each other. Furthermore, they seem to offer, in a negative reversal, a captivating image of the world so minutely elaborated in the 'great' plays. Both of

these plays, while retaining much that accounts for the interest of the major works, also indicate the new paths Cornelian dramaturgy trod in the thirty years that followed *Polyeucte*. They are representative of the abyss that sunders the Cornelian world and yet joins it together, too. On the the one side of this abyss stands the harmonious simulacrum of Classical perfection, and, on the other, its pallid reflection, peopled not with heroes but with the hero's Other, the monsters of Classicism's nether side.

As he states in the 'Examen' of *Nicomède*, Corneille, with this tragedy, felt the need to break new dramatic ground: 'Voici une pièce d'une constitution assez extraordinaire, aussi est-ce la vingt-unième que j'ai fait voir sur le théâtre; et après y avoir fait réciter quarante mille vers il est bien malaisé de trouver quelque chose de nouveau sans s'écarter un peu du grand chemin, et se mettre en hasard de s'égarer' (*Nicomède*, 'Examen', p. 417). The metaphors of traveling down unchartered paths and of getting lost are indication enough that Corneille, in his new period, was entering upon a dark continent, unexplored and fraught with pitfalls.

Nicomède is 'extraordinary' because Corneille attempts here to alter radically the very heart of the tragic situation. He eliminates any appeals to the 'passions' and essays a drama whose success stands or falls solely on the moral grandeur of its hero: 'La tendresse et les passions qui doivent être l'âme des tragédies n'ont aucune part en celle-ci. La grandeur de courage y règne seul et regarde son malheur d'un oeil si dédaigneux qu'il ne saurait arracher une plainte' ('Examen', p. 417).

This denegation of passion strikes us as particularly novel when we compare *Nicomède* with *Rodogune*. In the latter play, perhaps the most Senecan of all Corneille's theater, passion, rather than being contained, is exacerbated to a degree never before attained in Cornelian theater. At first glance nothing would appear more different than these two plays: the bloody horror of *Rodogune* contrasts with the poised equanimity of *Nicomède*. Yet, in spite of their very real differences, both these tragedies are subtended by a new set of dramatic imperatives that join them together and place them in direct contrast with the dramatic universe of the major plays.

The new path Corneille follows in both of these plays turns out to be a sexual deviation. From here on there is a crossing over, a strange reversal of roles, in the Cornelian world. The women become the standard bearers of the 'will to power', of the renunciation and the singleness of purpose that up until *Rodogune* had been the lot of Corneille's heroes.[1] The men become mired in meta-

physical dilemmas which reduce them to positions of indecision, passivity and, ultimately, to impotence. The essential traits defining sexual and, therefore, political difference, the separation of the Cornelian world into the well-ordered camps of masculinity and femininity, are blurred. It is from the blurring of these positions, from their 'perversion', that the monstrous, of which *Rodogune* is the first and perhaps the best example, is born and triumphs.

This monstrosity that suddenly appears with *Rodogune* strikes us as all the more horrific because as spectators we are implicated in what can only be termed Classicism's nightmare. All that the Classical stage banished, all that was contained and hidden in the mystification of a world poised in symmetrical reciprocity, is thrust into our view as a terrible parody of itself. This deformation of sexuality acts out the repressed fears and desires of the Absolutist State in the mise-en-scène of its own immolation. It does so by situating the origin of the tragic dilemma in the fear that haunted the world of Patriarchy as its nemesis and its desire – in parricide.

In the universe of order and Law that Corneille elaborated in the years 1636–41 parricide was the crime that remained forever an unthinkable impossibility and yet always a dim threat. In a patriarchal world parricide couples in its horror not only the sexual taboo of an incestuous desire for the father, but also the political threat of revolutionary upheaval: for Corneille's world, as perhaps for all western society, parricide is always also regicide.[2]

In *Rodogune* Cléopâtre's murder of her husband deprives her children of a father and the kingdom of its leader. Thus the dilemma of the play – Who is to replace the father and re-establish order in the land? What is explicit in *Rodogune* remains implicit in *Nicomède*. It is this difference that accounts for the blood of the one and the pallor of the other.[3] The potential for paternal bloodletting was not initially absent in *Nicomède*. In the sources of the play that Corneille cites, particularly Justinius, anecdotal material of sufficient tragic potential abounds: 'Prusias chassé du trône et délaissé même de ses domestiques, quelque soin qu'il prit à se cacher, fut enfin tué par ce fils et perdit la vie par un crime aussi grand que celui qu'il avait commis en donnant l'ordre de l'assassiner' ('Examen', p. 417). It is precisely this plot, the actual parricide, that Corneille chose not to stage: 'J'ai ôté de ma scène l'horreur d'une catastrophe si barbare, et n'ai donné ni au père ni au fils aucun dessein de parricide' ('Examen', p. 418).

In *Nicomède* Corneille balks at the sacrifice of the Father/King. The issue of parricide that is introduced in the play's preface is hid-

den in its elaboration. Yet, as in *Rodogune*, parricide serves as the invisible subtext of the tragedy. The murder of the father and the usurpation of his place throws the Classical universe into disarray. How this 'ritual' slaying takes place, who desires it and how society reacts to this transgression forms the nexus of both plays. Each offers a different and contradictory response to these questions. It is this final contradiction that best demonstrates the undermining of Corneille's Classical dream.

In the universe of *Rodogune* and of *Nicomède* the 'natural' order of the world has been turned on its head. Male hierarchy has been usurped and in the place of the Father/King now stands the frightening image of a deranged queen. *Nicomède* and *Rodogune* play out the hidden fears of Patriarchy by figuring the return of what the Father and his Law had tried so hard to repress: the devouring, chaotic figure of omnipotent femininity.

My readings of the four great plays made it obvious that this repressed image was constantly present 'en sourdine' in the familiar disguises of the Cornelian heroine; Chimène, 'dénaturée', Emilie, a 'furie', and Camille, 'criminelle', are all apotropaic talismans – both present and yet absent – who ward off the more dangerous, a-social, an-historical side of femininity. The narcissistic masochism of Corneille's most famous heroines was nevertheless contained by the very system of representation that gave birth to them. It was contained in the metaphorical relation – wife, daughter, sister – they assumed for their male counterparts.

After *Polyeucte*, however, the Mother, that most invested aspect of femininity denied in the great plays, returns to the Cornelian stage. She returns precisely in/as that ambivalent locus over which all the principles of male genealogy had glossed. *Rodogune* and *Nicomède* trace, in very different ways, the return of the woman as 'uteros'. The womb, that mystifying vessel in which new males are produced, was strategically ignored precisely because its 'indifference' was too threatening a reminder, in this world of division, of an ambivalence that contaminates patriarchal ideology. Strangely, however, when the woman returns as biological imperative, she is not marked as a nurturing, loving, protective force, but as an 'hysteric'. The Mother returns as a ghoulish devourer, a perverted 'unnatural' Mother who castrates her males and cannibalizes her offspring. The Mother re-emerges on the Cornelian stage as a figure/fantasy of dispersion and Death. The new 'hysteric' marks the reappearance in the tragic universe of Medea, the eternal female outcast who was left at the threshold of Cornelian Classicism.

149

Cléopâtre's entrance on stage (II, i) clearly and immediately shows her to be Medea's sister. Her first lines are incantatory, hypnotic. Their invocatory rhythms recall the sorceress' incantations and separate her from the world of order and logic to replace 'her' in the realm of inchoate matter:

> Serments fallacieux, salutaire contrainte,
> Que m'imposa la force et qu'accepta ma crainte.
> Heureux déguisements d'un immortel courroux,
> Vains fantômes d'Etats, évanouissez-vous!　　(II, i, 395–8)

Much less dramatic a presence than Cléopâtre, Arsinoé in *Nicomède* is, nevertheless, a member of Corneille's monstrous sorority. The world of *Nicomède* trembles on the brink of the tragic. The entire atmosphere of the court, the internal relations between the members of the royal family and the external relations between Bithynia and Rome are explosive primarily because the natural order of the universe has been perverted. Arsinoé, allied to Rome, attempts to undermine legality by replacing masculine genealogy (metaphoric substitution) with matrilineal descent (metonymic displacement). We are (once again) in the universe of a 'fisher king', in a wasteland where the father has been made a eunuch. (He, seeing only with female eyes, has been blinded/castrated.)[4] Prusias' thraldom, a form of impotence, has unsettling effects upon the entire kingdom. The play begins with an empty space where there should be a King. It is into this space that Nicomède, aided by Nature ('la voix du sang') in the person of his brother Attale, moves to save the universe of Law and Order, of Patriarchy, from its undoing.

Rallying to the aid of Patriarchy, 'Nature' saves *Nicomède* from disintegration and allows the play to end on a note of restored harmony. Nothing could be farther from the pessimism of *Rodogune*'s conclusion. Perhaps no other of Corneille's dramas ends so negatively. The dénouement is all the more bleak when we contrast it with the air of relief, the promise of new hope with which the play begins:

> Enfin, ce jour pompeux et heureux nous luit,
> Qui d'un trouble si long doit dissiper la nuit,
> Ce grand jour où l'hymen, étouffant la vengeance,
> Entre le Parthe et nous remet l'intelligence,
> Affranchit sa princesse et nous fait pour jamais
> Du motif de la guerre un lien de la paix.　　(I, i, 1–6)

The tragedy starts as an epithalamium. Despite, however, the promising tone of Laonice's initial speech, it immediately becomes

apparent to us, familiar as we now are with the dissonant echoes the word 'hymen' carries in Corneille, that this marriage is an impossible dream.

The world of *Rodogune* is perhaps the most uncanny in all Corneille. On whatever level we choose to dissect the play, we always return to a dyadic opposition that is formed along political and sexual lines. On the most obvious level of sexual difference Séleucus and Antiochus confront Rodogune and Cléopâtre as they all play out this 'partie carée de l'assassinat'. Not only is the sexual symmetry perfect in its simplicity but the imbrication of the sexual and the political reflects this perfection in the chiasmatic dilemma faced by all the participants in the tragedy: to Cléopâtre's ultimatum that the crown be given to that twin who eliminates Rodogune, responds Rodogune's imperious bargain of giving herself to that brother who kills the queen (Mother).

This perfect structural symmetry is informed by an absence and a perversion. As in *Nicomède*, but more radically, the Father/King has been eliminated and his place taken by the Mother. This perversion of the 'natural' political and sexual order can only produce 'monsters'. These monsters are all the more terrifying because they are so familiar. All the accustomed divisions of the Cornelian universe are maintained, but by their simple reversal they plunge us into a world of false illusions and deformations. The men are wimpering castrati and the women virilized harpies. It is this exchange of sexual essences that leads us into the crux of the tragic where the horrifying alternative — matricide or infanticide — appears as the only natural choice available to characters forced to live a symmetry that has become untenable.

In the final analysis the ultimate dilemma of *Rodogune* revolves around the question of sovereignty: who will be master, who slave, who will live and who die? In the strange chassé-croisé of inversion that this play represents the question of sovereignty is a question of who, in this universe of Amazons, is most masculine, that is, which of these two women, Rodogune or Cléopâtre, is less 'lacking', more given to sublimation, to wholeness, and less condemned to the realm of the 'in between'.

The essential and fatal distinction that separates Cléopâtre from Rodogune is that of an internal split that makes Cléopâtre susceptible to desire and renders Rodogune invulnerable. I do not want to suggest that Rodogune is without sexual desire, that she does not love. Her passion, however, is remarkable in that it is 'transcendental'. Rodogune's desire is always masculine — it idealizes love as

politics. The object of her passion is the throne, but the throne metaphorized as the King. What Rodogune accepts and what Cléopâtre cannot accept is that we can only approach the object of desire asymptotically; it is always a fantasmatic image, receding, never within our grasp. We can only settle for its metaphor in the world.

The secret and inexplicable passion that radically separates the protagonists does so in a particularly decisive way for the evolution of Rodogune's erotic history and for the political resolution of the dilemma facing the princes. Let us remember that Corneille by killing off Séleucus resolved *his* dilemma; he never has to inform his audience which of the two brothers was born first, which, in other words, in the genealogical imperative of Patriarchy bears the first and decisive mark of the Father: 'La mort de Séleucus m'a exempté de développer le secret du droit d'aînesse entre les deux frères, qui d'ailleurs n'eût jamais été croyable, ne pouvant être éclairci que par une bouche en qui l'on n'a pas vu assez de sincérité pour prendre aucune assurance sur son témoignage' (*Rodogune*, 'Examen', p. 356).

This mark, however, is recognized and validated not by the sons' mother but by a surrogate mother − Rodogune (new wife of the Father). It is she who recognizes Antiochus as the metaphoric substitute (the image) of the dead King. She refers to Antiochus as 'son vivant portrait'.

Antiochus is the 'living replica' of the King. In Absolute Monarchy, the King, we know, never dies; the essence of kingship is immediately passed on from one king to the next without any interruption.[5] Rodogune recognizes the difference between the brothers and articulates it, re-establishing dynastic descent. The new image also ratifies Rodogune's desire that unswervingly recognizes and names her mate, through whom and by whom she accedes to the sovereignty for which she is destined. Rodogune loves neither of the two men; she loves the King who makes her queen.

The tragedy's end echoes the note of ambivalence that has been associated with the wedding from the beginning. It is as if this marriage were a sacrifice in which the new Cornelian couple, a weak, ambivalent King and a strong determined queen, offer their negativity on the altar of a patriarchal system that has been perverted. Cléopâtre's curse:

> Puissiez-vous ne trouver dedans votre union
> Qu'horreur, que jalousie, et que confusion!
> Et, pour vous souhaiter tous les malheurs ensemble,
> Puisse naître de vous un fils qui me ressemble! (v, iv, 1821–4)

resounds in the empty theater even after the curtain falls. It warns us that, in the future, this perverted couple, Classicism's latest incarnation, can only generate new and more ominous monsters.

The contradictory resolutions of *Rodogune* and *Nicomède* are emblematic of the metaphysical quagmire into which late Cornelian tragedy has fallen. After *Polyeucte* the Cornelian world seems caught in the oscillatory indeterminacy of its own sado-masochistic fantasies. In the last analysis it appears that this oscillation is symptomatic of an ideological conflict, where the desire that has been repressed in the elaboration of what we could call an esthetic of totality (a totalitarian esthetic) seeks, but cannot find, structures that can accommodate it, that can 'naturalize' it in the world. The conflict between an emerging subjectivity no longer adequate to the esthetic of symmetry that spawns it and an excess that cannot be represented except as 'unnatural' condemns the Cornelian world to an irresolvable conflict.

It would perhaps be an error to ask Corneille to provide us with a resolution to the aporia his theater produced. Nevertheless, that a resolution – and here I do not mean a reassuring optimistic working out of the conflict – can be glimpsed in Corneille's last tragedy, *Suréna*, is not the least indication that Corneille, by taking leave of the theater, also points, beyond the death of his world, to the birth of another.

Suréna internalizes, as melancholy, the oscillatory ambivalence that marks the exhaustion of Cornelian dramaturgy and places it at the heart of its tragic dilemma. It is to this melancholy that we must turn if we wish to understand the new alignment of forces that emerges from the chrysalis of the old order and signals its end.

First staged in 1674, *Suréna* appears at the moment of Absolutism's triumph. If we are to believe the adulatory descriptions of Félibien's 'Divertissements de Versailles donnés par le Roy au retour de la conqueste de la Franche Comté', this triumph reached its zenith during the months of July and August.[6] In the sublime narcissism of a series of staged 'fêtes' the Monarchy figured its own apotheosis. Marked as a year of both military and artistic triumph, 1674 saw perhaps for the first time in history the coalescence of Absolutism's ethos and its esthetic into a closed circuit of reflexivity, into a seamless totality, One and Transcendent.

In the rising paean of universal adulation of the King, Corneille's *Suréna* strikes a strident note. The play's 'melancholy recitative'

echoes with the eerie knell of some distant funeral bell. More than twenty years ago, S. Doubrovsky told us that *Suréna* signaled the end of a world. This Cassandra-like tragedy does not, however, so much figure the demise of the Cornelian universe, a world that was already exhausted in *Polyeucte*, as it suggests the end of Absolutist hegemony. The unwelcome guest at the feast, *Suréna* intrudes as the 'memento mori' of Absolutism at the very moment its victory seems so firmly and universally acclaimed.

Traditionally *Suréna* has been seen as a capitulation to Racinian dramaturgy: love, which Corneille had always relegated to an ancillary position in the tragic plot, second always to matters of State, here comes to the fore and dominates the evolution of dramatic peripeteia. Like so many of the dichotomies that supposedly legislate the Cornelian canon, this one, as we have seen, proves to be neither operative in the great plays nor tenable in *Suréna*. Perhaps it is the genius of Cornelian dramaturgy to insist upon the imbrication of the sexual and political as the suture, the focal-vanishing point, the impossible join of Absolutist ideology.

Ideology is both elusive and illuding. Although reproduced materially – in the everyday gestures and rituals of a populace – ideology remains always beyond representation, informing its parameters, those invisible limits that makes representation possible.[7] Yet the forms of representation remain at an asymptotic distance from 'ideology', always supplementary and insufficient. L. Althusser's classic definition – 'L'idéologie représente le rapport imaginaire des individus à leurs conditions réelles d'existence'[8] – is particularly revelatory for our purposes. I would like to insist that it is this 'imaginary' (in the sense of unconscious) relation that we glimpse in the theater, and I would like to add that we glimpse it only as 'symptoms'. Ideology becomes apparent to us only in those strategic moments when the characters, who are offered to our gaze as 'subjects' (that is, both subjugated and subjected), become dramatic ('dramatis personae'), and this at that moment when their particular form of subjectivity is put into question. This questioning renders them discordant. In Corneille this discord is always situated at the interstice of sexuality and politics, at their join.

In *Suréna*, paradoxically, this discord, which we have come to expect as a kinesis, is a stasis. The play's 'atmosphere' (by which I mean both the configuration of the represented universe and the impression the confrontation of the internal world with its exterior

reality creates) has generally been described as 'melancholic'.[9] More than in any other of Corneille's plays we have the experience of watching the gradual but inexorable progression of ataraxia. The characters are overwhelmed by a situation in which they are frozen, passive, and which eventually submerges them. The 'moi' of the Cornelian protagonist can no longer resist the encroachments of the external world. It is undone by it, dissolved into it. Another way of presenting this startling situation would be to say that the division between 'ego' and external reality is no longer tenable, but that 'ego' and the world become confused. In this confusion – taking the world as a narcissistic extension of the self – both the world and ego are lost in indifference, in Death.

This atmosphere of passivity, of stasis, reflects the overwhelming aspect of pathological melancholia as described by Freud:

> The distinguishing mutual features of melancholia are a profoundly painful dejection, cessation of interest in the outside world, inhibition of all activity, and a lowering of the self-regarding feelings to a degree that finds utterances in self reproaches and self revilings and culminates in a delusional expectation of punishment.
>
> (*Mourning and Melancholia, Standard Edition*, XIV, p. 244)

What is obviously intriguing to us in *Suréna* is that these traits, rather than being concentrated in one character, are disseminated among all the participants in the tragedy. In this fashion, rather than lending themselves to what would be a reductive analysis of an 'individual', these traits reconstruct a picture of general unhappiness, a sense of political malaise. It is this 'malaise' that insists in *Suréna* as a symptom of an ideological breakdown. The melancholia of *Suréna* allows us an insight into the invisible workings of ideology where a conflict of subjectivity points to transition, to the erosion of what was a dominant system of illusion and to its replacement by another, as yet undefined, constellation of forces.

At the center of all melancholia is a loss, an essential void as elusive as it is pervasive. It is the inscrutability of this void that renders melancholia all the more opaque. It might be reasonably easy to ascertain what 'object' the melancholic thinks he has lost. Much more difficult would be the task of finding what in this object (an object which is always a metaphor for a more 'archaic' object, for an object that is always a fantasy for an object) has been given up. How, in other words, has the melancholic been abandoned by the object? In melancholia the question of *who* one has lost is always camouflaging the more pernicious enigma of *what* has been

lost in that loss.[10]

I would like to propose at the outset that at the heart of *Suréna* (as in *Nicomède*, in *Rodogune*) the central absence that gives impetus to all dramatic (tragic) action, while, at the same time, informing the parameters inside which this action takes place (an absence that is, therefore, both at the center and the circumference), is the ambivalent derogation of sovereignty, the sundering and therefore the destruction of the Ideal, of the One, the Integral Body of the Father/State that Corneille's great tragedies had so laboriously and steadily constructed.

The entire Cornelian endeavour has traced the 'incorporation' of the Monarchy as an Absolutist imperative. What this means essentially is that the icon of the Monarchy that emerges in the Cornelian world (in *Cinna*, in *Polyeucte*) is an image of the King which coalesces diachrony and synchrony (the containment in one body of both the historic essence of the nation's corporate structure, in the present, of the King's own being, a being which is both a transcendental essence and a particular example). This ironic Ideal posits a system of values in which materiality is subsumed in ideality, femininity in masculinity, and metonymy in metaphor. The 'King' subsumes in his person all the historical contradictions of society and transcends them.[11] This transcendence, whose symbol, paradoxically, is the Kingly Body – the Monarchy as narcissistic self enclosure – is what poses itself/is posed as the ultimate object of desire for the King's subjects. By the same token this desire is reflexive; by being the desired 'object' of all his subjects the King becomes, always is, the Subject of desire, the ultimate grounding of subjectivity as subjugation. He becomes the Subject to whom all the different individuals of the kingdom are subjected.[12]

The constitution of the Subject of desire is co-terminous with the subjugation of the (individual) subject. Sovereignty combines in itself the politics of repression and desire, confusing the already nebulous boundaries separating politics and love, and presents them as one. In a well-ordered and well-run State, that is, in a State where the King's two bodies are one, the Monarch emerges as the center, as the Sun (as God), from which flows all glory, all reward, all desire.

In *Suréna* this center does not hold. It has been rent and melancholy descends upon the represented universe.

> Qu'un monarque est heureux quand parmi ses sujets
> Ses yeux n'ont point à voir de plus nobles objets,

Qu'au dessus de sa gloire il n'y connaît personne
Et qu'il est le plus digne enfin de sa couronne!   (III, i, 723–6)

Orode's complaint articulates what he and everyone else in the play
realizes: there is a troubling, intolerable split in the Body Politic.
The King is dis-incorporated, fragmented (cf. *Rodogune, Nicomède*).
The rhyme of the verses quoted above demonstrates on the most profound level the mechanics of this division: first there is a split
between subjects and object, their reversibility is denied, then a division exists between the particular Monarch ('personne') and his transhistorical essence ('couronne').

On any level we choose to define the role of the King in *Suréna*,
we are confronted with the troubling image of division. Perhaps the
most revelatory split is in the doubling of the Kingly Body itself,
the split in the representatives of kingship in the play, between the
political ruler (Orode) and his sexual surrogate (his son, Pacorus).
In the political universe of Cornelian absolutism, this division is
always the sign of a derogation, a sexual derogation. (In Corneille's
world, as we have seen, division is always the mark of femininity.)
In *Suréna* Orode shares the 'partage des femmes'. The Body of the
King has been castrated, contaminated by a femininity it must abhor.

Orode is king through no merit of his own. It is only due to the
force of another, Suréna, that he retains his throne:

> Suréna de l'exil lui seul m'a rappelé;
> Il m'a rendu lui seul ce qu'on m'avait volé,
> Mon sceptre.   (III, i, 711–13)

Orode is not Absolute in any sense of the term. He is, in fact,
not a king at all, not in the Cornelian sense of a self-sufficient force.
Orode's knowledge of his own 'impotence' ('vos propres exploits
m'ont mis en impuissance') in military force leads to a denegation
of his sexual potency. Living in the borrowed halo of Suréna's
masculinity, he is no longer the object of desire of his subjects (of
Eurydice). In front of this triumphant power, Orode is reduced to
the bitter tears of a woman: 'Quand j'en pleurai la perte, il [Suréna]
forçait les murailles' (III, i, 717).

Orode's ambivalence – he needs Suréna to be King and yet this need
is a constant reminder that he is an impostor – traps Orode, as well as
all the other characters. None can act. They can only oscillate between
whatever two poles they articulate as defining their existential
dilemma.[13] For Orode these two poles are either the murder of Suréna,
or his recuperation, by marriage to Mandane, Orode's daughter. His
confidant Sillare clearly articulates his predicament:

157

Quoi qu'ait fait Suréna, quoi qu'il en faille attendre,
Ou faîtes-le périr, ou faîtes-en un gendre.

                    .   .   .

Il faut, il faut ou le perdre, ou vous en assurer;
Il n'est point de milieu.   (III, i, 729–30, 736–7)

Precisely because he is not sovereign, Orode remains lost in oscillation, lost, that is, in a 'both/and' desire which condemns him to stagnation.

The frozen oscillation we witness in Orode (but he is just an example of a generalized paralysis: Eurydice cannot choose between losing Suréna and seeing him married to Mandane; Pacorus cannot renounce Eurydice, but cannot accept her loving another; Suréna, finally, cannot opt between his desire for Eurydice and his political salvation) indicates a breakdown of subjectivity. The individual moves between two poles, poles which form the extreme limits of his/her articulated perception of individual reality, defining that stasis as the only choice available to them. This choice, however, in its inadequacy to their desire, indicates that the relation of the desiring subject to the model structuring his desire has been distorted. At the same time no change has intervened in the world (the 'real', the political domain) that could accommodate this disequilibrium, that could receive it into a new network of power and knowledge.

The limits of representation that inform the parameters of *Suréna* are available to us in the litany of injunctions (ritualized enunciations) which all the characters constantly repeat. These injunctions, all the accepted presuppositions of a monarchal, patriarchal State, are actualized in discourse, are actualized as a commonly held set of beliefs that are as intangible as they are binding.[14] Foremost among them are those limits that paradoxically subject desire to an Ideal, and yet, in this subjugation, allow the subjected the feeling of freedom – of being each invested with certain prerogatives that are the rewards of their own repression:

P. – Elle est fille, et de plus, dit-il, elle est princesse:

                    .   .   .

Je sais de ses devoirs l'indispensable loi
Je sais quel rude joug, dès sa plus tendre enfance,
Imposent à ses voeux son rang et sa naissance.
                    (I, ii, 186, 191–3)

P. – Je sais ce qu'à l'Etat ceux de votre naissance,
Tout maîtres qu'ils en sont doivent d'obéissance:

> Son intérêt chez eux l'emporte sur le leur,
> Et du moment qu'il parle il fait taire le coeur.
>
> (II, iii, 609–12)

> C'est bien traiter les rois en personnes communes,
> Qu'attacher à leur rang ces gênes importunes,
> Comme si, pour vous plaire et les inquiéter,
> Dans le trône avec eux, l'amour pouvait monter.
> Il nous faut un hymen, pour nous donner des princes.
>
> (III, iii, 1025–9)

This Absolutist imperative that echoes throughout the play is the most insidious form of repression in the totalitarian State; it brings the force of the State to bear in the subjugation of desire to Law, daughters to fathers, and sentiment to logic. This injunction echoes throughout the play and inscribes itself as the (rhetorical) locus of tragic potential. It crystallizes the political/sexual imbroglio as a taboo − the impossible transgression which must remain inviolate lest sovereignty, the imposition and acceptance of 'raison d'Etat', succumb. In *Suréna* this injunction which represents the 'voice' of masculine sublimation (the desire of/for genealogy) is as totalizing as it is totalitarian.

The hint of discord, the rumblings of a menace to the hegemony that this patriarchal injunction fears, is heard in the strange, enigmatic 'plainte' of the play's heroine, Eurydice. Her 'plainte' that echoes mysteriously throughout the play attacks both the edifice of Absolutism and her own being as part of that structure. In its monolithic simplicity it confounds the workings of Patriarchy and threatens its demise.

To the essential, unanswerable question that haunts the King in *Suréna*, the obsessive question both Orode and Pacorus continually ask − 'Whom does Eurydice love?' − she responds, simply, 'J'aime ailleurs.' Her very first speech in the play introduces this 'leit-motif' as the central troubling conundrum, the absent center, the symptom of the Sovereign's frustrated desire, of his loss:

> Mais que servent pour moi tous ces préparatifs,
> Si mon coeur est esclave et tous ses voeux captifs,
> Si de tous ces efforts de publique allégresse
> Il se fait de sujets de trouble et de détresse?
> J'aime ailleurs.   (I, i, 11–14)

Repeated by all the characters (Palmis, l. 230; Pacorus, l. 635; Suréna, l. 933; Eurydice, ll. 1133, 1415), this leit-motif forms the chorus of an anti-rhetoric opposed to the injunction of Absolutist prerogative.

Eurydice's response to the royal query is enigmatic in that instead of the answer one would expect, 'J'aime un autre' (a response with an object), she responds with an adverb, 'ailleurs'. By articulating her desire as an 'ailleurs' rather than as 'un autre' Eurydice situates herself beyond the gaze of the Monarch. Eurydice's echoing 'ailleurs' reflects and widens the breach in the integrity that subtends the idealized Absolute quality of Monarchy. Her 'spatial' metaphor poses a limit to the King's ubiquity. In an Absolute State, there is no 'ailleurs': the King is everywhere, and everywhere is (reflects) the King. What this means, simply, is that in a successful Monarchy there is no desire that is not the desire of/for the Monarch, no desire that would separate the universal Subject from his subjects.[15] In this perfect State, as in medieval theology, the Monarch, like God, is both the center and the circumference of the world, which is One. He is absolute, there is no other, no outside, no 'ailleurs'.

Eurydice's 'ailleurs' gives, therefore, the lie to this world, to its indivisibility, by introducing difference into Integrity. In this (further) sundering of the One we witness the decomposition of the Classical subject, the freeing of the subject(ed) from the Subject, and its reconstitution as a (temporally) unhinged 'individuality'.[16] We might even say that this is the first time in the Cornelian universe that a split between a public and private sphere is so radically accused. In a world that ignores the division of the universe into public and private spheres, that clings so desperately to the illusion of the self as disappearing into the State, in the metaphoric apotheoses of 'gloire' and 'devoir', metaphors that precisely underline the self's sacrifice to the State, we are here presented with a creation of difference. Could it be that this creation, impossible to represent, except as the foreign desire of a woman, is an attempt to represent the Other, the new force, the new desire that is unbound from the Sovereign Subject, that is coterminous with the Subject's loss of sovereignty, but which as yet cannot be supported by 'history'? Could this be the sign of the emergence of a new 'individuality' as an uncomfortable adversary to an entire order of aristocratic privilege, of, that is, the 'bourgeois'?

By enunciating her desire as an 'ailleurs' situated beyond the desire of the Monarch, Eurydice imposes a limit to that Sovereign will. At the same time that Eurydice posits herself as a political danger to her own world, a danger that is, rhetorically, metaphorical, her enigmatic answer to the King's inquiry also

establishes Eurydice, metonymically, as a sexual threat to that world. Eurydice's refrain 'j'aime ailleurs' functions as a metonymical displacement of the enigma women pose to patriarchal society. Hers is a riddle as mysterious and potentially as deadly as the Sphinx's to Oedipus. The answer to the question 'Whom does she love?' remains a puzzle, 'ailleurs'. Put another way, however, what is this question really asking? 'Who (that is *what*) is the object of her love (desire)?', or, if we reduce it even further, we realize that the question Orode and Pacorus continually ask, the question of the Ruler/Father put to Eurydice, is that old, unanswerable question, the sign of masculine anxiety: 'What does she (Eurydice) desire? What does (this) woman want?'

And Eurydice does not know. Or at least she doesn't say. That is, of course, her mystery. This mystery figures her narcissistic hold, in the world of masculine absolutes, of her 'femininity', of her being as 'pas toute'. Eurydice, in her inability to represent her desire in a world of absolutes, while still representing an absolute desire, is both in a metaphorical and a metonymical relation to her world. It is this confusion, we might say her perversion of distinction, her 'monstrosity', that situates her in the only position – as negation – available to her in the play. Eurydice internalizes her division, as enigma and as silence. She becomes a melancholic, the perfect monster – the 'dame mérencolyie' of Classicism:[17]

> Je veux qu'un noir chagrin à pas lents me consume,
> Qu'il me fasse à longs traits goûter son amertume;
> Je veux sans que la mort ose me secourir
> Toujours aimer, toujours souffrir, toujours mourir.

> (I, iii, 265–8)

Eurydice articulates, in her rhetoric, the position of melancholic ambivalence: withdrawn from the world, she is rendered impotent. She can conceive of no change, no tragic action that would allow her to leave her immobility. Eurydice is paralyzed by politics and by her own erotic history. She has lost a love – Suréna – not as he is in the world, but as she imagines him to herself, the object of her own narcissistic fantasties. Eurydice's fantasy life recasts Suréna in the role of King, replaces the defective Sovereign by another, 'real' one:

> il sait rétablir les rois dans leurs Etats.
> Des Parthes le mieux fait d'esprit et de visage,
> Le plus puissant en biens, le plus grand en courage,

Le plus noble: joins-y l'amour qu'il a pour moi,
Et tout cela vaut bien un roi qui n'est que roi.   (I, i, 60–4)

Strangely, hauntingly, the voice that is the most radically disruptive of Absolutism in the play dreams of despotism, desires to be subjugated to Suréna-as-King. This fantasy of Sovereignty (and subjugation) is Eurydice's own masochistic projection that is brutally denied by reality:

O. – Cependant, est-il roi, Madame?
E. –   Il ne l'est pas.   (I, i, 59)

Eurydice loves Suréna 'ailleurs' as 'King' in her father's court:

Tous deux, aussi qu'au roi, me rendirent visite.
Et j'en connus bientôt le différent mérite;
L'un fier, et tout gonflé d'un vieux mépris des rois,
Semblait pour compliment nous apporter des lois;
L'autre par les devoirs d'un respect légitime
Vengeait le sceptre en nous de ce manque d'estime.
      (I, i, 41–6)

Suréna is loved as surrogate, as supplementation. Paradoxically this same hero who is loved for his 'virility' is caught in Eurydice's love, a love that is sadistic, and unmanned. When he tells her 'Comme je n'ai plus d'yeux vers elles à tourner', he admits that Eurydice has deprived him of his desire (eyes) for (any other) women. Suréna, like Orode, has been blinded by his love, a love that traps him – emasculates him, makes him, in that love, always unavailable to Eurydice. Suréna's 'reality' is a constant denial of Eurydice's fantasy.

Suréna's love for Eurydice reduces him first to impotence and eventually to death. He shares with her the impossibility of a desire that is foreclosed to reality, and this foreclusion paralyzes him, making him the mirror reflection of Eurydice's melancholy. Suréna is described as a Saturnian presence, 'si froid, si retenu'. He constantly asks for death and can only reflect Eurydice's stance of rhetorical depossession:

Où dois-je recourir
O ciel! S'il faut toujours aimer, souffrir, mourir!
      (I, iii, 346–7)

Suréna and Eurydice are trapped in their narcissistic mirroring, and reduced to a mutually self-reflective narcosis. Neither of them can move to satisfy their desire without bringing down the entire edifice of Absolutism inside which they dwell. The stultifying torpor of their desire is its profound sense of loss. For them no

'ailleurs' exists except the 'ailleurs' of foreclusion by the ideology which informs this desire, gives it its transgressive rebellious attraction and forever denies it.

Caught in the paralysis of their impossible desire, Suréna and Eurydice attempt, in a form of passive reversal, to construct for themselves an 'outside' at the very center of Orode's court. Their refusal to name the object of their love, their silence, joins them together, enfolds them both in its eloquence and separates them (temporarily) from the all-embracing demand of Orode.

> L'amour dans sa prudence est toujours indiscret;
> A force de se taire, il trahit son secret.　　(IV, iv, 1275–6)

Silence's indiscretion (the refusal to mirror the desire of the Sovereign) effectively widens the chink that has appeared in the Absolute edifice, radically sundering the political predicates upon which desire rests. Silence articulates in its hollow absence the conjunction of sexual and political treason:

> Un sujet qui se voit le rival de son maître
> Quelque étude qu'il perde à ne le point paraître
> Ne pousse aucun soupir sans faire un attentat;
> Et d'un crime d'amour il fait un crime d'Etat.
> 　　　　　　　　　　　　　　　　(IV, iv, 1329–32)

In the closed world of totalitarianism cracks have appeared that send out shock waves with profoundly unsettling consequences for the future of Monarchy.

The split in Orode, his jealousy/dependence as it is frustrated and exaggerated by the silent refusal of his subjects to speak their desire, subjugates Orode to this silence, while at the same time turning his subjects from him. Orode's initial mistrust of Suréna becomes complete paranoia, while Suréna's abnegation of him turns to resentment. He allows himself to give voice to a rhetorical stance that is the first indication that his desire, frustrated, turns him into a rebel:

> Mon crime véritable est d'avoir aujourd'hui
> Plus de nom que mon roi, plus de vertu que lui;
> Et c'est de là que part cette secrète haine
> Que le temps ne rendra que plus forte et plus pleine.
> Plus on sert des ingrats, plus on s'en fait haïr:
> Tout ce qu'on fait pour eux ne fait que nous trahir.
> 　　　　　　　　　　　　　　　　(V, ii, 1511–16)

The silent frustration of their sexuality has an ambivalent effect

on the structures of their world: it allies them to each other, binds them together as an 'ailleurs', an 'Other' of sovereign desire. By the exact same token, and simultaneously, their desire, as other, causes a return of the repressed in the ideological apparatus of Absolutism: it turns the Sovereign into a tyrant.

In the perfect Absolute State the immense dissymmetry that exists between Sovereign and subject remains always implicit, available, if at all, in the specially ritualized ceremonial of royal largesse, or of Death (execution).[18] In *Suréna* this implicit difference returns in explicit action. Orode, perhaps in spite of himself, in front of a desire that so radically puts into question his own place in the hierarchy that rules his world, is driven to treachery, to assassination, to the use of his power to control, to force obedience from what escapes him.

The wedge that separates Eurydice/Suréna from Orode/Pacorus widens inevitably and dialectically as the tragedy runs its course. The very existence of their love, as a denial of Sovereignty, causes sovereignty to exercise its repressive power. Needless to say, the death of Suréna spells the end to the entire world of the play: Eurydice dies from loss; Orode/Pacorus and their kingdom will surely fall to prey to forces they can never control without Suréna.

In extreme melancholia, the 'ego' no longer can perceive of its separation from external reality. This outside becomes part of it, a negative hated part. It is the disintegration of the ego that precipitates its shocking self-destruction, its suicide. The world of *Suréna* does not, cannot escape the same fate. Caught at the aporia of a desire that de-subjugates them, that denies them their subjectivity as subject of the King's desire, Suréna and Eurydice can but move into the only 'ailleurs' that is available to them, that is adequate to their desire. That space exists, however, outside the confines of representation, outside their world's ability to articulate itself. It exists in the secret, silent indifference of Death.

Their death, however, the death of *Suréna*, is paradoxically a beginning. The step out of 'duty' ('un pas hors du devoir'), a duty that has defined the Absolutist schema, leads them (us) down a very long road. The road which begins in *Suréna* leads from the sumptuous 'Divertissements de Versailles' to the 'fête révolutionnaire'. The path we have traced in the Cornelian universe ends, in the new space, the 'ailleurs' of Absolutism, at the Place de la Concorde, at the foot of the guillotine. Corneille's world has traced for us the parabola of seventeenth-century Absolutism, of Patriarchy as desire, and finally of desire as rebellion. At the end of this road,

Sovereignty, which at its beginning was disguised behind its own exercise of power, behind the theater as a veiled space of Absolutist prerogative, is finally sundered. The return of all that Absolutism must repress surfaces in the final, spectacular parricide − the execution of the King. In this parricide an entire order of desire and representation, structured around 'le père du peuple', comes to an end, and a new order, only dimly but correctly perceived in *Suréna*, begins its own meanderings.

NOTES

Preface

1 A. de Vigny, *Cinq-Mars*, in *Oeuvres complètes* (Paris: Gallimard, 1948), II.

2 See M. Foucault, *Surveiller et punir: naissance de la prison* (Paris: Gallimard, 1975), chap. 2, 'L'éclat des supplices', pp. 36–72.

3 *Ibid.*, p. 52: 'Le supplice a donc une fonction juridico-politique. Il s'agit d'un cérémonial pour reconstituer la souveraineté un instant blessée . . . Son but est moins de rétablir un équilibre que de faire jouer, jusqu'à son point extrême, la dissymétrie entre le sujet qui a osé violer la loi, et le souverain tout puissant qui fait valoir sa force.'

4 S. Doubrovsky, *Corneille ou la dialectique du héros* (Paris: Gallimard, 1963), p. 268: 'L'histoire cornélienne est une histoire de "philosophe" . . . l'instrument d'une prise de conscience pratiqué par l'homme de l'histoire concrète où il se trouve engagé; de l'histoire en train de se faire et de le faire, en bref, de l'histoire vécue ou "constituante" par opposition à l'histoire reconstituée. L'histoire cornélienne n'est pas une matière, dans laquelle le drame puiserait, elle est la "matière même" du drame, au sens où la conscience ne peut faire un objet d'étude pour la psychologie que dans la mesure où elle porte ce psychologue lui-même à l'existence.'

5 The major proponent of Corneille's theater as a representation of its immediate historical moment is, of course, G. Couton. See, for example, *Corneille et la Fronde* (Paris: Belles Lettres, 1955) and *La Vieillesse de Corneille* (Paris: Maloine, 1949).

6 M. de Certeau, *L'Ecriture de l'histoire* (Paris: Gallimard, 1975), p. 60.

Introduction

1 Among the many studies one could cite, several particularly intriguing ones must be mentioned: for the esthetics of the period, J. Rousset, *Circé et le Paon, la littérature de l'âge baroque en France* (Paris: Corti, 1953) and S. Sarduy, *Barocco* (Paris: Seuil, 1975); for the development of social attitudes, R. Mandrou, *Introduction à la France moderne, 1500–1640: essai de psychologie historique* (Paris: Albin Michel, 1961) and V. L. Tapié, *Baroque et classicisme* (Paris: Plon, 1957); for epistemology, the work of M. Foucault, see below, n. 2.

2 See M. Foucault, *Histoire de la folie à l'âge classique* (Paris: Gallimard, 1966) and *Les Mots et les choses* (Paris: Gallimard, 1966), esp. chap. 3, 'Représenter'.

3 See A. Ubersfeld, *Lire le théâtre* (Paris: Editions sociales, 1978), p. 265: 'Tout texte théâtral est la réponse à une demande du public, et c'est sur ce point que se fait le plus aisément l'articulation du discours théâtral avec l'histoire et l'idéologie.'

4 For a discussion of the relation between theatrical text, history and ideology, see Ubersfeld, *Lire le théâtre*, esp. chaps. 1, 'Texte et représentation', and 6, 'Le discours théâtral', and also M. H. Huet, *Rehearsing the Revolution* (Berkeley: University of California Press, 1982).

5 Besides the works of G. Couton already mentioned in the preface, other major studies that deal with this interrelation are S. Doubrovsky, *Corneille*, P. Bénichou, *Morales du grand siècle* (Paris: Gallimard, 1948), B. Dort, *Pierre Corneille, dramaturge* (Paris: L'Arche, 1957), and R. J. Nelson, *Corneille, his Heroes and their Worlds* (Philadelphia, University of Pennsylvania Press, 1963).

6 A. d'Aubigné, *Oeuvres*, ed. H. Weber (Paris: Gallimard, 1969).

7 E. Kantorowicz, *The King's Two Bodies, a Study in Medieval Political Theology* (Princeton: Princeton University Press, 1957).

8 This desire is articulated in d'Aubigné's *Tragiques* around the rhetorical and political figure of Henri IV.

9 'Everything in the state . . . was vaguely familiar, but nothing was recognizably the same. Little had been lost on the way; little undeniably new had been added, but all had changed.' M. Oakesholt, *On Human Conduct* (Oxford, 1975), part III, p. 198, quoted in N. Keohane, *Philosophy and the State in France* (Princeton: Princeton University Press, 1980), p. 10.

10 Three recent works use and elaborate on Kantorowicz's study, each, of course, with its own critical perspective. All center their analyses on the Absolutism of Louis XIV. These are L. Marin, *Le Portrait du roi* (Paris: Minuit, 1981), J.-M. Apostolidès, *Le Roi machine* (Paris: Minuit, 1981), and the latter's recent *Le Prince sacrifié: Théâtre et politique au temps de Louis XIV* (Paris: Minuit, 1985).

11 N. Keohane, *Philosophy and the State*, p. 16. For my discussion of Absolutism I am indebted to this thorough study as well as to: R. Mousnier, *Les XVI et XVII siècles* (Paris: P.U.F., 1967), chap. 4, 'Les nouvelles structures de l'Etat'; O. Ranum, *Paris in the Age of Absolutism* (New York: John Wiley, 1968); E. Kantorowicz, *The King's Two Bodies*; P. King, *The Ideology of Order* (New York: Barnes and Nobel, 1974); and W. F. Church, *Richelieu and Reason of State* (Princeton: Princeton University Press, 1972).

12 R. Mousnier, *Les XVI et XVII siècles*, p. 249.

13 J. Derrida in his 'La Pharmacie de Platon', in *La Dissemination* (Paris: Seuil, 1972), pp. 84–108, discusses the metaphoric connection between the images of the Sun, the Father and power in western philosophy.

14 See M. Foucault, *La Volonté de savoir, histoire de la sexualité* (Paris:

Gallimard, 1976), p. 143: 'La famille est l'échangeur de la sexualité et de l'alliance: elle transporte la loi et la dimension juridique dans le dispositif de la sexualité: et elle transporte l'économie du plaisir et l'intensité des sensations dans le régime de l'alliance.'

15 See Ubersfeld, *Lire le théâtre*, pp. 14–15.

16 *Ibid.*, p. 14: 'Plus que tout autre art – de là sa place dangereuse et privilégiée – le théâtre se démontre pratique sociale, dont le rapport à la production, donc à la lutte des classes, n'est jamais aboli, même s'il apparaît estompé par moments, et si tout un travail mystificateur le transforme au gré de la classe dominante en simple outil de divertissement.'

17 Besides Ubersfeld, see O. Mannoni, *Clefs pour l'imaginaire, ou l'autre scène* (Paris: Seuil, 1969), chapters entitled 'Je sais bien mais quand même . . .' and 'L'Illusion comique'; A. Green, *Un oeil en trop: le complexe d'Oedipe dans la tragédie* (Paris: Minuit, 1969); and J. F. Lyotard, 'Oedipe juif' in *Dérive à partir de Freud et Marx* (Paris: 10/18, 1973).

18 See Freud's *Interpretation of Dreams*, The Standard Edition of the Complete Psychological Works of S. Freud, ed. J. Strachey, A. Freud and A. Strachey (London: the Hogarth Press and the Institute of Psychoanalysis, 1981), v. G. Bataille in his *Erotisme* (Paris: 10/18, 1967) bases his analysis on precisely such a paradox.

19 Ubersfeld, *Lire le théâtre*, p. 47.

20 This point is stressed by all the theoreticians of the theater mentioned above, Ubersfeld, Lyotard and Huet.

21 Besides Freud, Lyotard and Green already mentioned, the reader should also consult P. Lacoue–Labarthe's 'Theatrum analyticum' in *Glyph II* (Baltimore: Johns Hopkins University Press, 1977).

22 It is practically impossible to consider 'Classicism' in general. The term has for centuries been the subject of debate, as an esthetic, a philosophy, even as an historical period. Nevertheless, if we consider 'French Classicism' as an 'Ideology', we can see beyond the great and varied internal contradictions of the period to certain imperatives that insist in art, politics, philosophy. 'Symmetrical' structuring is, I would argue, one of these insistent symptoms. For general debate on the term I would refer the reader to the classic works: H. Peyre, *Qu'est-ce que le classicisme?* (Paris: Nizet, 1965); R. Bray, *La Formation de la doctrine classique en France* (Paris: Nizet, 1957); R. Fernandez, 'De l'esprit classique', *Nouvelle revue française* (184, Jan. 1929); E. B. O. Borgerhoff, *The Freedom of French Classicism* (Princeton: Princeton University Press, 1950); J. Schérer, *La Dramaturgie classique en France* (Paris: Nizet, 1959); and, of course, E. R. Curtius, *European Literature and the Latin Middle Ages* (trans. W. Trask, New York: Pantheon Books, 1953). More recent works that also examine Classicism as containment (besides Foucault, Marin and Apostolidès already mentioned) are E. Harth, *Ideology and Culture in Seventeenth*

Century France (Ithaca: Cornell University Press, 1984); T. Reiss, *The Discourse of Modernism* (Ithaca: Cornell University Press, 1982); and the introduction to M. Greenberg, *Detours of Desire: Readings in the French Baroque* (Columbus: Ohio State University Press, 1984).

23 Bénichou, *Morales du grand siècle*, p. 20: 'Le groupe social au nom duquel s'accomplit chez lui l'acte héroïque n'est jamais plus vaste que la famille, l'Etat n'étant lui-même autre chose que la famille.'

24 Doubrovsky, *Corneille*, p. 133: 'Contrairement à ce qu'on a pu dire, Corneille ne confond jamais les hommes et les femmes. Bien mieux, il semble accorder à chaque sexe une "nature" propre.'

25 S. Kofman, *Freud et l'énigme de la femme: la femme dans les textes de Freud* (Paris: Galilée, 1981), p. 171: 'C'est cette rupture par le refoulement d'une évolution qui ne saurait donc être aussi linéaire ni logique que celle de l'homme qui est une des causes des illusions de la métaphysique, de sa croyance en une essence féminine ou masculine pure.'

26 See M. Montrelay, *L'Ombre et le nom: sur la femininité* (Paris: Minuit, 1977), p. 66: 'La femininité fait échec à l'interprétation dans le mesure où elle ignore le refoulement.' We should also consider the comment of Kofman's *Freud et l'énigme de la femme*, p. 171: 'Et parce que "refouler" n'est pas oublier rien ne sera jamais joué définitivement: la sexualité "masculine" de la femme peut faire retour de multiples manières: dans les rêves, dans les symptômes hystériques, dans l'idéal masculin de la femme.'

27 See, for example, Kofman, *Freud et l'énigme de la femme*, p. 160: 'En dépit de l'affirmation principale d'une bisexualité originaire commune aux deux sexes, de fait prédomine un seul sexe, le sexe mâle: le pénis est toujours déjà la zone érogène directrice – pour les deux sexes.'

28 L. Irigaray, *Speculum de l'autre femme* (Paris: Minuit, 1975), p. 26.

29 *Ibid.*, p. 27.

30 This is a term used by J. Lacan in his seminar *Encore* (Paris: Seuil, 1975). One should also consult S. Heath's dense article 'Difference' (*Screen*, 1978, pp. 51–113), which discusses Lacan's analysis of femininity as well as the theories of female representation put forth in the studies of Lemoine-Luccioni, Irigaray and Montrelay.

31 E. Lemoine-Luccioni, *Partage des femmes* (Paris: Seuil, 1976), p. 9: 'L'homme est un, par la grâce du significant de son manque, "le phallus" qui se trouve être le symbole de son organe sexuel, le pénis . . . L'homme est, et reste, en tant qu'homme – et à supposer qu'il existe en tant qu'un homme qui ne serait pas aussi une femme – un.'

32 *Un oeil en trop*, p. 39.

33 For the emergence of the modern subject see F. Jameson, *The Political Unconscious* (Ithaca: Cornell University Press, 1981) and R. Mandrou, *Introduction à la France moderne*. Also P. Ariès, ed., *Communication 35: Sexualités occidentales* (1982).

34 Heath, 'Difference', p. 106.

35 *Ibid.*, p. 107. Cf. Huet, *Rehearsing the Revolution*, chap. 2, 'The Spectator' and Mannoni, *Clefs pour l'imaginaire*, p. 174: 'Si le théâtre met d'une certaine façon en mouvement nos capacités d'identification et les libère, en même temps, par ses conventions, par son institu-tionalisation, il renforce les protections et les défenses.'

36 Mannoni, *Clefs pour l'imaginaire*, p. 174.

1. Mythifying matrix: Corneille's *Médée*

1 C. Lévi-Strauss, 'Structure du mythe', in *Anthropologie structurale* (Paris: Plon, 1958).

2 *Ibid.*, p. 229: 'Tout peut arriver dans un mythe: il semble que la suc-cession des événements n'y soit subordonée à aucune règle de logique ou de continuité. Tout sujet peut avoir un quelconque prédicat, toute relation concevable est possible.'

3 The following works, which all deal with the mutual involvement and investment of theater as spectacle and the audience – collective and individual – have guided my thinking: Green, *Un oeil en trop*; Man-noni, 'L'illusion théâtrale', in *Clefs pour l'imaginaire*; Ubersfeld, *Lire le théâtre*, esp. chaps. 1, 'Texte et représentation' and 6, 'Le discours théâtral'.

4 Green, *Un oeil en trop*, p. 96.

5 *Ibid*, p. 18.

6 See J. – J. Goux, 'Différence de sexes et périple de l'histoire', in *Les Iconoclastes* (Paris: Seuil, 1978), p. 191: 'C'est en questionnant la division mythique des apports du mâle et de la femelle dans la procréa-tion qu'il est possible . . . de reconstituer l'archéologie de l'idéalisme. L'idéalisme est d'abord *une conception de la conception*. L'homme dans la procréation apporte la *forme* de la progéniture, la femme ap-porte la *matière*. C'est ce que disent tous les discours mythiques sur la procréation.'

7 Corneille, *Discours de l'utilité et des partis du poème dramatique*, p. 13: '[la] dignité [de la tragédie] demande quelque grand intérêt d'Etat, ou quelque passion plus noble et plus mâle que l'amour . . . il faut qu'il [l'amour] se contente du second rang dans le poème, et laisse [à la politique] le premier'.

8 See A. Artaud, *Le Théâtre et son double* (Paris: N.R.F., 1964), p. 38: 'Et c'est ainsi que tous les grands Mythes sont noirs et qu'on ne peut imaginer hors d'une atmosphère de carnage, de torture, de sang versé toutes les magnifiques Fables qui racontent aux foules *le premier par-tage sexuel* et le premier carnage d'essence qui apparaissent dans la création.'

9 The characters, on one level, function as allegories of impulses. Impulses, as Freud talked about them, are marked by their ability to revert into their opposite (manifestations). See 'Instincts and their Vicissitudes' (*Standard Edition*, XIV).

10 See Goux, 'Différence de sexes', p. 191: 'Or, les métaphores d'Aristote et de Platon attestent que l'opposition philosophique entre la matière et l'idée puise directement à cette archéologie mythique de la conception avec la dimension du désir qu'elle implique. Aristote dit clairement "la matière désire la forme comme la femelle désire l'homme".'

11 Irigaray, *Speculum*, p. 89.

12 All references to *Médée* are to the edition by A. de Leyssac (Geneva: Droz, 1978).

13 Also for the definition of 'epiclery' in Greek law one could consult W. K. Lacey, *The Family in Classical Greece* (Ithaca: Cornell University Press, 1968).

14 For an analysis of the role of marriage and maternity and the exchange value of women within the ideological parameters of Patriarchy, and particularly the slippage from femininity to maternity, see Irigaray, *Speculum*, esp. pp. 97–129.

15 A. Green, 'Sur la mère phallique', *Revue française de psychanalyse*, jan.–fév., 1968, p. 2.

16 See Freud's brief essay on Medusa (*Standard Edition*, XVIII).

17 It is interesting to note that in his *La Toison d'or*, written in 1660, Corneille insists on the fact that although Jason accomplishes (with Médée's help) the preliminary tasks allowing him to reach the Golden Fleece, it is Médée who actually takes it and brings it to the Greeks:

> M. – Ne laissons pas ainsi la victoire imparfaite:
> Par le milieu des airs, courons à leur defaite;
> Et nous-mêmes portons à leur témérité
> Jusqu'à dans ce vaisseau ce qu'elle a mérité . . .
>
> (V, V, 2100–3)

18 See F. Nietzsche, *The Birth of Tragedy*.

19 See W. Goode, 'Medea and Jason: Hero and Non-Hero in Corneille's *Médée*', in *French Review* (51, May 1978) and also de Leyssac's introduction to his edition of *Médée*.

20 Freud, 'On Narcissism: an Introduction' (*Standard Edition*, XIV).

21 At least in G. Dumézil's definition: 'Souveraineté et fécondité sont des puissances solidaires et comme deux aspects de la Puissance.' Quoted in Green, *Un oeil en trop*, p. 24.

22 See Irigaray, *Speculum*, p. 63: 'Or, pour que ce moi soit valeureux il faut bien qu'un "miroir" le rassure, réassure sur sa validité. La femme étayera ce redoublement spéculaire renvoyant à l'homme "son image", le répétant comme "même . . . La femme donc sera le même à une inversion près . . . comme, *en tant que mère*, elle permettra la répétition de même." '

23 Irigaray, *Speculum*, p. 98.

24 See Goux, 'Différence de sexes', p. 200: 'En tant qu'il est le garant de la permanence du "même" dans la reproduction, c'est le père et

non la mère qui a à répondre de la vie et de la tendresse essentielles du vivant. Il sera le représentation de la reproduction, le signifiant de la perpétuation vitale, voire donc aussi, par un pas de plus, le granat de l'éternité.'

25 'L'exécution de la peine est faite pour donner non pas le spectacle de la mesure, mais du *déséquilibre et de l'excès*. Il doit y avoir dans cette liturgie de la peine une affirmation emphatique du pouvoir et de sa *suprématie intrinsèque*.' Foucault, *Surveiller et punir*, p. 12.

26 *Ibid.*, p. 39: 'Dans les *excès* des supplices toute une économie du pouvoir est investie.'

27 For a reading of the Medea myth that stresses its socio-political implications, corroborating my own interpretation, see C. Alvaro, *La lunga notte di Medea* (Milan: Bompiani, 1949). For a more anthropologico-psychoanalytical reading see G. Carboni and D. Nobili, *La Mauvaise Mère* (trans. R. Myjori, Paris: Petite Bibliothèque Payot, 1977). See also B. d'Astorg's 'Médée, mère, meurtrière', in his *Les Noces orientales* (Paris: Seuil, 1980).

2. *Le Cid*: Father/Time

1 See the standard reference works: A. Adam, *Histoire de la littérature française au XVII siècle*, I (Paris: Del Duca, 1956); R. Bray, *La Tragédie cornélienne devant la critique* (Paris: Hachette, 1927) and *La Formation de la doctrine classique*; G. Reynier, *Le Cid de Corneille* (Paris: Mellottée, 1929), and, of course, J. Chapelain, *Les Sentiments de l'Académie française sur la tragi-comédie du Cid* (Paris, 1637), repr. in M. Pelisson, *Histoire de l'Académie française* (Paris, 1700).

2 All references to the *Cid* are to the M. Rat edition, *Théâtre choisi de Corneille* (Paris: Garnier, 1961).

3 Cf. Freud, *The Interpretation of Dreams* (*Standard Edition*, V), p. 349: 'dreams take into account in a general way the connection which undeniably exists between all the portions of the dream-thoughts by combining the whole material into a single situation or event. They reproduce logical connections by *simultaneity in time*.'

4 Both Doubrovsky (*Corneille*) and Bénichou (*Morales du grand siècle*) analyze, in different but complementary terms, the importance of the 'noble' or 'aristocratic' essence as it is represented and informs Corneille's theater. My own discussion is indebted to theirs.

5 See Doubrovsky, *Corneille*, pp. 89–105, for his discussion of the 'race of heroes' that the *Cid* articulates.

6 For my discussion of this male linking in a generational chain I will be following (as it will soon become apparent) G. Rosolato's essays, particularly his 'La Différence des sexes'; 'Du père'; and 'Trois générations d'hommes dans le mythe religieux et la généalogie', in his *Essais sur le symbolique* (Paris: Gallimard, 1969).

7 See Doubrovsky, *Corneille*, p. 95: 'Avec *Le Cid* et le "meurs ou tue"

172

de don Diègue, le noble découvre à nouveau, dans l'affrontement de la mort inévitablement donnée ou reçue, sa vérité et sa justification.'

8 See Irigaray, *Speculum*, p. 122: 'le relais par la femme permettrait de voir ce qui d'habitude s'occulte dans son évidence: la prégnance de l'homosexualité masculine'; and Deleuze and Guattari, *L'Anti-Oedipe* (Paris: Minuit, 1977), p. 194: 'soulignant le fait universel que le mariage n'est pas une alliance entre un homme et une femme, mais "une alliance entre deux familles", "une transaction entre hommes à propos des femmes", G. Devereux en tirait la juste conclusion d'une motivation homosexuelle de base et de groupe'.

9 Irigaray, *Speculum*, p. 152: 'L'accord, en tout cas, sera conclu entre deux hommes pour le passage de la femme d'une "maison" à une autre, liée désormais à un autre "cercle" de famille.'

10 Doubrovsky, *Corneille*, p. 90: 'Voilà donc, tout comme l'éblouissement amoureux était vicié en son essence par la possibilité du change, la vertu et la portée de la "vaillance" atteintes au coeur par le temps. Don Diègue découvre dans l'horreur et l'humiliation que le passé est tout entier en suspens dans le présent.'

11 Without wishing to stretch a comparison too far, it is intriguing to note how Corneille's theater can be seen to trace the same evolution of civilization as imagined by Freud, especially in *Totem and Taboo*. The reader should also consult the interesting study of J.-M. Apostolidès, *Le Prince sacrifié* (esp. chap. 3, 'L'univers historique'), which offers, in a more sociological perspective, a similar interpretation of *Le Cid*.

12 For the 'political' implications of narcissism the reader would do well to consult *Narcisses* (Nouvelle revue de psychanalyse, no. 13, 1976), in particular the articles of G. Rosolato ('Le Narcissisme') and A. Green ('Un, Autre, Neutre: valeurs narcissiques du Même'). At the same time a similar point (Gomès' recalcitrance) has been analyzed by G. Couton in *Réalisme de Corneille* (Paris: Les Belles Lettres, 1953).

13 Rosolato, 'Trois générations'.

14 'La thèse que nous défendons ici est que le fantasme du meurtre du père soutient le passage du triangle oedipien du cycle fermé oedipien, à la linéarité indéfinie des générations d'hommes où s'insère le sujet. Ceci n'est possible que par l'accès à la figure de père-Mort.' Rosolato, 'Trois générations', p. 60.

15 'Il est vrai que, dans ce sujet il faut se contenter de tirer Rodrigue de péril, sans le pousser jusqu'à son mariage avec Chimène. Il est historique, et a plu en son temps, mais bien sûrement il déplairait au notre; et j'ai peine à voir que Chimène y consente chez l'auteur espagnol, bien qu'il donne plus de trois ans de durée à la comédie qu'il en a faite. Pour ne pas contredire l'histoire, j'ai cru ne me pouvoir dispenser d'en jeter quelque idée, mais avec incertitude de l'effet; et ce n'était que par là que je pouvais accorder la bienséance du théâtre avec la vérité de l'événement' ('Examen', pp. 13–14).

16 For the imbrication of the brother/sister couple see Lemoine-Luccioni, *Partage des femmes*, pp. 103–25, and Irigaray, *Speculum*, pp. 266–82.

17 Lemoine–Luccioni, *Partage des femmes*: 'Le frère et la soeur ordonnent le sexe par leur seule opposition à partir de leur ressemblance postulée (même origine) en scotomisant une plus fondamentale différence . . . Nés à des moments differents, ils sont nés de parents différents. Mais ils veulent leurs parents, tels des essences, immuables' (p. 113); 'La chose encombrante et cachée dans la relation du frère et de la soeur, c'est le sexe de la soeur, et même sa vulve' (p. 115).

18 For this term and its use in feminist writing and theory, see J. Gallop 'Writing and Sexual Difference: the Difference Within', in *Critical Inquiry*, 8, no. 4, 1982.

19 Doubrovsky, *Corneille*, pp. 195–291.

20 For a fuller development of this idea of the woman as 'split', 'not-whole', see chap. 3.

21 As we have been studying it, Patriarchy, structured around the evolution of three generations of men, allows the male less ambivalence, or, to express it another way, subjects males to a greater and more complete repression of hostility directed toward the State in which he is inscribed. If the young boy is to become a 'normal' man and is to assume his place in the line of men he must have internalized as 'conscience' an overriding obeisance to ideals that inform a sense of 'polis'. The ambivalence that males might feel is (according to Freud) less great and its sublimation more complete than the female's because in a system that validates an integral subject, the young male having but one highly invested erotogenic zone does not have to accommodate (as Freud posits the female must) a transference of pleasure from one erotic zone to another. The penis was and remains the 'normal' area of (sexual) pleasure for the male. The young girl's development, however, is more ambivalent. During her 'normal' evolution from infancy to adulthood, she must transfer the locus of her pleasure from the essentially 'masculine' organ (the clitoris) to a 'truly' feminine one (the vagina). This oscillation between two erotogenic zones is navigated, if it is navigated, with great resistance, and constant ambivalence. The result of this internal splitting, division of unresolved conflict between two powerful sources of pleasure, will be, again according to Freud, that this conflict, and therefore, in essence, the female, always remains unresolved. Even Freud's 'Normal' female is always less resolved, less unified than her male counterpart. She is always oscillating from one zone to another, from a masculine type of pleasure to a feminine. She is, in this sense, more truly 'bisexual', less able to support repression and therefore less likely to support sublimation. She remains in an inherently more ambivalent relation to patriarchal values, values of the One, of the State, and can never as completely accept the idealization that defines the State as an ade-

quate substitute for the memory/desire of a more total, more immediate and more cataclysmic pleasure.

22 The expression is Doubrovsky's (*Corneille*, p. 91): 'Nous voici arrivés à un passage qui, depuis trois siècles, a fait couler des océans d'encre.'

23 A point that is driven home with the greatest force in O. Nadal's *Le Sentiment de l'amour dans l'oeuvre de Corneille* (Paris: Gallimard, 1948).

24 This is the first of a series of internalized 'dead fathers' that haunt Corneille theater (Gomès, Emilie's father, Polyeucte (as father), etc.). For the importance of this fantasmatic object, see Rosolato, 'Du père', p. 42: 'cet échange [the relation between men] implique une dette contractée par un père mort . . . et dont le règlement, exigé par les lignées du système y ont recours'.

25 'Le père, à chaque étape, est celui en qui et par qui advient la différence' (Rosolato, 'Du père', p. 43).

26 For a full discussion of this point see chap. 3.

27 Rosolato, 'Du père', p. 64; 'Il faut remarquer la proximité que Freud suggère entre cette imago et la forme sociale du matriarcat; ceci confirme un autre trait du Père Idéalisé: d'être une image composite où, sous la dominance du Père peut se révéler l'image de la mère-au-pénis.'

28 'All Ears: Nietzsche's Otobiography', in *The Pedagogical Imperative, Teaching as Literary Genre*, Yale French Studies (New Haven; Yale University Press, 1982).

29 Although the ultimate reference to this 'pre-Oedipal' presence, rhythm or non-representable force is to M. Klein and Kleinian analysts, J. Kristeva has expanded on its significance for literature (and music) in *Polylogue* (Paris: Au Seuil, 1977) in her discussions of the 'chora' and of its link to the body of the Mother.

30 For the relevance of these terms, 'bad' and 'good' Mother (object), see M. Klein, *Envy and Gratitude* (London: Hogarth Press and the Institute for Psychoanalysis, 1953).

31 For the importance of the name and the way in which it inscribes the child within a signifying network of economic, social, political and sexual values, see Rosolato, 'Du père', p. 45: 'La particularisation de sujet passe par un terme générique. De sorte que le nom signifie l'appartenance . . . à une communauté qui, elle, se nomme dans l'individu.' When, therefore, Rodrigue accepts another 'name' not only does he become other, but the community in which he is inscribed is also transformed; all the structures must re-align to accommodate this new member. See also Starobinski, 'Sur Corneille', *Temps moderne* (Nov. 1954; repr. in *L'Oeil vivant*, Paris: Gallimard, 1961), p. 716: 'Selon la ''psychologie de Corneille'' . . . le ''grand nom'' résulte des actes; le héros crée sa renommée à partir de ses hauts faits. Le nom glorieux vient unifier les exploits discontinus, les rassemblant à la cime de leur trajectoire . . . Selon l'idéologie que Corneille partage avec les nobles . . . tout commence par un grand nom: les grands actes résultent

infailliblement. L'ordre suivi par la psychologie se trouve exactement renversée . . . En face d'une telle idéologie, de structure typiquement féodale, la psychologie cornélienne semble définir au contraire l'attitude des grands bourgeois qui se font un nom à force d'exploits et de services rendus au roi de France . . . Cette attitude rejoint l'idéologie féodale dont elle évince le prestige.'

32 See above, note 30.

3. *Horace*, Classicism and female trouble

1 All references to *Horace* are to the edition by P. Lelièvre in *Théâtre complet* (Paris: Gallimard, 1950).

2 For a dense discussion of this point of Lacanian theory see Heath, 'Difference', p. 65: 'Sexuality is not given in nature but produced; the individual subject is not constructed from sexuality, sexuality is constructed in the history of the subject with difference a function of that construction not its cause'; also, p. 59: 'Male and female differ in consequence of the phallic function in castration, are in the position of a different relation to phallus and castration.'

3 This is, of course, one of Freud's main arguments presented to explain the 'difference' between masculinity and femininity in both *Totem and Taboo* and *Civilization and its Discontents*.

4 'La féminité la plus réussie ne peut prétendre à l'idéalité, ne peut en rien se conférer un idéal' (Irigaray, *Speculum*, p. 129).

5 Irigaray (*Speculum*, p. 151) defines marriage in the following terms: 'Tout cela sera monnayé entre les deux chefs de famille en fonction des biens et intérêts idéologiques respectifs. L'accord en tout cas sera conclu entre deux hommes pour le passage de la femme d'une maison à l'autre, liée désormais à un autre "cercle de famille".'

6 'Et c'est dans les (encore) "entre" du devenir de l'être ou des êtres que quelque chose de son aspécificité pourrait se repérer' (Irigaray, *Speculum*, p. 207).

7 See Doubrovsky's discussion of the masculine and feminine essence, their evolution in Cornelian society and the metaphors and images that subtend them (*Corneille*, pp. 131–5).

8 *Ibid.*, p. 92.

9 For the importance of 'blood' for the economy of femininity see Irigaray, *Speculum*, pp. 156–67.

10 This is, of course, one of Irigaray's main arguments in her analysis of the 'mirroring' of desire and of how females are recuperated in a male scheme of desire that is always desire for the 'same', in other words, a 'homosexual' desire.

11 Jacques Derrida in 'La double séance' (*Dissemination*, Paris: Seuil, 1972, p. 106) has waxed poetic on the ambiguity, the polemic possibilities of 'hymen' in his work on Mallarmé. See his evocation of the 'hymen' as 'entre/autre' (pp. 237–45).

12 At least that is what Kofman's gloss of Freud would have us deduce; 'être héros, pouvoir résoudre les énigmes, implique d'abandonner toute foi et toute croyance, de "tuer" le père et de coucher avec la mère sans crainte de la castration et de la mort' (*Freud*, p. 107).

13 'Examen', p. 783: 'Il passe pour constant que le second acte est un des plus pathétiques qui soient sur la scène et le troisième un des plus artificieux. Il est soutenu de la moitié du combat des trois frères.'

14 See Lemoine-Luccioni, *Partage des femmes*, p. 100: 'Voilà la femme telle que nous l'avons décrite, toujours partagée, toujours privée de la moitié d'elle-même, divisée narcissiquement entre sujet et objet, orpheline de toute façon. En un mot narcissique de structure et vouée à un destin de partition.'

15 See Heath (quoted above, note 2) as well as J. F. Lyotard, who in his article 'Some of the Things at Stake in Women's Struggles' (*Sub-Stance*, no. 2, 1978), accepting Lacan's use of the 'phallus' as the ultimate signifier, writes: 'The body has no sex before being traversed by "the defiling of signifier", the threat of castration, or death, a mark of Oedipal Law.'

16 This description is more radical than I have the place to analyze here. Suffice to say, when Horace returns from his immersion in blood, his sense of 'self' as an integrity is shattered. He speaks only in metonymical corporal displacement. His body is in pieces:

> Ma soeur, voici le bras qui venge nos deux frères,
> Le bras qui rompt le cours de nos destins contraires
>
> (IV, v, 1251–2)

and addresses Camille also as 'detachable parts', rather than as a whole:

> O, d'une indigne soeur l'insupportable audace!
> D'un ennemi public dont je reviens vainqueur
> Le nom est dans ta bouche et l'amour dans ton coeur!
> Ton ardeur criminelle à la vengeance aspire!
> Ta bouche la demande, et ton coeur le respire.
>
> (IV, v, 1268–72)

In his discourse they are both confounded, an intermingling of parts, an indistinction of bodies rather than distinction of two 'sexed beings'.

17 'Examen', p. 783: 'Tout ce cinquième est encore une des causes du peu de satisfaction que laisse cette tragédie; il est tout en plaidoyers et ce n'est pas là la place des harangues ni de longs discours.'

18 'Cadavériser la femme, c'est tenter une ultime fois de maîtriser son caractère, énigmatique, et atopique, de fixer en une position définitive et immuable l'instabilité et la mobilité même' (Kofman, *Freud*, p. 269).

* An earlier version of this chapter appeared in *Romanic Review* (74, May 1983), pp. 271–93.

4. *Cinna*: empty mirrors

1 Letter of January 17, 1643, quoted in *Cinna*, ed. B. Grillet (Paris: Larousse, 1965), pp. 115–16.
2 All references to *Cinna* and to the 'Examen' are to *Théâtre choisi de Corneille*, ed. M. Rat (Paris: Garnier, 1961).
3 Doubrovsky, *Corneille*, p. 220: 'Cinna est une grande pièce politique parce que nous y trouvons en quelque sorte des "prolégomènes à tout Etatisme futur". Car tout ce qui est dit de l'Etat monarchique reste vrai de tout Etat totalitaire.'
4 Quoted in Grillet, ed., *Cinna*, p. 117.
5 The expression is M. Foucault's; see *La Volonté de savoir*, p. 62.
6 For my use in this chapter of the terms 'narcissism' and 'narcissistic' I am indebted to G. Rosolato's article 'Le narcissisme', where he establishes a connection, that I find rich, between the literary myth of Narcissus and the clinical definition of this most protean of psycho-sexual phenomena. At the outset I would like to quote Rosolato's definition (p. 8) as a grounding for my own uses of this term in this chapter:

> Surtout il importera de bien préciser les *cinq courants* qui sont à la base de sa structure: *le retrait libinal, l'idéalisation, le dédoublement, la double entrave et l'oscillation métaphoro-métonymique*, en sachant que chacun étaie les autres, enrichit leur compréhension dans la réciprocité de leur articulation . . .
> Au demeurant elle (= analyse plurifocale) s'illustre par les traits mêmes du mythe qui en a fixé l'immémoriale figure: (1) Narcisse repousse Echo, ou Ameinias; (2) il découvre son reflet dans une source ou selon la version de Pausanias, il reconnaît en lui sa soeur jumelle morte; (3) cette image de lui-même idéalisé le fascine; (4) il reste entravé dans sa stérilité, son impuissance, entre la vie et la mort; (5) et quand il s'éteint une métamorphose s'accomplit, une plante qui porte son nom apparaît, l'oscillation se déporte métaphoriquement sur le souvenir ainsi perpétué par la création d'une fleure qui évoque la beauté corporelle défunte . . . Et ce sera sans oublier que pour chacun d'eux, dans sa problématique, propre, la mort est un repère basal, toujours présent. Narcisse se mirait encore jusque sur les eaux du Styx.

Of course, in my own analysis of *Cinna* I will be concentrating on only some of these five aspects signalled out by Rosolato.
7 See L. Bersani, 'The Subject of Power' (*Diacritics*, Sept. 1977), p. 5: 'Relations of power include by definition the adversary role; they are inconceivable without the points of resistance present everywhere in a power network. The subjugation of others is never a stable achievement of power.' Likewise Foucault, *La Volonté de savoir*, p. 113: 'Ce pouvoir, ce n'est pas une certaine puissance dont certains seraient

dotés, c'est le nom qu'on prête à une situation stratégique complexe dans une société donnée . . . Ce pouvoir s'exerce à partir des points innombrables et dans le jeu de relation inégalitaires et mobiles.'

8 For the term 'Sovereign' as I use it in this chapter I refer the reader to G. Bataille's essay 'L'homme souverain de Sade', in *L'Erotisme* (Paris: 10/18, 1967), where sovereignty is defined as a total depossession of the self in front of the very limits of that self. Freeing oneself from the conditions linking one to others, one enters the realms of the 'sacred', of the divine, as the object of all desire. Bataille traces the evolution from the 'historical' sovereign to Sade's Sovereign: 'le souci de la puissance infléchit la souveraineté réelle (historique). La souveraineté réelle n'est pas ce qu'elle prétend être, jamais elle n'est plus qu'un effort ayant pour fin de dégager l'existence humaine de son asservissement à la nécessité. Entre les autres le souverain historique échappait aux injonctions de la nécessité. Il y échappait au maximum à l'aide de la puissance que lui donnaient ses fidèles sujets. La loyauté réciproque entre le souverain et les sujets reposait sur la subordination des sujets et sur le principe de participation des sujets à la souveraineté du souverain . . . Sade, à l'intention des autres, des lecteurs, a décrit le sommet auquel la souveraineté peut accéder: il y a un mouvement de la transgression qui ne s'arrête pas avant d'avoir atteint le sommet de la transgression' (p. 123).

9 This mirroring – or double – corresponds to an ambivalent narcissistic stance that Rosolato defines in the following way: 'Le double et l'image spéculaire se caractérisent par leur bi-polarité. D'un côté ils évoquent la prédestination et l'anticipation d'une permanence et d'une immortalité avec le superfétatoire qui menace l'unicité d'où l'agression et les actions de destruction qui en découlent' ('Le Narcissime', p. 18). In M. Foucault's analysis the same apparent bipolarity marks the psycho-sexual as just a part of a larger network of power: 'que les relations de pouvoir ne sont pas en position d'extériorité à l'égard d'autres types de rapports (processus économiques, rapport de connaissances, relations sexuelles), mais qu'elles leur sont immanentes; elles sont les effets immédiats des partages, inégalités et déséquilibres qui s'y produisent, et elles sont réciproquement les conditions internes de ces différentiations; les relations de pouvoir ne sont pas en position de superstructure, avec un simple rôle de prohibition ou de reproduction; elles sont, là où elles jouent un rôle directement producteur' (*La Volonté de savoir*, p. 123).

10 Doubrovsky (*Corneille*, p. 203) describes the relation of Cinna and Emilie as the 'descente aux enfers du couple'.

11 'Examen', p. 151: 'Comme les vers de ma tragédie *Horace* ont quelque chose de plus net et de moins guindé pour les pensées que ceux du *Cid*, on peut dire que ceux de cette pièce ont quelque chose de plus achevé que ceux d'*Horace*.'

12 Here, Emilie rejoins her sisters, Camille and Chimène, guardians of

the excluded, of the negated position of femininity, of femininity as Death which in their own sado-masochistic relation to the world of Patriarchy surfaces in the ambivalence of rebelling while remaining within the structures that negate them. Irigaray discusses this paradox in *Speculum*, pp. 146–7: 'Valeurs "mystiques" auxquelles la femme serait *prédisposée*: par le suspens, la censure, de ses pulsions; par ce qui de sa petite enfance, du "stade pré-oedipien" restera énigmatique, obscur, "continent noir"; par la révélation aussi de l'organe mâle comme signifiant de la toute-puissance . . . Dût-elle en mourir, la femme aura rempli sa mission. Vièrge? Son geste n'en sera que plus exemplaire. Condamnée par le roi? Elle aura, d'autant mieux, fait éclater les contradictions du système. Ce que la colère assez peu digne du souverain démontre. Car si la femme religieusement, aveuglément, ne soutient pas les attributs de la puissance du roi, juge ou guerrier, celle-ci risque fort de décliner ou encore d'être inutile, puisqu'il s'agit toujours d'arbitrer des rivalités entre hommes pour le pouvoir. Cela dit, qu'Antigone proclame aussi haut ce qu'il en est de l'empire "phallique" de la mère, des droits du sang, au mépris du sceptre du roi, et du pénis de son héritier, était difficilement tolérable en régime patriarcal!'

13 Quoted in Grillet, ed., *Cinna*, p. 156.

14 See Doubrovsky, *Corneille*, p. 200: 'Emilie apparaît comme l'aristocrate qui s'entête et s'aveugle à ne considérer les problèmes de la Maîtrise que sous l'angle des rapports individuels; c'est la conscience aristocratique originelle, restée figée dans l'épreuve initiatique'.

15 See two definitions in the Oxford English Dictionary: 'One of the avenging deities, dread goddesses with snakes twisted in their hair, sent from Tartarus to avenge wrong and punish crimes'; 'Fierce passion, disorder or tumult of mind, approaching madness'.

16 Freud in 'On Narcissism, an Introduction' (*Standard Edition*, XIV, pp. 88–9) talks about the particular narcissism of beautiful women: 'Women, especially if they grow up with good looks, develop a certain self-contentment which compensates them for the social restrictions that are imposed upon them in their choice of love object. Strictly speaking, it is only themselves that such women love.' He goes on to say that it is precisely this narcissistic stance of being self-absorbed that makes her attractive to men: 'The importance of this type of women for the erotic life of mankind is to be rated very high. Such women have the greatest fascination for men, not only for aesthetic reasons, since as a rule they are the most beautiful, but also because of a combination of interesting psychological factors. For it seems very evident that another person's narcissism has a great attraction for those who have renounced part of their own narcissism and are in search of object love . . . It is as if we envied them for maintaining a blissful state of mind, an unassailable libidinal position which we ourselves have since abandoned.'

17 For the relation of sado-masochism to narcissism see J. Laplanche, *Vie et mort en psychanalyse* (Paris: Flammarion, 1970), esp. chaps. IV, 'Le moi et le narcissisme', and V, 'Agressivité et sado-masochisme'.

18 Doubrovsky, *Corneille*, p. 191.

19 These are, of course, traditional rhetorical tropes to describe civil disorder (from Juvenal and Martial to Ronsard and d'Aubigné).

20 In the sense in which we are elucidating Corneille's Auguste, he could be an example of the totalitarian leader as presented by Freud in his *Mass Psychology and the Ego*. See also Apostolidès, *Le Prince sacrifié*, pp. 63–7.

21 'The only absolute escape from power is to escape from relations themselves. The most sophisticated resistance to power, a resistance which, however, produces unattackable power, is a denial of the conditions which generate power' (Bersani, 'The Subject of Power', pp. 19–20). It is, of course, the characters' inability to 'escape' from the relations that define them that condemns them to a perpetual return of the same.

22 M. Foucault argues this point in *Surveiller et punir*, pp. 51–2: 'l'aveu est un rituel de discours où le sujet qui parle coincide avec le sujet de l'énoncé; c'est aussi un rituel qui se déploie dans un rapport de pouvoir, car on n'avoue pas sans la présence au moins virtuel d'un partenaire qui n'est pas simplement, l'interlocuteur, mais l'instance qui requiert l'aveu, l'impose, l'apprécie et intervient pour juger, punir, pardonner, consoler, reconcilier; un rituel où la vérité s'authentifie de l'obstacle et des résistances qu'elle a eu à lever pour se formuler; un rituel enfin où la seule énonciation, indépendamment de ses conséquences externes, produit chez qui l'articule de modifications intrinsèques: elle l'innocente, elle le rachète, elle le purifie, elle le décharge de ses fautes, elle le libère, elle lui promet le salut.'

23 In *Surveiller et punir*, Foucault discusses at great length the role of the execution as part of a strategy that is one of dissymmetry in which the power of the Sovereign comes down upon the offender to show the greater force, the divinity, of the State: 'D'un côté elle (public execution) clôt solennellement entre le criminel et le souverain une guerre dont l'issue était jouée d'avance; elle doit manifester le pouvoir démésuré du souverain sur ceux qu'il a reduits à l'impuissance. La dissymétrie, l'irréversible déséquilibre de forces, faisaient partie des fonctions de supplice' (p. 54).

24 Foucault also points out that the sovereign can equally establish his power by his grace, by refusing the death penalty and choosing not to kill: 'Présent le souverain l'est dans l'exécution non seulement comme la puissance qui venge la loi, mais comme le pouvoir qui peut suspendre et la loi et la vengeance. Lui seul doit rester maître des offenses qu'on lui a faites' (p. 57).

25 A future that is already hinted at in the play when we learn that since 'Auguste' began his reign Rome has recovered her wealth and peace. Cinna tells Auguste:

Rome

. . .

reçoit maintenant de vos rares bontés
Sous vous, l'Etat n'est plus en pillage aux armées,
Les portes de Janus par vos mains sont fermées.

(II, i, 549, 552–4)

5. *Polyeucte*: seeing is believing

1 See *Le Cid*, I, iii: 'Cet hyménée à trois également importe.'
2 See le père Caffaro, 'Lettre d'un théologien' (Paris, 1694); Bossuet, *Maximes et réflexions sur la comédie* (Paris, 1694); Massillon, 'Serment XVIII sur l'injustice du monde envers les gens du bien'; and Bourdaloue, 'Serment pour le septième dimanche après la Pentecôte sur l'hypocrisie'. These are all quoted in H. Phillips, *The Theater and its Critics in Seventeenth Century France* (Oxford, 1980).
3 'Nous ne devons qu'une croyance pieuse à la vie des saints, et nous avons le même droit sur ce que nous en tirons pour le porter sur le théâtre, que sur ce que nous empruntons des autres histoires; mais nous devons une foi chrétienne et indispensable à tout ce qui est dans la *Bible*, qui ne nous laisse aucune liberté d'y rien changer. J'estime toutefois qu'il ne nous est pas défendu d'y ajouter quelque chose, pourvu qu'il ne détruise rien de ces vérités dictées par le Saint Esprit. Buchanan ni Grotius ne l'ont pas fait dans leurs poèmes, mais aussi ne les ont-ils rendus assez fournis pour notre théâtre . . . Heinsius a plus osé qu'eux dans celui que j'ai nommé' ('Examen', pp. 213–14). All references to *Polyeucte* and to the 'Examen' are to *Théâtre choisi de Corneille*, ed. M. Rat (Paris: Garnier, 1961).
4 See J. Lacan, *Seminaire XI*, 'Les quatre concepts fondamentaux de la psychanalyse' (Paris: Seuil, 1973), pp. 161–2: 'Si tout est embrouilli dans la discussion des pulsions sexuelles c'est qu'on ne voit pas que la pulsion sans doute représente, mais ne fait *que* représenter, et partiellement, la courbe de l'accomplissement de la sexualité chez le vivant. Comment s'étonner que son terme soit la mort? Puisque la présence du sexe chez la vivant est liée à la mort.'
5 J. Starobinski, *L'Oeil vivant* (Paris: Gallimard, 1961), pp. 14–15: 'Le regard, qui assure à notre conscience une issue hors du lieu qu'occupe notre corps, constitue, au sens le plus rigoureux, un excès. D'où la severité des Pères de l'Eglise. De tous les sens, la vue est le plus faible, le plus naturellement coupable. Toutefois, ceux-là mêmes qui font grief au regard mondain de son indiscrétion et de sa dispersion en appellent à ce même pouvoir pour le diriger vers la "lumière surnaturelle" et les formes intelligibles. L'outrance naturelle du regard, à leur gré, cesse d'être coupable si elle se dirige vers l'autre monde.' See also

Irigaray, *Speculum*, p. 116.

6 Freud, 'Instincts and Their Vicissitudes' (*Standard Edition*, XIV, pp. 129–32).

7 Lacan, *Seminaire XI*, p. 71: 'des êtres regardés dans le spectacle du monde'.

8 *Ibid.*, pp. 94–5.

9 See my *Detours of Desire*, chap. 5, 'Corneille's Sexual Politics: The Perils of Pauline'.

10 Catherine Clément talks about the actual image of the female criminal who kills her beloved/hated victim in *Vies et légendes de J. Lacan* (Paris: Grasset, 1981), p. 87.

11 'Le désir de la femme ne se dirait qu'en rêves.' Irigaray, *Speculum*, p. 156.

12 'A moins que toute la puissance et la différence (?), se soient là déplacées dans le(s) regard(s)? . . . D'où l'envie de la toute puissance de ce regard, de ce savoir? Sur le sexe. L'envie, la jalousie de l'oeil-pénis, du regard phallique' (Irigaray, *Speculum*, p. 53). See also, for the importance of the look as an active, phallic possession, Heath's 'Difference', pp. 55–8, and L. Mulvey's 'Visual Pleasure and Narrative Cinema', *Screen*, 16, no. 3, Autumn, 1975.

13 This is the point Lacan makes (*Ecrits*, p. 579): 'Plus loin encore la relation du père à cette loi doit-elle être considérée en elle-même, car on y trouvera la raison de ce paradoxe, par quoi les effets ravageants de la figure paternelle s'observent avec une particulière fréquence dans les cas où *le père a réellement la fonction de législat* ou s'en prévaut, qu'il soit en fait de ceux qui font les lois ou qu'il se pose en pillier de la foi, en paragon d'intégrité ou de la dévotion, en vertueux ou en vir-tuose, en servant d'une oeuvre de salut, de quelque objet ou manque d'objet qu'il y aille de nation ou de natalité, de sauvegarde ou de salubrité, de legs ou de légalité, du pur, du pire ou de l'empire, tous idéaux qui ne lui offrent que trop d'occasions d'être en posture de mérite, d'insuffisance, voire de fraude, et pour tout dire d'exclure le Nom-du-Père de sa position dans le signifiant.' This is precisely the aporia of Pauline's and Félix's relation. See my *Detours of Desire*, chap. 5.

14 This would seem to corroborate the eternal structure of all chivalric love. See Lacan, *Seminaire XX* (Paris: Seuil, 1975), p. 65: 'L'amour courtois, qu'est-ce que c'est? C'est une façon tout à fait raffinée de suppléer à l'absence de rapport sexuel, en feignant que c'est nous qui y mettons obstacle.'

15 Freud, of course, analyzes this important ritual in his 'The Taboo of Virginity' (*Standard Edition*, XI).

16 'La "castration" pour la femme serait de n'avoir rien à donner à voir, de n'avoir rien. De n'avoir rien de pénis, de voir qu'elle (n')a rien. Rien de même que l'homme. Donc *rien* de sexe qui se montre dans une forme susceptible d'en fonder la réalité; d'en re-produire la vérité.

Rien à voir équivaut à n'avoir rien' (Irigaray, *Speculum*, p. 54). See also Heath, 'Difference', pp. 53–5.

17　See Freud's 'The Taboo of Virginity', p. 203: 'The husband is never anything but a proxy, never the right man; the first claim upon the feelings of love in a woman belongs to someone else . . . to her father; the husband is at best a second.'

18　See Lemoine-Luccioni, *Partage des femmes*, pp. 88–9: 'Privée d'objet extérieur d'amour, la femme erre "comme une âme en peine", et se retourne en effet vers son Père: le seul homme qui l'ait aimée, ou qu'elle ait pu aimer. C'est en lui seul qu'elle trouve son idéal, c'est à dire cette unité qui lui fait défaut puisqu'elle est partagée. Et quand elle aime un autre homme, elle l'aime comme elle a aimé son père. Elle en fait un Père. Elle attend tout de lui.'

19　*Ibid.*, p. 161: 'Qu'une femme puisse être l'unique pour un homme . . . fait de cet homme l'objet absolu, comme elle est le "corps absolu", mythe idolâtre où le sujet propre s'abîme; tant vaut franchir le pas du mystique. Mais de même la femme qui fait d'un homme l'"unique" est une mystique.'

20　At least this is what Lacan would have us (perhaps) believe: 'Cette jouissance qu'on éprouve et dont on ne sait rien, n'est-ce pas ce qui nous met sur la voie de l'ex-sistance? Et pour quoi ne pas interpréter une face de l'Autre, la face Dieu, comme supportée par la jouissance féminine?' (*Seminaire XX*, p. 71).

21　'Male or female, the subject is implicated from and in the phallus, phallic jouissance, but differently, there is a male and a female way of failing relation. In other words, the structure of a subject is a division in the symbolic; that division is not the fact of some immediately given sexual difference, men and women are not complementary to one another, two halves that could be joined in union, both are produced in division; the phallus is the term of that production inasmuch as it functions as the signifier in the articulation of castration; male and female differ in consequence of the phallic function in castration, are in the position of a different relation to phallus and castration; thus there can be no sexual relation, only a relation to phallic jouissance, in the woman as in the man' (Heath, 'Difference', p. 59).

6. *Nicomède, Rodogune, Suréna*

1　'Rodogune constitue . . . une coupure radicale. Encore quelque temps à égalité avec les hommes . . . les femmes prendront la succession des hommes pour le maintien de l'éthique héroïque.' Doubrovsky, *Corneille*, p. 292.

2　*Ibid.*, p. 151: 'Ce n'est pas par hasard si l'acte privilégié du théâtre cornélien est précisément celui auquel nous sommes arrivés: le parricide. Comme la libido dans le psychodrame freudien, le "parricide", sous une forme ouverte ou voilée, directe ou symbolique, est au centre de

la dramaturgie cornélienne'. See also Green, *Un oeil en trop*, p. 239.

3   For a discussion of the 'un-tragic' aspect of Cornelian tragedy, see J. Maurens, *La Tragédie sans tragique: le néo-stoïcisme dans l'oeuvre de P. Corneille* (Paris: Colin, 1966).

4   See G. Carloni and D. Nobili, *La Mauvaise Mère*, trans. R. Maggiori (Paris: P.B.P., 1977).

5   'Suivant la loi, le roi ne meurt jamais, c'est à dire que, par la seule force de la loi, toute l'autorité royale est transmise incontinent, après la mort du monarque, à celui qui a le droit de lui succéder', art. xxx, chap. II, of 'Projet des premiers articles de la Constitution, lu par M. Mounier, 28 juillet 1789', quoted in *La Tribune française*, I (Paris: Aux presses de la Tribune française, 1840), p. 67. See also Kantorowicz, *The King's Two Bodies* and Apostolidès, *Le Roi machine*.

6   See Marin, *Le Portrait du roi*, 'Troisième entrée', pp. 207–61.

7   L. Althusser, 'Idéologie, et appareils idéologiques d'Etat' in *Positions* (Paris: Editions Sociales, 1976), p. 105: 'une idéologie existe toujours dans un appareil, et sa pratique, ou ses pratiques. Cette existence est matérielle'.

8   *Ibid.*, p. 101.

9   See, for instance, the introductory comments of M. Rat in his edition of the play, p. 485: 'Mélancolique constat d'un grand poète . . . '.

10 Freud, *Mourning and Melancholia* (*Standard Edition*, XIV), p. 241: 'one feels justified in maintaining the belief that a loss . . . has occurred, but one cannot clearly see what has been lost . . . he (the patient) knows *whom* he has lost but not *what* he has lost in him'.

11 See Kantorowicz, *The King's Two Bodies*, and also Marin, *Le Portrait du roi*.

12 See Althusser, 'Idéologie', pp. 119–20: 'Nous constatons que la structure de toute idéologie interpellant les individus en sujets au nom d'un Sujet Unique et Absolu est spéculaire . . . Ce qui signifie que toute idéologie est centrée, que ce Sujet Absolu occupe la place unique du centre, et interpelle autour de lui l'infinité des individus en sujets dans une double relation spéculaire telle qu'elle assujettit les sujets au Sujet, tout en leur donnant, dans le Sujet où tout sujet peut contempler sa propre image . . . la garantie que c'est bien d'eux et bien de lui qu'il s'agit . . . '

13 Ambivalence is one of the determining causes of melancholia; see Freud, *Mourning and Melancholia*, p. 251: 'This conflict due to ambivalence, which sometimes arises more from real experiences, sometimes more from constitutional factors, must not be overlooked among the preconditions of melancholia.'

14 See Althusser, 'Idéologie', p. 107: 'Dans tous les cas l'idéologie reconnaît donc, malgré sa déformation imaginaire, que les "idées" d'un sujet humain existent dans ses actes . . . nous parlerons d'actes insérés dans des pratiques. Et nous remarquerons que ces pratiques sont réglées par des rituels dans lesquels ces pratiques s'inscrivent, au sein de l'existence matérielle d'appareil idéologique.'

15 See Marin, *Le Portrait du roi*, p. 82: 'L'absolu du pouvoir est l'absolu du pouvoir agir, l'absolu d'un agir qui n'a pas d'autre source qu'interne', and again, p. 176: 'ce que le pouvoir toujours désire . . . la secrète demande de la toute puissance, être le seul en soi-même, l'absolu souverain.'

16 The concept 'individual' as opposed to 'subject' is analyzed by Althusser, 'Idéologie', pp. 110–16; 'L'idéologie interpelle les individus en sujets'.

17 This term, of course, comes from the entire medieval tradition of rhetorical and iconographic representations of 'melancholy'. See Klibansky, Panofsky and Saxl, *Saturn and Melancholy* (New York: Basic Books, 1964).

18 Foucault in *Surveiller et punir*; see Introduction.

Index

Index

Gallop, J., 174 n. 18
genealogy, 19, 20, 30
  as temporality, 39, 40
  as history, 52
Goode, W., 171 n. 19
Goux, J. - J., 170 n. 6, 171 n. 10, n. 24
Green, A., 12, 20, 168 n. 17, 170 n. 3, 171 n. 15, n. 21, 173 n. 12, 184–5 n. 2
Greenberg, M., 168–9 n. 22
Grillet, B., 178 n. 1, n. 4, 180 n. 13
Grotius, 120, 182 n. 3
Guattari, F., 173 n. 8

Hamlet, 8
Harth, E., 168–9 n. 22
Heath, S., 13, 169 n. 30, n. 34, n. 15, 176 n. 2, 177, 183 n. 12, 183–4 n. 16, 184 n. 21
Heinsius, 120
history, xiii
  as unconscious, 40
Hobbes, T., 4
homo-eroticism, 42, 135–6
homosexuality, 75
Huet, M. H. 7, 167 n. 4, 170 n. 35
hymen, as oscillation, metaphor-metonymy, 76–7, 84–5, 151
  as tragic locus, 119–20, 132–3, 137–8

ideology, as subjectivity, 154
Irigaray, L., 11, 169 n. 28, 171 n. 11, n. 14, n. 22, n. 23, 173 n. 8, 174 n. 16, 176 n. 4, n. 5, n. 6, n. 9, n. 10, 179–80 n. 12, 182–3 n. 5, 183 n. 11, n. 12, 183–4 n. 16

Jameson, F., 169 n. 33
Juvenal, 181 n. 19

Kantorowicz, E., 3, 167 n. 7, n. 11, 185 n. 5, n. 11
Keohane, N., 4, 167 n. 9, n. 11
King, as Father, 4–5
King, P., 167 n. 11
Klein, M., 60, 175 n. 29, n. 30
Klibansky, R., 186 n. 17
Kofman, S., 11, 169 n. 25, n. 26, n. 27, 177 n. 12, n. 18
Kristeva, J., 175 n. 29

Lacan, J., 169 n. 30, 177 n. 15, 182 n. 4, 183 n. 7, n. 13, n. 14, 184 n. 20

Lacey, W. K., 171 n. 13
Lacoue-Labarthe, P., 168 n. 21
Laplanche, J., 181 n. 17
Lemoine-Luccioni, E., 169 n. 31, 174 n. 16, n. 17, 177 n. 14, 184 n. 18, n. 19
Lévi-Strauss, C., 16, 170 n. 1
Leyssac, A. de, 171 n. 12, n. 19
Louis XIII, xi, 4, 9
Louis XIV, 4, 9
Lyotard, J. F., 168 n. 17, 177 n. 15

Machiavelli, 4
Mandrou, R., 166 n. 1, 169 n. 33
Mannoni, O., 168 n. 17, 170 n. 35, n. 36, n. 3
Marin, L., 167 n. 10, 185 n. 6, 186 n. 15
marriage, as center of tragedy, 6
  as appropriation, 46–8, 72
  as tragic dilemma, 49
  as public ritual, 135, 137–8
Martial, 181 n. 19
masochism, 9
masculinity, 10–13
  as reproductions of same, 20
Massillon, 182 n. 2
Maurens, J., 185 n. 3
melancholia, 153–5, 164
Monarchy, as icon, 156
  as desire, 160
Montaigne, M. de, 2
Montmorency, Duc de, xi
Montrelay, M., 169 n. 26
Mousnier, R., 167 n. 11, n. 13
Mulvey, L., 183 n. 12
myth, and sexuality, 19
  as mediation, 16–18
  as paradox, 19
  as tragedy, 32

Nadal, O., 50, 175 n. 23
narcissism, 14, 27–8, 173 n. 12, 178 n. 6, 180 n. 16
  as political conservatism, 44
  and masochism, 62
  as closure, 120
Narcissus, myth, 91
Nelson, R. J., 2, 167 n. 5
Nietzsche, F., xiv, 171 n. 18
Nobili, D., 185 n. 4

Oakesholt, M., 167 n. 9
Oedipal conflict, 12, 45
Oedipus, 8

Index

Panofsky, E., 186 n. 17
parricide, as regicide, 148–50, 165, 184–5 n. 2
Peyre, H., 168–9 n. 22
pharmakos, 30
phallic mother, 23, 33
Phillips, H., 182 n. 2
Plato, 171 n. 10
pleasure, theatrical, 9
 as masochism, 12
 as narcissism, 16
politics, as sexuality, 6

Ranum, O., 167 n. 11
Rat, M., 172 n. 2
Reiss, T., 168–9 n. 22
Religious Wars, 2
Reynier, G., 172 n. 1
Richelieu, J. – A. Duplessis, Cardinal de, xi–xii, 4
Ronsard, P. de, 2, 181 n. 19
Rosolato, G., 45, 172 n. 6, 173 n. 12, n. 13, n. 14, 175 n. 24, n. 25, n. 27, 175–6 n. 31, 178 n. 6, 179 n. 9
Rousset, J., 166 n. 1

sado-masochism, 101, 127, 130, 153
Sarduy, S., 166 n. 1
Saxl, F., 186 n. 17
Schérer, J., 168–9 n. 22

self, modern, origins of, 13
Sovereign, xii, 3
 as object of desire, 4
sovereignty, as subjugation, 156
spectator, and pleasure, 13
 as multiple instance, 13
Starobinski, J., 124, 175–6 n. 31, 182–3 n. 5
subjectivity, and representation, xiv, 7
symmetry, as essentialization, 9–11, 27, 48–52, 66

Tapié, V. L., 166 n. 1
Theater as desire, 2
 and audience, dialectic, 2
 as spectacle, 7
 as dream, 8
theatrical illusion, 14
theatrical pleasure and politics, 7
time, unity of, 38
tragedy, as familial closure, 6
 as desire, 6–7
 as politics, 18
Trinity, Holy, of Classicism, 41–5

Ubersfeld, A., 9, 167 n. 3, n. 4, 168 n. 15, n. 19, 170 n. 3

Vigny, A. de, xii, xiii, 166 n. 1
voyeurism and exhibitionism, 125